Manager's Portfolio of Model Memos for Every Occasion

Revised and Expanded

Cynthia A. Barnes

PRENTICE HALL

Library of Congress Cataloging-in-Publication Data

Barnes, Cynthia A.
    Manager's portfolio of model memos for every occasion / Cynthia A.
Barnes.—Revised and Expanded.
      p. cm.
    Includes index.
    ISBN 0-13-242520-3 (cloth).—ISBN 0-13-242512-2 (paper)
    1. Memorandums—Handbooks, manuals, etc.   I. Title.
HF5726.B237 1996   96-34632
651.7'55'0202—dc20   CIP

Printed in the United States of America

10 9 8 7 6   10 9 8 7 6 5

ISBN 0-13-242520-3 (C)   ISBN 0-13-242512-2 (P)

ISBN 0-13-010699-2 (W/CD)

10 9 8 7 6 5 4 3

PRENTICE HALL
Paramus, NJ 07652

On the World Wide Web at http://www.phdirect.com

Acknowledgments

Many people and forces made this revised and expanded edition possible. I'd like to thank God, who makes all things possible, and my parents, Theadore and Mary Drew, who made me possible.

This book could never have been written without the loving support and continued tolerance for benign neglect of my special husband and desktop publishing consultant, Martin Barnes, and my son, Martin II.

Thanks also to Carter Drew, President and Managing Director of McDonald's South Africa, and Cordelia Callaway, Senior Quality Consultant at the University of Illinois, Chicago. My special brother and sister, they have had a lot to do with my ongoing growth and development.

As the eldest of the fourth generation of my family, I acknowledge a host of family members (especially my grandfather, Mr. Eddie Pulliam) who set high expectations for me and then helped me achieve them.

Tom Power, Mariann Hutlak, and the staff of Prentice Hall helped me enormously. "Ike" Lanier and Dr. Mary Davis reviewed the manuscript and provided their expertise. Allen and Suzanne Hopkins, my computer consultants, provided invaluable technical assistance. Special thanks to Joyce Batson, my "fan club" president, and to Emily Young, Ted May, Bob Grigsby, Kathy Scott, Charlene Brown, Sue Pinsonat, Nancy Wallis, Dr. Leonard Baca, Gil Davis, Marilyn Hoskins, William Martinez, Ronald Strachan, and William and Doris Beary.

Thanks, too, to good memo writers everywhere.

About the Author

Cynthia A. Barnes, Ph.D., earned her doctorate in Human and Organizational Systems from The Fielding Institute, Santa Barbara, California. She also has a Master's Degree in Organizational Development from The Fielding Institute; a Master's Degree in Teaching (English Education) from Northwestern University; and a Bachelor's Degree in Psychology/English from the University of Illinois at Chicago.

Learning Evocateur for Learning . . . for Change, Denver, Colorado, Dr. Barnes provides developmental therapy for individuals and organizations. Also Creative Consultant and Co-owner of Write On (a desktop publishing firm), Dr. Barnes writes memoranda, letters, proposals, reports, and brochures for organizations, large and small.

Cynthia A. Barnes was formerly Dean of Educational Development and Faculty Services, Director of Faculty/Staff/Organizational Development, and Professor of Business Communications at the Community College of Aurora, Colorado (CCA). While at CCA, Dr. Barnes wrote grant proposals that earned CCA's Professional Development Program a Program of Excellence Award from the State of Colorado, and a U.S. Department of Education award for funds to design professional development for college faculty of color. Cynthia's writing secured more than $1.2 million in grant funds for CCA.

Dr. Barnes's list of clients includes the U.S. Postal Service; American Telephone and Telegraph (AT&T); the Mayo Clinic/Foundation; Denver Regional Transportation District (RTD); the City of Aurora, Colorado; the Lowry Air Force Base Reserve Personnel and Accounting and Finance Centers; the Minnesota and Virginia Community College Systems; Humber College, Toronto, Canada; and Guam Community College, among others.

Cynthia A. Barnes also edited *Critical Thinking: Educational Imperative* (Jossey-Bass, Spring 1992) and authored "Straight Talk," a contemporary issues column, for *Far Northeast News,* formerly a community newspaper. She is a renowned public speaker and has given presentations and facilitated seminars at international, national, and regional conferences and conventions.

A former Distinguished Faculty Member of the Year at CCA, Dr. Barnes received the National Teaching Excellence Award from the National Institute of Staff and Organization Development at the University of Texas at Austin, and the John Fry Individual Merit Award for outstanding contributions to the field of professional development from the National Council for Staff, Program, and Organizational Development. She was a quarter-finalist in the *Chicago Sun-Times* search for an advice columnist to replace Ann Landers, is a graduate of Leadership Aurora (Colorado), and has been cited in *Who's Who of American Women, Who's Who in American Education, Who's Who of Women Executives,* and *Who's Who of Emerging Leaders.*

About This Revised and Expanded Edition

In the six years since the first edition of *Manager's Portfolio of Model Memos for Every Occasion* was published, your organization has probably undergone changes of monumental proportions. Gripped by challenges imposed by a global economy, your workplace may have undergone a takeover, a downsizing, or a reorganization. As a leader, manager, or supervisor, you have probably been involved in at least one innovation—reengineering, team management, or continuous service improvement—in order to remain solvent and competitive.

In this dynamic environment, skillful communication is critical. Communicating effectively about a variety of topics has become one of your most valuable assets. In the midst of all the change around you, however, "executives still spend at least 22 percent of their time writing and reading memos," reports Robert Half International, a New-York-City-based recruiting firm.

Twenty-two percent—that's a lot of time; time you could spend getting the product made, closing the sale, balancing the books, managing organizational change. Instead, you're now spending that time—roughly, one full month per year—writing, rewriting, and revising your memoranda or deciphering the memos of others. Communicating your ideas to those in your organization is costing you time, but more than that, it's costing you money.

Meanwhile, your boss and your customers expect results. You know only too well how hard you work to produce those results. Would that you could telephone a subordinate or call an employee into your office each time a job must be done. But the resulting traffic jam would be unmanageable, not to mention the fact that your verbal instructions would vanish, literally, into thin air.

To get the results you want, only a permanent record—black marks on a page—will motivate your subordinates to meet deadlines, follow instructions, and get the work out. Spoken words will work in some situations. But in others, getting results means writing a clear, concise memo that says what you mean and means what you say.

This revised and expanded edition of *Manager's Portfolio of Model Memos for Every Occasion* can help you do just that! Choose one from the hundreds of sample memoranda and phrasing alternatives, and use each "write touch" memo as is, or tailor it to your specific needs with the stroke of a pen or the touch of a keyboard.

This comprehensive collection of memoranda, suitable for even more occasions, can help you manage subjects ranging from absenteeism to scheduling; from cost approval to training; from total quality management to management information systems: the issues you care about, the issues that can make or break your efforts, especially in today's climate of perpetual change.

In addition to the more than 750 model memos in the original version, this updated edition includes brand new chapters addressing the challenges faced by today's organizations: *organizational change, team functioning and management, information technology,* and *diversity issues.* New memoranda on day-to-day operations, training, sensitive workplace concerns, and quality-of-life issues have been added as well.

Model Memoranda in Action (designated by an asterisk) are memos contributed to this volume by busy professionals just like you. These memos got results for them; they can get results for you, too.

WHO CAN USE THIS BOOK

This portfolio includes sample memos for cutting-edge supervisors, managers, leaders, and staff:

- Executives
- Mid-level Managers
- First-line Supervisors
- Organizational Development Consultants
- Executive and Administrative Assistants
- Office Managers
- Support Staff
- Project Managers and Directors
- Training Officers
- Diversity Managers
- Accountants, Budget Officers, Controllers
- Professional, Administrative, and Technical Personnel
- Account Executives

- Information/Data Processing Personnel
- Quality Consultants
- Team Leaders, Coaches, and Members
- Organizational Change Agents

Your organizations are gripped by perpetual change. Only leaders and managers like you—those who embrace this shift to horizontal, customer-centered (external and internal), and openly communicative workplaces—will continue to thrive. And with the continued proliferation of information technology, effective, efficient communication will be a major key to your success.

If you correspond with executives, management, co-workers, and subordinates, chances are you'll find a memo just right for most occasions. Whether you deal with products or services, work in the public, private, or nonprofit sector—whatever your business—this guide can take some of the time, cost, and aggravation out of the business of writing memos.

USING THESE MEMOS TO GET RESULTS

Hundreds of memoranda and phrasing alternatives have been indexed to meet your needs. During the course of your busy day, you can let your fingers do the working by selecting memos that help you:

- Delegate assignments, complete paperwork and reports, get equipment repaired, request supplies—plan and organize your day-to-day operations.
- Deal with sick-leave abuse, publicize vacation work schedules, grant and deny requests for leave, correct paycheck errors for workers—manage the salary and benefit side of the house.
- Spell out work assignments and duties, announce promotions, assign projects with deadlines—direct the work activities of your section, unit, or department.
- Commend subordinates, follow-up on customer complaints, recommend termination—control the performance and progress of those who help you get the job done.
- Discuss total quality management initiatives, organizational vision, downsizing, rightsizing, outplacement, and reengineering—handle organizational change.

- Implement company policy, write foolproof procedures, change work hours—inform your workers of changes, elicit their "buy-in" and help them through the change process.

- Establish self-directed work teams, communicate team mission, determine team structure—manage horizontally by effecting team results.

- Announce meeting and training dates.

- Announce an electronic network, discuss computer security, describe management information systems, and manage information overload—meet the challenges of information technology.

- Follow up on money matters, approve travel expenses, deal with overages, justify an expenditure.

- Define diversity, address diversity-related conflict, or request adaptations for disabled workers—support diversity initiatives.

- Write about sensitive issues like mandatory drug testing, AIDS, or costly employee errors.

The memos, you'll find, mirror the broad range of issues you handle each day, from the early-shift whistle to the close of business, to after-hours electronic mail.

This handy resource has just given you one full month per year, one less thing to worry about, and new communication tools for the age of constant change. Spend this time—and the money you'll save—finding creative approaches for a host of global challenges and possibilities. In a world in flux, managers and supervisors need to communicate on solid ground. This new *Manager's Portfolio of Model Memos for Every Occasion* provides you with hundreds of tools to do just that. Devote your time to taking care of business; the business of memo writing has now been taken care of for you.

Contents

*Model Memos in Action

*Model Memos in Action

---

*Model Memos in Action

---

*Model Memos in Action

4. MODEL MEMOS ABOUT WORK PERFORMANCE ISSUES 113

*Model Memos in Action

*Model Memos in Action

7. MODEL MEMOS ABOUT TEAMS 204

8. MODEL MEMOS ABOUT INFORMATION TECHNOLOGY 224

---

*Model Memos in Action

*Model Memos in Action

12. MODEL MEMOS FOR MONEY MATTERS 328

*Model Memos in Action

13. MODEL MEMOS ABOUT SENSITIVE ISSUES 358

---

*Model Memos in Action

*Model Memos in Action

1

Model Memos for Day-to-Day Operations

Operating effectively from day to day, sometimes moment to moment. That's what makes—or breaks—your business, whatever your business. The short-term, day-to-day actions you take will determine your organization's long-term bottom line.

But you know all too well, that you'll have to take a new short-term action just as soon as you've handled the last problem or challenge. And you'll have to communicate your ideas to your boss, your co-workers, or your subordinates. Whether you're announcing a job opening, cancelling an appointment, delegating a work assignment, getting equipment or supplies, collecting time cards, or hiring a new worker, writing memoranda to describe your short-term actions steals valuable time from your day: each day, every day.

Now, writing those routine memoranda doesn't have to rob you of valuable time. The memoranda in this chapter will communicate your ideas about routine matters. Turn to the page you need, have the memo typed, and send it out: another day-to-day matter gets resolved. Use one of the phrasing alternatives or add a few words, if needed, to say what you mean and mean what you say.

Day-to-day memoranda writing has been done for you. So you can spend time with the more important business of working or managing the work of others. You can now spend your time where it counts: improving your organization's bottom line.

ANNOUNCING A JOB CHANGE

To:
From:
Date:
Subject: Job Change

Effective Monday, January 5, 19/20_____, the following job changes will take effect. These changes reflect the job-audit information you furnished Personnel Services.

    The Clerk-Typist position will be classified as Administrative Assistant I. The position of Senior Clerk-Typist will be converted to Administrative Assistant II. The Senior Secretary position will be converted to Administrative Assistant III. Staff Assistants I, II, and III will now be classified as Executive Assistant I, II, or III.

    Results from the salary survey will be used to determine new salary ranges for each classification. No salary changes will take place until next fiscal year, October 1, 19/20_____. Details about this conversion will follow. If you have questions about your specific job class, contact your human resources manager.

MEMO WRITER TIPS

1. Describe the job change.
2. Give an effective date.
3. Provide reasons for the change.

PHRASING ALTERNATIVES

Paragraph 1

    Lay-off reorganization has required certain job changes. Effective immediately, the Quality-Control Clerk position will be changed to Product Service Technician.

    Bonnie Kay's job has been changed from Production Supervisor to Quality Control Manager. She will assume her new duties on Monday, August 1, 19/20_____.

Paragraph 2

Product Service Technicians will perform their previous duties and add functions previously handled by the Customer Service Representatives. This change will broaden the scope of PSTs. Feedback they receive from customers will also help them determine how product quality can best be enhanced. PSTs will receive a salary increase to compensate for additional duties.

Bonnie's experience and expertise can best be used to monitor overall quality of products. Since she is thoroughly familiar with production personnel and operations, she should readily make the transition to management and help us improve our product as well.

Paragraph 3

This job change should help balance workload and improve service. If you have any questions, see your supervisor.

I know I can count on each of you to give Bonnie your full support.

ANNOUNCING A JOB VACANCY

To:
From:
Date:
Subject: Job Vacancy

Qualified employees are encouraged to apply for the Management Analyst II position (Job Announcement #20371) currently open in the Finance Department. October 1, 19____, marks the closing date for applications.

This position is vacant because of Ms. Susan Capra's recent promotion to Analyst III. Consistent with our company's policy of promoting from within whenever possible, interested employees need to submit the following information to the Personnel Department, no later than 5:00 p.m., October 1, 19____:

1. an updated application form
2. a letter of application, outlining your qualifications for the position
3. a current resume

Before you apply, stop by the personnel office to review the job announcement. The new Analyst II should be notified by October 21, 19____. Best of luck to all applicants.

MEMO WRITER TIPS

1. Name the job and department in the very first sentence. Those who are interested can read on; those who are not may stop here.

2. Be sure you include deadline information in the first paragraph.

3. It's a good idea to explain why this vacancy has occurred. This will short-circuit rumors and may provide potential applicants with additional motivation to apply.

4. Make sure you provide details about what information must be submitted by when, and encourage readers to review the job announcement before they apply. This way, employees won't waste valuable time applying for a position if they are not fully qualified.

PHRASING ALTERNATIVES

Paragraph 1

If you meet the qualifications for Sheet Metal Worker II, please submit your application for this job by Friday, August 2.

A vacancy in the Credit Collections Division is scheduled to occur on November 14, 19____. All interested and qualified employees are encouraged to apply by November 26.

Qualified workers interested in applying for Radiology Technician should submit application materials to the personnel office no later than July 17, 19____.

Paragraph 2

Max Larson has accepted a position in the Charlotte office, creating this vacancy. If you are interested in this position, send an updated application form and letter of application to Sue Knowles, Room 206, by 4:30 p.m., August 2.

Budget allocations have enabled us to hire an additional Collections Representative. Those who meet the qualifications should send the following to the personnel office by November 14:

1. Form 3405
2. A current resume
3. A letter of recommendation from your immediate supervisor

Paragraph 3

A job description is available on the Job Vacancy Announcement Board, Suite 706. Review this carefully before submitting your application package.

Contact the personnel department for a copy of Job Announcement #34566. Make sure you meet the qualifications before you apply. Good luck!

ANNOUNCING A LAY-OFF

To:
From:
Date:
Subject: Lay-Off

Sales of door fasteners have steadily declined for the past two years. This decline makes it impossible for the company to continue to manufacture these items without, ultimately, affecting sales in other areas.

For this reason, all workers on the fastener production line will be laid off, effective Friday, April 4, 19____, at 4:00 p.m. Your final paycheck, including two weeks' severance pay, will be ready by that date. Pick your check up in the payroll office on April 4.

I am very sorry this lay-off could not be avoided. I want to thank you all for the hard work you've given to this company. As openings become available in other areas, you may be called back to work, according to applicable personnel policies.

MEMO WRITER TIPS

1. Explain why the lay-off has become necessary.

2. Tell workers who will be laid off, when.

3. Discuss any procedures for recalling workers, applicable union policies, unemployment insurance benefits, etc.

PHRASING ALTERNATIVES

Paragraph 1

Company profits have dwindled by 35 percent this year. These dwindling profits have prompted me to study areas where we might cut back on personnel, in order to preserve some jobs.

House Bill 1136 passed on March 5 mandated a reduction in force of Health and Human Services counselors.

The holiday season has ended. This means Abbott Department Store must return to pre-holiday personnel levels.

Paragraph 2

Much to my regret, you will be laid-off at the end of your shift on Friday, March 3, 19_____ . Your last check, including one month's severance pay, will be mailed to you no later than March 10.

Counselors hired within the last year will either be offered other positions within the agency or laid off, based on job performance and seniority factors. These status changes will begin on Monday, October 9, 19_____ . Human Resources will schedule an appointment with each counselor affected by this action within the next 30 days.

Seasonal employees hired within the past 90 days will be laid off after Friday, January 15, 19_____ . You may pick up your final paycheck before you leave work on that date.

Paragraph 3

Thank you for all your hard work. I wish we could have avoided this lay-off, but declining profits simply make that impossible at this time.

I appreciate your service and dedication. Union guidelines specify that employees may be called back to work, if additional work becomes available, according to seniority rights. The personnel office will provide you with information about filing your unemployment insurance claims.

Your loyalty and outstanding performance are greatly appreciated. Perhaps you'll have the opportunity to work for us again next season.

ANNOUNCING RECALL FROM A LAY-OFF

To:
From:
Date:
Subject: Recall Notice

Work volume has increased dramatically. Therefore, you are being recalled to work as a Production Associate, effective Monday, January 21, 19/20_____ , 7:30 a.m. If you are unable to return to work on this date, call Susan Whitaker, HR, at (206) 888-9009, by Wednesday, January 16.

If you do not call Susan by January 16 or report to work on January 21, the next associate on the recall list will be contacted.

If you return to work on January 21, see Susan Whitaker in Human Resources, Room 100, before reporting to your section.

MEMO WRITER TIPS

1. Provide the effective date of the recall.

2. Discuss the process for returning to duty and information about failure to report.

ANNOUNCING A PROMOTIONAL EXAMINATION

To:
From:
Date:
Subject: Promotional Examination, Clerk-Typist

The promotional examination for Clerk-Typist will be given on Monday, February 3, 19_____, from 8:00 a.m. to 12:00 noon in Room 1238. Employees who plan to take the examination must register with the personnel office by 4:00 p.m., Friday, January 1.

No materials, including briefcases, handbags, etc., can be taken into the examination room. No one will be admitted to the examination room after 8:00 a.m. SHARP.

Study booklets are available in the personnel office.

MEMO WRITER TIPS

1. The first sentence should include what, when, and where specifics about the promotional examination.

2. Discuss any restrictions or special conditions in the second paragraph so employees come properly prepared on exam day.

3. Provide information about available study materials, etc.

PHRASING ALTERNATIVES

Paragraph 1

The examination for Occupational Health Nurse has been scheduled for Saturday, April 11, 19_____ . The exam will begin promptly at 9:00 a.m. and last until 1:00 p.m. To register, contact Marge Miller at ext. 410 no later than Wednesday, April 8.

Now is the time to register for the upcoming promotional exam for Supervisor I, Production. The test will be given on Monday, May 4, from 7:30 a.m.–10:30 a.m. You must sign up in the human resources office by April 22 if you plan to test.

Paragraph 2

You will be permitted to use pocket calculators and dictionaries during the exam, but no other articles, even handbags or briefcases, will be allowed in the testing room. Arrive by 7:30 a.m. or you will not be allowed to take the examination.

Plan to bring #2 pencils with you, but no other supplies can be brought into the examination rooms. Doors to the testing room will be locked at 8:55 a.m. If you do not arrive before then, you will not be permitted to test.

ANNOUNCING A SALES CONTEST

To:
From:
Date:
Subject: Sales Contest

Land five new accounts this month and win an all-expenses-paid vacation for two to Hawaii. The Hawaiian Feast Sales Contest begins today. The winner will be announced on Friday, May 13th.

Here are the contest rules:

- Accounts must be ones Landmark Enterprises has never handled before. Prospects you are currently working are okay.
- Each new account must place at least a $500.00 order by May 11.
- A completed "New Account Data Sheet" must be submitted to your Account Manager for each new account.

The lucky winner and his/her companion will fly to Hawaii for a three-day stay at the Honolulu Hilton on Maui. In addition, the winning go-getter will take along $500.00 spending money.

Go get those new accounts and get yourself a well-deserved vacation—on us. A real Hawaiian Feast is just five new accounts away.

MEMO WRITER TIPS

1. Describe what sales personnel have to do and what they can win in the first sentence. Use a sales pitch to get their attention right away.
2. Be sure to include a deadline so people know how long they have to achieve the goal.
3. Outline contest rules and/or restrictions.
4. Close the memo by offering additional details about the prize and a few motivational words.

PHRASING ALTERNATIVES

Paragraph 1

Sell $2,000 or more in products this month and win yourself a two-day stay at the Copper Junction Lodge. Our quarterly sales contest begins May 3 and runs through May 31.

The Peak Achiever Sales Contest starts next Monday and ends on November 20. All you have to do is generate 25 new leads and get at least one new account. Your prize . . . $150.00 in cash!

Paragraph 2

Contest rules are outlined below:

The easy-to-follow contest regulations are outlined below:

Paragraph 3

Getting new leads can now earn you a substantial cash award. Start making those phone calls now!

A few new sales will entitle you and your guest to an all-expenses-paid vacation valued at more than $500. Sell big! Win big!

CANCELLING AN APPOINTMENT

To:
From:
Date:
Subject: Appointment Cancellation

Unfortunately, I won't be able to keep our Friday, November 18 appointment for 3:00 p.m. The General Manager will be flying in from the coast, and we'll be touring each job site Friday afternoon.

I'll call you Monday and reschedule.

> **MEMO WRITER TIPS**
> 1. Put all pertinent facts in the first sentence: day, date, time.
> 2. Briefly explain why you're cancelling.
> 3. Say how, when, and whether you plan to reschedule.

PHRASING ALTERNATIVES

Paragraph 1

I'm sorry I'll have to cancel our 8 a.m. appointment on August 3. I'm really backlogged on the Hammerfield Project, so I'll have to reschedule.

Can we reschedule our April 14 appointment? When I made it, I didn't realize I had another appointment scheduled for the same day and time.

Paragraph 2

I'll have my secretary call and reschedule.

Let's plan it for later that same week. I'll call to set up another time.

COMMUNICATING SECTION GOALS*

To:
From:
Date:
Subject: Performance Goals For 1989

Provided below are suggested goals for the 1989 Performance Plan.

1. Develop and implement an accountability structure that clearly defines each senior manager's authority and responsibility in carrying out District goals and programs.
2. Implement employee selection and performance management programs that maximize the productivity of all employees in accomplishing district goals and programs.

---

*This memorandum was written by the Director of Administration of a metropolitan transportation district.

3. Develop a district-wide healthcare benefits cost containment program.
4. Develop an operational plan with timelines for implementing the Affirmative Action Plan.

MEMO WRITER TIPS

1. List the goals for your unit or section, beginning with the most ambitious goals.
2. Detail each in one to two sentences.

PHRASING ALTERNATIVES

Paragraph 1

Below are listed this year's goals for our department.

The 19____ goals for the Utilities Department are as follows:

The goals and objectives below describe the plans and undertakings I would like to see us achieve over the coming year.

DELEGATING ASSIGNMENTS

To:
From:
Date:
Subject: New Assignment: Great Falls Project

You've been selected to monitor work on the Great Falls Project. When a job needs to get done—and get done well—your name is one of the first to come to mind. Your skills will most assuredly make this project a successful one.

Plan to update me bi-weekly on the project's progress. If you have any questions about the file I've attached, let's meet next Wednesday to discuss specifics.

MEMO WRITER TIPS

1. "You've been selected" or "You have been chosen" lets your reader know he/she brings special talent to the new assignment. In the same sentence, name the project or new assignment.
2. Address what role you plan to play and how you plan to support their efforts.

PHRASING ALTERNATIVES

Paragraph 1

I'm turning over to you the follow-up on the job we did for Knowlton and Company. I know you'll make sure they're satisfied with our services.

Because you've had previous training experience, you have been chosen to provide orientation for the three new employees in our section.

Paragraph 2

Let me know when the job is complete. If you need anything from my office, just let me know.

Laura Brigham can provide you with technical support. I'll check back with you in a few weeks to see what progress you've made.

DISTRIBUTING THE ORGANIZATIONAL CHART TO NEW PERSONNEL

To:
From:
Date:
Subject: Organizational Chart

Your job is an important one and fits into our company as outlined on the attached organizational chart. Discuss problems, questions, suggestions, etc. with your immediate supervisor, Mr. Rand. When necessary, he'll communicate your concerns to upper management.

Welcome aboard!

MEMO WRITER TIPS

1. The organizational chart establishes "chain of command." Let your new employees know this, while welcoming them to the organization.

2. Spell out how problems should be addressed, and close on a positive note.

PHRASING ALTERNATIVES

Paragraph 1

Attached is a copy of the organizational chart for our agency. Your immediate supervisor is your link to management, as you are the link to subordinates under your direction. Use the chain of command outlined when you have problems or questions.

Here is the organizational chart for our operation. It will acquaint you with our structure and where you fit in the overall management hierarchy.

ENCOURAGING WORKERS TO MAKE CHARITABLE CONTRIBUTIONS*

To:
From:
Date:
Subject: United Way Campaign

The United Way is once again asking for our support. Let's give generously again this year. Our agency goal is $5,000, one thousand dollars more than last year's total contributions.

Return the attached card to the Personnel Department if you decide to contribute through payroll deduction. Give until it helps! Thank you for your continued support.

MEMO WRITER TIPS

1. Include a company or department goal as an incentive. Employees like feedback on where their money has gone.

2. Keep this memo short, as it is one employees are accustomed to receiving.

PHRASING ALTERNATIVES

Paragraph 1

Once again, it is time to give to those less fortunate than ourselves, through your tax-deductible donations to the United Way Campaign. The $23,000 you donated last year went to fund a variety of helpful projects in your community.

Please give—and give generously—to this year's Charitable Fund Campaign. We raised $1,700 last year and should be able to raise at least $2,000 this year.

---

*This memorandum was written by the Personnel Director of a community-based, job training program.

Paragraph 2

Completed payroll deduction cards should be returned to Employee Relations by March 31. Give whatever you can afford. Every little bit helps.

Payroll deduction forms will be included in next week's pay envelopes. Fill out your form and return it to Rhonda by April 1. Thank you for your donations to this worthy organization.

THANKS FOR CHARITABLE CONTRIBUTION

To:
From:
Date:
Subject: Thanks for a Charitable Contribution

Thanks to staff members like you, this year's Metro Charities Campaign was a phenomenal success. The company met its goal of $50,000 in contributions. Your contribution helped us achieve our objective. Metro Charities thanks you and so do I.

MEMO WRITER TIPS

1. Name the charitable organization.
2. Discuss total contributions, if appropriate.
3. Express your thanks to staff.

EXPLAINING AN ORDER DELAY TO SUBORDINATES

To:
From:
Date:
Subject: Order Delay

The piping ordered for the Valve Assembly Unit has not yet arrived. I checked with purchasing, and according to the supplier, the pipe should arrive by this Thursday. The supplier has been instructed to ship the supplies overnight delivery, since I know you can't begin reconstruction of the unit until this material arrives.

MEMO WRITER TIPS

1. Outline what order has been delayed and why.
2. Let the reader know when the shipment can be expected.

PHRASING ALTERNATIVES

Paragraph 1

The chip we need to complete the interface of our new telephone system will arrive by 5:30 p.m. tomorrow. In the interim, we are limited to receiving incoming calls on the main switchboard number (333-3333). Advise all your clients to use this number until further notice.

The drill bit you need is not in stock at Abrams Company. I am checking with other vendors to find the part and will deliver it to you as soon as it comes in.

The test kits you ordered on 2/6 are on back-order. In order to have enough kits for this week, I am issuing a purchase requisition today so we can get kits from a local supplier. This supplier has promised delivery by Monday.

EXPLAINING HOW TO COMPLETE ELECTRONIC TIME CARDS

To:
From:
Date:
Subject: Procedure for Electronic Time Cards

When you report for work, insert your passcard in the electronic time clock below the red arrow in the center of the machine. You will hear a "beep" when your passcard has been inserted correctly.

When you leave work, follow the same procedure. Your time will be computed electronically for pay purposes. Since this is the official record of your time worked, it is critical that you remember to check in and check out each day. Failure to do so will result in lost pay.

Under no circumstances should you check in or out for other employees. Both parties will have their pay docked in this event.

If you have questions about electronic time-card information, contact the personnel office immediately.

MEMO WRITER TIPS

1. List the steps sequentially.
2. Discuss how discrepancies are resolved.
3. Stress the importance of following the procedure.

FILLING TIME CARDS/SHEETS OUT CORRECTLY

To:
From:
Date:
Subject: Time Cards

Please fill out your time cards as follows:

1. Write in your employee number.
2. Record the number of hours you work each day.
3. Total your hours for the week at the bottom of the card.
4. Sign and date the card at the bottom.
5. Place completed time cards in the box marked "payroll" next to the time clock.

A sample time card is attached.

Completing time cards properly saves us time and reduces the chances for errors in calculating your paychecks.

MEMO WRITER TIPS

1. List the steps involved in completing the time card or sheet.
2. Attach a sample so employees can see how to fill the cards out correctly.

PHRASING ALTERNATIVES

Paragraph 1

Time sheets should be filled out according to the following procedure:

If you fill out your time cards as outlined on the attached sample, we can eliminate many of the payroll errors we have had recently.

GETTING A JUMP ON THE OFFICE RUMOR MILL

To:
From:
Date:
Subject: Rumor Control

The rumor mill has been at it again. There is no truth—I REPEAT, NO TRUTH—to the rumor that the impending merger may shut down this plant.

I have asked section supervisors to schedule meetings with their teams, to discuss what, when, how, and why this merger will affect each of you. Write down any questions you have, and come to your meeting prepared to get the facts.

MEMO WRITER TIPS

1. Acknowledge that rumor mills do exist, but do so in a light, non-threatening tone.

2. Dispel the inaccurate information and present the facts, or detail what arrangements have been made to communicate the facts.

3. Don't belabor the point or alienate subordinates by scolding them for using (or abusing) one of the oldest forms of communication known to organizations.

PHRASING ALTERNATIVES

Paragraph 1

I am writing this memo to present you with factual information about our "rumored" move to the Minneapolis area.

This memorandum, contrary to what the "rumor mill" may say, will outline the details of the new classification study results.

GETTING EQUIPMENT INVENTORIED

To:
From:
Date:
Subject: Equipment Inventory

Please inventory all office equipment in your department by 5:00 p.m., Friday, January 15. Provide the following information for each piece of equipment (see note below) in your section:

- Year purchased
- Type
- Model number
- Serial number
- Condition (excellent, satisfactory, defective)

Your input will help us determine next year's equipment needs more accurately. Thanks for your help.

OFFICE EQUIPMENT: typewriters, word processors, computers, monitors, printers, adding machines, calculators, desks, chairs, file cabinets, bookcases.

MEMO WRITER TIPS

1. Be specific about the type of equipment to be inventoried and the date the inventory is to be completed.
2. Define what you mean by "equipment."
3. Tell your reader why the inventory is necessary.
4. Provide your reader with an inventory form, whenever possible.

PHRASING ALTERNATIVES

Paragraph 1

Conduct an inventory of all repair tools in your area and return the results to me by Friday, June 10.

This year's equipment inventory will begin on June 15. Someone from the facilities department will be visiting your work area during that week.

Paragraph 2

Thanks for helping me get an accurate count of our machinery.

Your cooperation in preparing your inventory report is appreciated.

GETTING EQUIPMENT REPAIRED

To:
From:
Date:
Subject: Equipment Repair

The micrometer in Engineering Lab #3 needs repairs. Please send someone to repair this equipment today.
Thanks.

MEMO WRITER TIPS

1. Explain what kind of equipment is in need of repairs and, if possible, what kind of repairs you believe are needed.
2. Let the reader know when you would like to have the repairs completed.

PHRASING ALTERNATIVES

Paragraph 1

Our microfilm reader (Serial #S-19844) is on the blink. Could you send someone to repair it as soon as possible?

Please have someone in maintenance take a look at the printer on Barb Walters's desk. For some reason, it's not printing properly. Thank you.

Repairs are needed on the Novak bookkeeping machine in my office. Please have someone look at it today. We're right in the middle of a billing cycle and need the machine fixed ASAP.

GETTING SUBORDINATES TO COMPLETE REQUIRED FORMS

To:
From:
Date:
Subject: Expense Voucher Form

You submitted your receipts for your Dallas trip (3/14) but failed to complete the necessary Expense Voucher Form. Your request for reimbursement cannot be completed until you have done so.

Please complete the form (sample and blank form attached) and return it to my office in order to expedite your claim.

Thank you.

Attachments

MEMO WRITER TIPS

1. Tell the employee what form needs to be completed and explain why this is necessary.

2. Attach a sample of how the form should be filled out, if necessary.

3. If a deadline is involved, let the employee know when the completed form is due and to whom the form should be returned.

PHRASING ALTERNATIVES

Paragraph 1

Please complete Form #99-1 (petty cash reimbursement) and return it to my office no later than Friday. Checks will be cut on this date, and your request cannot be processed until the form has been completed.

Your healthcare benefits claim will be submitted as soon as you have submitted a copy of Form 303 (attached). Claims cannot be processed without this form.

Forms are "necessary evils." I need a completed W-4 form in order to include your hours on the 9/14 payroll run. Please complete the form and return it to Room 204 by noon tomorrow.

HANDLING A SUBORDINATE WHO DISAGREES WITH A DECISION

To:
From:
Date:
Subject: Implementing the Cane Decision

In follow-up to our meeting today, I know you weren't quite satisfied with the decision I made to have both you and Jean make the Cane presentation. Be assured that I made this decision because you have the accounting expertise, while Jean has excellent presentation skills and is also familiar with the ins and outs of the medical research industry.

Together, I thought the two of you would make a much more convincing presentation than either of you would alone. Though you don't agree with my decision, I know you'll do everything you can to get this account.

MEMO WRITER TIPS

1. Acknowledge that the subordinate does not agree with the decision you have made.

2. Briefly explain why you made the decision and close by disclosing your confidence in the fact that the employee will carry out the decision even though he/she does not agree with it.

PHRASING ALTERNATIVES

Paragraph 1

Even though you disagree with the construction estimates I presented today, I'm certain my figures will prove to be correct in the long run. Instead of dwelling on who's right, let's just get the job done. If you turn out to be right, I'll be the first to admit it.

You've been assigned to head the audit review team, in spite of your objections. You have the experience to conduct this audit, and I'm confident you'll lead the team without any major problems. Thanks for carrying out this responsibility even though you don't like doing so.

Moving Harry Stern to the marketing group just makes sense at this time. I heard your objections and took them into consideration, but trust me, I have a better overall picture of the operations than you do and am sure this is the best move under the circumstances.

Paragraph 2

Work with me on this. The entire department will benefit in the long run.

I know you're professional enough to implement a decision, even one you don't agree with. Feel free to tell me, "I told you so" if you're proven right in the future.

I think Harry Stern's the best applicant for the position. Though you don't agree, I hope you'll support me in my choice and make Harry's transition to this department as smooth as possible.

HANDLING A SAFETY VIOLATION

To:
From:
Date:
Subject: Safety Standards

Welders must always wear safety goggles while operating their torches. While I was on the floor yesterday, I noticed two operators working without protective eye covering.

Safety standards may seem unnecessary, since all of you are experienced workers. But, believe me, standards have been designed for YOUR protection. Let's continue to do a quality job, but let's do it safely.

MEMO WRITER TIPS

1. Point out which safety rule has been violated.

2. Including information about how you came to know about the violation gives your reminder more "teeth," but avoid phrases like, "It has come to my attention."

3. Threatening employees is not likely to get the results you want. This memo should sound as though you're confident they'll comply.

PHRASING ALTERNATIVES

Paragraph 1

Protective shoe covers must be worn at all times on the processing floor. I had to remind three handlers to wear this safety gear yesterday.

Bulk mail bins should be pushed, never lifted. This will prevent back and leg injuries.

Paragraph 2

Safety standards protect you. Please follow them carefully.

Adhere to safety procedures at all times. Failure to do so may result in lost time and lost wages.

INSPIRING WORK ON AN URGENT PROJECT

To:
From:
Date:
Subject: Rushhhhhhhh Project

Sorry to "put you under the gun" again, but I need the figures on the Amorti account within the next two days. Without them, we may not be able to hang on to their account.

You always manage to come through in the clinches, and I'm counting on you to do it again. If you need someone to cover your own accounts till this project's completed, let me know right away.

MEMO WRITER TIPS

1. Say what you need and when you need it, but acknowledge that you're asking for extra effort.

2. Explain why you need the work in a hurry. People often work more quickly when they fully understand the ramifications of failing to do so.

3. Offer assistance IF you are able to provide it.

PHRASING ALTERNATIVES

Paragraph 1

I would appreciate it greatly if you could rush the review of the merchant files and get them to me by tomorrow noon.

Would you please process the film marked "urgent" right away. I know you're already behind in your work, but I need these photos to show to the client at our morning meeting.

Paragraph 2

You can always be counted on to work quickly and efficiently. Thanks for your help once again.

Thank you for lending your assistance in this crisis. You are a real asset to this department.

ITEMS IN SHORT SUPPLY

To:
From:
Date:
Subject: Supply Shortage

We're quickly depleting our supply of form-fed computer paper. What we have must last through the end of the month. I'll have to ration the available supply until our order comes in.

Please take only what you need. We should have new stock no later than February 20.

MEMO WRITER TIPS

1. Let employees know what item is in short supply and when new supplies can be expected.
2. Tell them what procedure you'd like them to follow with existing supplies.

PHRASING ALTERNATIVES

Paragraph 1

I'll be dispensing the last of the computer diskettes we currently have available this week. If you need diskettes, pick them up in my office. New ones should arrive within 10 days.

Our stock of legal pads is just about gone. Holly will be distributing what we have left, and when those are gone, we'll just have to "make do" until our new order comes in, some time around the first of the year.

I've completely run out of Form J-221s. Do you have any extras you could spare until the printing office releases its new edition?

MAKING A HIRING
RECOMMENDATION TO PERSONNEL

To:
From:
Date:
Subject: Hiring Recommendation

Margaret O'Bannion is my choice for the Marketing Representative position. While the other applicants are qualified, Margaret has the mobile telephone sales experience I think this position requires.

   Since we need this person yesterday, I hope you'll be able to speed up the process so Margaret can start by Monday, July 15. Thanks for all your help. You guys did a super job.

MEMO WRITER TIPS

1. State who you'd recommend for what position.

2. If possible, be definitive about why you chose this candidate over other applicants. In the event one of the other applicants questions your decision, this memorandum may be used to document your choice.

3. Say when you'd like the applicant to start.

4. Build bridges with your personnel department by thanking them for the work they've done.

PHRASING ALTERNATIVES

Paragraph 1

   I recommend we hire Mr. Lance Smith for the equipment operator position. He has five more years of experience than either of the other two applicants.

   Please notify Ms. Helen Craft that she has been selected to fill the scheduler position in our department. Her previous background in conference planning made her the obvious choice for this job.

Paragraph 2

   I'd like her to begin work by July 31. Thank you for your assistance.

   See if he can begin work on September 3rd. I'd like him to begin then so he can train with Dirk for at least two weeks.

MOVING THE OFFICE OR SECTION

To:
From:
Date:
Subject: Office Move

Your section will be moved to Suite 406 over the weekend. Please meet with your employees and complete the attached floorplan. Leave it with my secretary before you leave on Friday.

Have employees label their boxes, furniture and equipment with the stickers provided by the movers. Sketch how furniture should be arranged on the floorplan; correspond numbers on the sketch with those you've affixed to the furniture.

By working together, we can make this move as painless as possible. I'm sure you'll enjoy your new space.

MEMO WRITER TIPS

1. Tell when the move is to take place.

2. Describe the procedure employees should use to identify furniture and equipment.

3. Since people generally become territorial about their workspace, reassure them that the move will go smoothly and be beneficial.

PHRASING ALTERNATIVES

Paragraph 1

You will be moved to Room 304 on Monday, as planned. Facilities staff will move your equipment. Let them know where you want items placed in your new office.

All offices will be moved to Troy Towers, 18th and Grant Streets. The move will begin on Monday, September 14, and everyone should be in the new building by September 21.

Paragraph 2

Label your equipment with the stickers provided by the movers. Your supervisor will show you a diagram of the new floorplan.

Packers will label and pack material on Friday. The move should be complete by the time you arrive for work on Monday morning.

Paragraph 3

The new facilities are attractive and spacious. You'll be very comfortable there, I'm sure.

You'll begin a new week in new surroundings. Your efforts can help make this move a smooth, pleasant one.

PARKING IN ASSIGNED SPACES

To:
From:
Date:
Subject: Assigned Parking Spaces

People, park in your assigned spaces. Beginning Monday, the license plate numbers of cars in unassigned spaces will be written down. Owners will be asked to leave work, move their cars, and make up the time involved.

We went to great lengths to mark and assign parking spaces so we could avoid these problems. Please extend the courtesy to your fellow employees of parking your car in its designated space. Thank you.

MEMO WRITER TIPS

1. Get right to the point. Employees know they are breaking the rules, so they're probably just waiting for you to take action.
2. Be clear about what the consequences of their actions will be, and then follow through.

PHRASING ALTERNATIVES

Paragraph 1

Please park your vehicle in the space assigned to you. Ample parking exists if everyone uses his/her designated parking area.

Visitor parking spaces are reserved for guests of the company. Do not park your vehicle in these spaces.

Vehicles parked in Drexel Industries reserved spaces will be ticketed and towed. Park your car in the spaces designated for Judson, Inc.

Paragraph 2

Please respect the rights of your co-workers by parking in your assigned space.

Violators will lose their reserved parking spaces and be asked to park in the all-purpose lot.

RELAYING INFORMATION ABOUT SALES PROSPECTS

To:
From:
Date:
Subject: Sales Prospects

Add the following names to your prospect list:

1. Allied Precast, Inc. Contact Jake Dewitt 333-4456
2. Continental Forms Co. Contact Angela MacFarlane, 448-3178
3. Universal Preforms, Inc. Contact Leonard Atwood, 758-1098
4. Macallister Concrete, Inc. Contact Florence Jones, 777-8889

Allied and Macallister are interested in delivered pre-mix concrete at prices less than $6.95 per square foot. Continental and Universal want forms. They're satisfied with their current supplier, but you may be able to sway them because the supplier has been late on several key deliveries.

All these firms are in the process of bidding on major projects, so a call this week would be right on target.

MEMO WRITER TIPS

1. List the prospects by company, contact name and phone number.

2. Include information about any special requirements or tips that will make a sale more likely.

PHRASING ALTERNATIVES

Paragraph 1

I thought you might be interested in this list of sales prospects:

Here are some sales prospects for your files:

REQUESTING ADDITIONAL PERSONNEL—PERMANENT

To:
From:
Date:
Subject: Request for Permanent New-Hire

Request you initiate hiring of one full-time order-filler for my department. I need the person by the end of the month but will take the help whenever I can get a qualified person on board.

Use the job description I gave you for the last person we hired. Thanks.

MEMO WRITER TIPS

1. Let the person who will be doing the hiring know what category of employee you want to hire.
2. Provide a job description, if one is not already on file.
3. Let them know when you would like the new-hire to begin work.

PHRASING ALTERNATIVES

Paragraph 1

Please begin search and screen procedures for a Clerk-Typist II in the Contracting Division. I need someone yesterday but will take a qualified applicant as soon as you can find one.

I need a permanent, full-time licensed practical nurse in urology. A job description should be on file in your office. I need the person by September 12.

Could you advertise and screen for a printing press operator for my department as soon as possible? John Lee will be leaving at the end of the month, and with the backlog of work we currently have, I need someone right away.

REQUESTING ADDITIONAL HELP—
SHORT TERM

To:
From:
Date:
Subject: Seasonal Help Request

I will need three (3) additional gift-wrap clerks during the holiday season, November 30 to December 31, 19_____. Please advertise for the positions, forward a list of qualified applicants to me, and I will interview as soon as you can get some names to me.

Thanks for your help.

MEMO WRITER TIPS

1. Say what kind of help is needed and for how long.
2. Briefly explain why you need the additional short-term help.
3. Close by thanking the reader for his/her assistance.

PHRASING ALTERNATIVES

Paragraph 1

Please begin hiring for a six-month contract for a Nurse Practitioner for my office. Judy will be taking a six-month leave of absence, and I'll need someone as soon as possible to replace her. Judy's last day of work is April 12, and I'd like to get someone at least two weeks before then, so the new person can be properly trained.

The warehouse operation will need two (2) forklift operators for the period 4/6–6/30. This will help me complete inventory and close out the books for the end of the year. Whatever help you can give in getting these people on as soon as possible will be appreciated.

Contact a temporary agency and find a clerk-typist for the drafting department as soon as possible, but no later than May 11. I need someone to prepare invoices and do other clerical duties so we can process our standing orders. Thanks.

REQUESTING EQUIPMENT

To:
From:
Date:
Subject: Equipment Request

Please send a portable ventilator to the nurses' station, 3rd floor, by the start of the 3 p.m.–11 p.m. shift.

    Thanks for your assistance.

MEMO WRITER TIPS

1. Specify what equipment is needed and by when.
2. Thank the reader for his/her cooperation.

PHRASING ALTERNATIVES

Paragraph 1

    Housekeeping needs a floor buffer for this evening's crew. Please deliver it to the storage room, 4th floor, by 5:00 p.m. Thanks.

    Could you deliver a memory typewriter to the customer relations department by 9:00 a.m. tomorrow? We have a new typist starting and need this equipment so he'll have something to work with.

    Equipment is needed in Room 304, Section 4. Our x-ray machine went out on last night's shift, and we need a replacement.

REQUESTING EXPENDABLE SUPPLIES

To:
From:
Date:
Subject: Supply Request

The Legal Department needs the following supplies by Thursday, May 9, 19____:

1. 10 reams 8½″ × 11″ bond paper, white
2. 6 boxes #2 pencils

3. 3 boxes felt-tip pens, black ink, fine
4. 6 packages 8½″ × 14″ ruled legal pads

Charge the supplies to cost center number 23459-4456. Thank you.

MEMO WRITER TIPS

1. Let the supply department know which department needs the supplies by when. Your "as soon as possible," may be different from theirs.

2. List the supplies. Include quantity and a description of the items. Lists are easier to read and will often prompt speedier results.

PHRASING ALTERNATIVES

Paragraph 1

Please deliver the following expendables to data processing by Friday, June 4:

I need the supplies listed below by October 14. Thanks.

REQUESTING INFORMATION FOR THE SECOND TIME

To:
From:
Date:
Subject: Second Request

This is my second request for your quarterly report, originally due last Friday. Please make sure you get the report to me by Friday, May 12, 19_____ . The quarterly sales figures cannot be computed without your input.

If you cannot meet this deadline, call me today.

MEMO WRITER TIPS

1. Notice the word "I" is conspicuously absent from this memorandum. This helps to shift the responsibility from the writer to the worker whose information is late.

2. The memo explains why the figures are needed and opens the way for the writer to make the reasons for delay known.

PHRASING ALTERNATIVES

Paragraph 1

Please send the inventory list—due last Thursday—to me no later than 5:00 p.m. tomorrow. The final inventory cannot be completed until your list is in.

This is the second time you've been asked for the draft of the Comtex User Manual. Make sure you get it to me by this afternoon.

Paragraph 2

Call me if you feel you cannot comply with this second request.

Let me know when you can provide information.

REQUESTING TIME SHEETS*

To:
From:
Date:
Subject: Time Sheets

Time sheets for the period ending April 15 must reach the payroll office by April 18, 12:00 noon. Any time sheets received after this deadline will not be processed for the April 30 payroll run.

MEMO WRITER TIPS

1. State the period ending date for time sheets.
2. Tell when the time sheets must be delivered to the payroll office and what the consequences will be if they are not.

PHRASING ALTERNATIVES

Paragraph 1

I need all time sheets for part-time employees no later than 8:00 a.m. Friday, August 1 for processing. Please forward your time sheets to my office by then.

---

*This memorandum was written by a payroll clerk for a construction company.

Checks for November 30 will be run on November 21. All time sheets must be in my office by then. If they are not, employees will not receive payment for that pay period until the next payroll period.

Please remind your employees that their time sheets need to be completed and returned to my office by Friday, June 3. Time sheets received after this date will be processed for the June 30 paycheck.

REQUESTING TECHNICAL ASSISTANCE

To:
From:
Date:
Subject: Technical Assistance Request

Word processors need additional Wordspeak software training. While the tutorials provide the basics, training targeted at our specific functions is required.

The following companies can provide the training we need:

Vendor	Hours	Cost
Acme Computer Training	40 hours	$195/participant
Compuworld	40 hours	$175/participant
Universal Software	60 hours	$295/participant
Avon Community College	80 hours	$125/participant

I suggest we contract with Avon Community College because they are the only vendor who agreed to tailor training to our specific needs. Training could begin within 30 days, and the total cost would include training development costs.

Could I have your decision by Friday, December 18? The new equipment, though installed, cannot yield maximum results until we provide adequate training for our personnel.

MEMO WRITER TIPS

1. Tell who needs what kind of technical assistance.

2. Explain why technical assistance is needed.

3. To make the decision easier, do background work on potential vendors and costs, if appropriate.

4. Finally, suggest a possible vendor and explain why this company can supply the technical assistance you need, if necessary.

PHRASING ALTERNATIVES

Paragraph 1

Could your department provide me with technical assistance on getting our computers up and running?

Your technical expertise is needed as we reinstall the ceiling wires in the new wing.

Paragraph 2

Though we received basic training from the manufacturer, there are still a number of features we do not understand how to operate. I have surveyed the operators in my section, and a list of the features they need help with is attached.

None of our installers is certified to rig the wires according to code. The last time we attempted to install them, all our work had to be torn out when the building inspectors found code violations.

Paragraph 3

Let me know when you could provide us with technical assistance, how long you think it would take, and how much it would cost. If you cannot help right now, please send me the name of a contractor whose work you trust.

Your help would really come in handy. Any labor costs would, of course, be paid out of our departmental budget.

RESCHEDULING AN APPOINTMENT

To:
From:
Date:
Subject: Rescheduling Our Appointment

Can we reschedule our Thursday appointment for Friday at 2:00 p.m.? The regional manager will be in the area on Thursday and wants me to meet him at our Flora Park store.

In this instance, no news is good news. If this time isn't convenient for you, call my secretary and we'll see what else we can work out.

> **MEMO WRITER TIPS**
>
> 1. Mention both the current meeting day and the day and time you'd like to meet. Phrasing your request as a question will probably net you a response right away.
>
> 2. Explain why you must reschedule the appointment.
>
> 3. Give the reader information about what action to take if the appointment can't be rescheduled.

PHRASING ALTERNATIVES

Paragraph 1

I would like to reschedule our Tuesday appointment (8:00 a.m.) for Wednesday at the same time. My return flight from Boston won't arrive until Tuesday at 6:00 p.m.

Paragraph 2

Let me know if this time is not convenient.

RESPONDING TO AN EMPLOYEE'S SUGGESTION

To:
From:
Date:
Subject: Suggestion

Your suggestion for revamping the check processing procedure could, potentially, save the company considerable time and money. After the review committee has studied your suggestions carefully, I will let you know whether, how, and when your suggestion can be implemented. You will be contacted if the committee has additional questions.

Thank you for taking the time to suggest this new procedure. Efforts that go above and beyond your work requirements are always appreciated. Expect to hear from me within the next two weeks.

MEMO WRITER TIPS

1. Make sure you respond to employee suggestions within two to three days.
2. Outline what will be done with the suggestion.
3. Thank the employee for submitting the suggestion.
4. Let the employee know when he/she can expect a reply. This way, you can avoid unnecessary phone calls, and the employee won't wonder about the status of his/her suggestion for weeks.

PHRASING ALTERNATIVES

Paragraph 1

Thank you for suggesting a new method for logging incoming mail. When I've had a chance to study your recommendations and talk to other mailroom personnel, I'll let you know whether your system will be implemented.

Employee suggestions are always welcome. The ideas you have for streamlining our credit analysis methods will be studied closely.

Paragraph 2

I should make a final decision within the next 30 days.

You will be notified about the results of this study within 14 days.

RESPONDING TO A VERBAL/ TELEPHONE INQUIRY

To:
From:
Date:
Subject: Telephone Inquiry

As we discussed this morning, the figures for the Coscow Account are attached. If you need additional calculations, let me know.

Attachment

MEMO WRITER TIPS

1. Review what was discussed in the verbal or telephone conversation.
2. Provide the reader with the information that was requested.

PHRASING ALTERNATIVES

Paragraph 1

In follow-up to your questions, the budget for the Heathfaire Construction project is $1.3 million dollars. So far, construction costs are well under budget, and the job is proceeding on schedule.

Attached is the information you requested last week. If you need anything else, just let me know.

The relocation is scheduled for March 8. I wasn't sure of the date when we spoke this morning. If I can help in any way, don't hesitate to let me know.

REVAMPING A FAULTY DECISION

To:
From:
Date:
Subject: Correction

Hindsight is always 20-20. Therefore, I am changing the implementation date of the new billing procedure to September 1. We simply don't have enough time to provide all employees with adequate training, and your objections pointed this out to me.

I think this new date will allow us to introduce the new system more efficiently and avoid costly errors.

MEMO WRITER TIPS

1. Admit that an error was made and state what it was.
2. Tell what the change in decision will be and when the change is to take place.

PHRASING ALTERNATIVES

Paragraph 1

Okay, I made a mistake. I thought two people could process incoming insurance claims just as quickly as three, but I see that I was wrong. Go ahead and hire a new claims clerk.

The new tracking procedure I initiated last month was obviously done without thorough study of the results. Therefore, I am asking you to adopt the old procedure until the "bugs" can be ironed out of the new system. Thanks.

Hotel customers are complaining about the new room-service hours of operation, just as you said they would. Let's institute the old hours until further notice.

SENDING F.Y.I. (FOR YOUR INFORMATION) MEMOS*

To:
From:
Date:
Subject: F.Y.I.

Attached is a copy of the proposed training schedule for employees in your branch, for your information. If you have questions, let me know.

Attachment

MEMO WRITER TIPS

1. This a brief memo used to cover some attachment or information you'd like the reader to have.

2. Let the reader know what the information is and where additional details can be obtained, if necessary.

PHRASING ALTERNATIVES

Paragraph 1

Here's something F.Y.I. Let me know what you think about it.

For your information, the following statistics outline the costs we've projected on your latest project.

Picked this up at the annual convention. Thought you'd be interested.

---

*This memorandum was written by a clerk-typist in the training section of a governmental agency.

SOLICITING EMPLOYEE SUGGESTIONS

To:
From:
Date:
Subject: Employee Suggestions

All employees are asked to provide me with suggestions about which computer system will best meet our graphics needs. Drop whatever suggestions you have in the suggestion box or send me a note outlining your recommendations.

I'll need your input no later than Friday, January 21. Thanks.

MEMO WRITER TIPS

1. Tell employees what suggestions you would like and what you intend to do with this information.
2. Let them know when the suggestions are needed.

PHRASING ALTERNATIVES

Paragraph 1

A suggestion box has been placed in the cafeteria. Any recommendations you have for saving money or improving operations will be greatly appreciated.

I need your input about the purchase of the new standardized processing equipment. Get your suggestions to me by next Friday, before we initiate purchase. Thanks.

Your suggestions regarding the qualifications for the new banquet sales manager are needed. Hall Franklin in Sales and Marketing would like to get your input before the position is announced. We've had problems in the past and think you can provide valuable input to keep us from making the same mistakes again.

SURVIVING A HIRING FREEZE

To:
From:
Date:
Subject: Hiring Freeze

A year-end deficit prevents us from hiring any new personnel until next fiscal year. This will pose a major challenge for many departments, especially those for whom additional positions had been budgeted.

Thank you for continuing to produce quality work, in spite of this temporary personnel shortage. Our difficulties should ease when new funds become available July 1. Until then, know your extra effort has not gone unnoticed.

MEMO WRITER TIPS

1. Announce the hiring freeze, give a brief explanation for it, and indicate when it might be lifted.

2. Acknowledge the fact that this poses an additional burden on personnel, but call it a challenge (to be overcome), rather than a problem (one that can't currently be solved).

3. Use the body of the memorandum to "stroke" employees for holding up under trying conditions.

4. The use of "we" and "our" make the hiring freeze a joint challenge, rather than the isolated problem "I" or "you" would connote.

5. Close on a positive note.

PHRASING ALTERNATIVES

Paragraph 1

Until further notice, no new personnel can be hired to fill existing vacancies. Actual revenues did not match projections.

A hiring freeze is necessary until the reorganization of management ranks has been completed.

Paragraph 2

Your quality work is appreciated. I'm certain it will help us get through the next two months.

I am as disappointed as you that this action had to be taken, but until additional funds are available, we will have to maintain current levels of production with existing personnel.

THANKING ANOTHER DEPARTMENT

To:
From:
Date:
Subject: Thanks for Your Cooperation

We could never have gotten the newsletter out on time without your assistance. Thank you for all the hard work you put in on it. If we can ever return the favor, just let us know.

MEMO WRITER TIPS

1. Let the other department know what they did that you appreciate.
2. Thank them for their help and offer future assistance, should they need it.

PHRASING ALTERNATIVES

Paragraph 1

Thanks so much for helping us fill our vacancy ahead of schedule. If I can ever return the favor, just let me know.

Please extend my sincere thanks to each member of your department for the overtime they put in to close out this fiscal year. We could not have finished our work on time without your help.

I thank you for loaning us your van for transportation to last weekend's conference. Your help enabled me to get our staff there on time. Just let me know when I can return the favor.

TOO MUCH WORK,
TOO FEW WORKERS

To:
From:
Date:
Subject: Personnel Shortage

Because of my backlog of work and shortage of personnel, I will not be able to prepare the report you requested before August 1. By then, I should have additional personnel on board and should have our end-of-year work completed.

Thanks for your patience during this shortage.

MEMO WRITER TIPS

1. Spell out specifically who/what is short and how this shortage will affect production.
2. Let the reader know when circumstances should improve.

PHRASING ALTERNATIVES

Paragraph 1

All the claim agents in my section have been working 10-hour days for the past three weeks. In spite of this, we have been unable to clear out our backlog of claims. We will continue to work overtime until all claims have been processed and hope to have this accomplished by October 1.

A 35 percent increase in orders and a shortage of personnel have resulted in a 7-day delay in filling requests. My people are working as hard as they can, but until we get additional help, our 3-day order cycle will be delayed.

THE TRANSMITTAL MEMORANDUM

To:
From:
Date:
Subject: Cost Accounting Projections

Attached for your information are the projections you requested on the Nash Consulting Job (#458). If you need additional information, just let me know.

Attachment

MEMO WRITER TIPS

1. The transmittal memorandum is a cover memorandum used to send reports, data, computer printouts, and other information.

2. The purpose of the transmittal memorandum is to briefly let the reader know what information is attached.

PHRASING ALTERNATIVES

Paragraph 1

Recommendations for improving the process we use to maintain quality control operations is attached. Please review them and return them to my office within two weeks. Thanks for your input.

I am sending you copies of the Overton file, as you requested. This file will document the transactions we have already had with Overton and should provide you with the information you need to determine whether or not we should continue doing business with them.

The following documents are enclosed, as per your request:

1. A list of qualified applicants.
2. A copy of the job announcement.
3. Proposed interview questions.
4. Names of others who might serve on the interview panel.

Call me if you need other information.

UPDATING SUBORDINATES

To:
From:
Date:
Subject: Update—Teller Interviews

I have screened 54 applications for the teller trainee position. Eight candidates will be interviewed on Wednesday, November 4.

After these interviews, the two best candidates will be selected, and I'm hoping we can hire these people by November 15.

Thanks for covering during this personnel shortage.

MEMO WRITER TIPS

1. Let employees know what you're updating them about in the first sentence.
2. Detail what progress has been made.
3. If there are a number of details, list or bullet each.

PHRASING ALTERNATIVES

Paragraph 1

I wanted to update you on the progress that's been made so far about our upcoming move to new offices.

Contract negotiations have been taking place for the past two weeks, and I wanted to let you know what progress has been made so far.

I've been reviewing the suggestions you made for making your work area safer, and I'd like to update you on the status of your requests.

Paragraph 2

The lease for our new offices should be signed by Friday of this week. The offices will have to be remodeled slightly to meet our needs. We'll probably be moving during the week of October 3.

Concessions have been made on the hourly rate. The union wants an eight percent increase, and management has agreed to a four percent increase.

So far, these steps have been taken:

- A safety captain has been appointed for your area.
- Equipment has been rearranged.
- Safety goggles have been ordered for all personnel.

I am still working with several of you to develop safety presentations for all workers in the unit.

WELCOMING A NEW EMPLOYEE*

To:
From:
Date:
Subject: Personnel Announcement

Atworth Development Corporation is pleased to announce that effective July 15, 1989, Mr. Conté Perez has joined the corporation as Manager of Finance. In his new position, Mr. Perez will be responsible for the analysis and coordination of all financial affairs of the corporation.

Mr. Perez is a graduate of the Horton School of Business and, most recently, was a consultant for Peter Rubloff and Associates.

Please join us in welcoming Conté to our staff.

MEMO WRITER TIPS

1. Announce when the new employee will begin.
2. Give the new employee's job title and briefly describe what his/her duties will be.
3. Include a one-sentence description of the new employee's past work experience.
4. Invite the members of the organization to welcome the new employee to the staff.

---

*This memorandum was written by the Vice President of Finance of an educational corporation.

PHRASING ALTERNATIVES

Paragraph 1

I am happy to announce the appointment of Harriet Larson to the position of Senior Consultant. Ms. Larson will begin work with the company on February 1. She will oversee the work of consultants.

Please welcome our newest employee, George Havier. Mr. Havier will begin work on Monday, July 5 and will supervise our collections department.

Our new telemarketing representative will begin work on March 22. Hazel Reed, with more than 10 years of telemarketing experience, will make a fine addition to our staff, I'm sure.

Paragraph 2

George comes to us from Knowles, Hamblin and Associates, one of the premier accounting firms in the city.

Ms. Larson has a B.A. from DeWitt University and a M.S. in Information Management from Brighton College. With 15 years of expertise in this area, I know she'll bring a vast wealth of expertise to our company.

Hazel was recently promoted and is being transferred from the Houston office. There, she supervised a staff of 55 and received last year's Outstanding Employee award.

Paragraph 3

Welcome, Hazel.

Take a moment to meet Mr. Larson and welcome him to our office.

I know you'll make George feel right at home.

WRITING A MEMORANDUM FOR RECORD*

To:
From:
Date:
Subject: Memorandum for Record

Gene Callis, my supervisor, called me in to his office today at 8:15 a.m. He told me he was "writing me up" for being five minutes late to work this morning.

---

*This memorandum was written by a Contract Specialist for the federal government.

When I asked about the five-minute "grace period," he said, "This is the second time you've been late in the last two weeks, so the grace period doesn't apply to you." When I asked him why other members of the department had been more than five minutes late, but had not been written up, he said, "Don't worry about them; just worry about getting yourself here on time."

I signed the counseling statement and left his office, but I told him, "I'm signing this but I don't agree with it."

MEMO WRITER TIPS

1. Memoranda for record are used to document conversations or situations that occur in your workplace, situations you don't want to forget.

2. When you want to document the specifics of a conversation, be sure to write a memorandum for record. You may think you'll remember what happened, but you will not be able to remember details weeks or months after the incident has occurred.

3. Write this memorandum as soon after the incident occurs as possible.

4. Write specific details of what happened and use quotation marks to indicate the exact words spoken by the parties involved.

5. Your memorandum for record becomes a permanent record of information you may need at a later date.

2

Model Memos about Salary, Benefits, and Compensation

Personnel costs probably consume the greatest portion of your budget. Writing about salary, benefits, and compensation, therefore, consumes a significant amount of your time. New employees must be told what salary and benefits they have. Other employees will want to know about the latest tax shelters and annuity plans. Personnel about to retire will need information about what their retirement options will be.

The model memoranda in this chapter tell workers what you want them to know about:

- Medical and dental coverage
- Insurance plans
- Vacation leave
- Sick leave
- Compensatory and overtime pay
- Salary increases
- Holiday pay
- Pension plans
- Changes in benefit options
- Leased vehicles

Use these memoranda to say "yes" or to say "no." You can approve a leave request or deny it; approve a raise request or turn one down.

When you need to tell employees in your department or in other departments about how/if they'll be compensated for doing the work you want done, the memoranda in this chapter will do your talking for you. The time you save writing about compensation issues pays YOU—with dividends.

ANNOUNCING A CHANGE IN EMPLOYEE BENEFITS

To:
From:
Date:
Subject: Change in Employee Benefits

Effective March 21, 19_____, employees with Medi-Health coverage will be asked to select another medical insurance plan. Our company must choose the most cost-effective coverage available, and since Medi-Health has increased its group rate steadily over the past three years, we regret we can no longer offer employees this option.

Please be assured that a program of comparable coverage will be made available to you. A meeting has been scheduled for Friday, March 3, 19_____, 3:00 p.m., to explain the plans of other healthcare carriers. Join us in Conference Room A to hear this information so you can select a new health-care plan.

MEMO WRITER TIPS

1. Describe the change and indicate the effective date in the very first sentence.

2. Next, explain why the change is necessary.

3. Assure employees that infringement on the benefits currently being provided is not taking place, and close by spelling out specifically what employees need to do to make the change.

PHRASING ALTERNATIVES

Paragraph 1

Those employees with Majestic Health Plan coverage will be required to select a new health care provider, effective July 1, 19_____. Majestic Health will no longer be providing coverage in this area, so this requires us to find other avenues for offering employees these benefits.

Paragraph 2

We are confident you will find adequate medical coverage with one of our other insurers. Contact the Personnel Office by March 15, 19____ , to find out about your options and select a new plan.

ANNOUNCING A MEETING ABOUT ANNUITIES AND TAX SHELTERS*

To:
From:
Date:
Subject: Annuity/Tax Shelter Presentation

A representative from the Copeland Companies will be at the college to discuss tax-sheltered options and benefits. The presentation will be on Thursday, January 7, 19____ , at 1:00 p.m., in Room 212C.

MEMO WRITER TIPS

1. Tell the reader the meeting is about tax shelters and/or annuities in the first sentence. If this subject holds no interest for the reader, he/she has no reason to read on.

2. Provide details about when and where the meeting is to take place.

PHRASING ALTERNATIVES

Paragraph 1

Come find out about tax shelters and annuities that may save you tax dollars and help you prepare for a solid financial future. Copeland Companies will be in Room 212C on Thursday, January 7, 19____ , at 1:00 p.m., to provide you with this information. Please plan to attend. The presentation should last no more than one hour.

Copeland Companies will present information about tax shelters and annuity plans on Thursday, January 7, 19____ , at 1:00 p.m., Room 212C. Please plan to join us for this hour-long informational presentation.

---

*This memorandum was written by a Director of Personnel Services in state government.

ASKING SUBORDINATES TO COMPLETE LEAVE FORMS

To:
From:
Date:
Subject: Completing Leave Forms

No leave form—no leave! Please complete the attached leave form and return it to your supervisor today. Thank you.

MEMO WRITER TIPS

1. Tell the reader what form must be completed and give specific guidelines about who forms should be submitted to and by when.
2. Keep this memo short and to the point.

PHRASING ALTERNATIVES

Paragraph 1

Please complete a "Leave Request" Form and return it to the Personnel Office by this Friday.

Complete the attached "Leave Request" and give it to your section chief by close of business today. Filling out leave forms promptly helps us track your leave benefits more efficiently. Thanks for your help.

COMMUNICATING ABOUT LEASED VEHICLES

To:
From:
Date:
Subject: Leased Vehicles

Your leased vehicle in now available for pick-up at our fleet distributor, Karl Van Hamp Buick. The dealership is located at 6129 Pine Avenue, Framewood, and is open from 10:00 a.m. until 10:00 p.m., Monday through Saturday.

Get your vehicle authorization slip from the accounting section. Be sure to familiarize yourself with our lease agreement and guidelines.

MEMO WRITER TIPS

1. Specify where and when the leased vehicle can be picked up.
2. Include information about any documents that must be taken for vehicle release.

PHRASING ALTERNATIVES

Paragraph 1

Pick up your leased vehicle at Fleet Maintenance anytime this week. Fleet Maintenance hours are 7:00 a.m.–4:00 p.m., Monday through Friday.

Your leased vehicle is ready for pick-up. Pick up your vehicle release form from Accounts Payable and take it with you to Odyssey Ford when you go to get your car. Accounts Payable will provide you with directions to the dealership, as well as information about their hours of operation.

Paragraph 2

Pay special attention to our leased vehicle guide. If you have any questions, contact the AP section.

Read the information about leased vehicles carefully. These policies have been developed for your and the company's protection and driving safety.

DEALING WITH LEAVE ABUSE

To:
From:
Date:
Subject: Leave Abuse

Our success depends on the committed efforts of each and every member of our team. That's why the company recognizes the need for leave privileges and extends these privileges to employees when there is legitimate need.

Abuse of leave privileges is another matter, however. Until further notice, you will be on leave restriction. Vacation and/or personal leave will not be granted. Sick leave will be approved only if you bring a doctor's statement to work the day following your absence. In no cases will sick leave be granted without a doctor's statement.

These leave restrictions will be in effect for the next sixty days. At that time, your leave status will be reevaluated, and if no further leave abuse has occurred, your leave restriction may be discontinued.

MEMO WRITER TIPS

1. Use the introductory paragraph to affirm the employee's value to the company.

2. In the second paragraph, make it clear that leave abuse will not be tolerated and specify what action is being taken to correct the employee's leave abuse problem.

3. In the last paragraph, tell the employee how long these corrective measures will be in place. At this point, write as though you expect the problem to be corrected, so omit any discussion of what may happen if leave abuse continues.

PHRASING ALTERNATIVES

Paragraph 1

You are a valued employee. That's why it's important for you to be at work every day, unless unavoidable emergencies arise.

Consistent attendance patterns allow members of your department to perform at full strength.

Your service to the company is an important part of our efficient functioning.

Paragraph 2

You have taken sick leave eight separate days in the past month and have been warned that this constitutes a pattern of leave abuse. All sick leave that you take for the next 60 days will be monitored closely and will not be approved unless you return to work with a doctor's statement.

Your recent pattern of taking excessive sick leave affects your work unit's functioning and morale and cannot, therefore, be tolerated. If you take sick leave at any time during the next 30 days, you will be required to report to your supervisor. Proper evidence of illness will be required, and you will be charged for leave without pay should your documentation of illness prove unsatisfactory.

Paragraph 3

Correcting this attendance problem now will eliminate any need for disciplinary action. If you would like to discuss this issue with me, please let me know at once.

These steps are unfortunate, but necessary. If you correct the situation now, we can all go back to building a solid work team—with you as a member in regular attendance.

DENYING A LEAVE REQUEST

To:
From:
Date:
Subject: Leave Request Denial

Your request for vacation leave cannot, regrettably, be granted now. Your help is vital, if we are to fill all current back-orders for equipment by the end of the month.

When we have recovered from this backlog, you'll be able to take the vacation you most certainly deserve.

MEMO WRITER TIPS

1. Give the reader the bad news right away; why prolong his/her disappointment? Be sure to use passive voice in this instance: "Your request has been denied," rather than "I have denied your request" or "I cannot approve your request." This will take some of the "sting" out of the message and keep you from becoming the "villain" here.

2. Be sure to give a reason for the denial and offer praise since you can't offer leave.

3. Give the employee some idea of when leave might be granted.

PHRASING ALTERNATIVES

Paragraph 1

Unfortunately, your leave request cannot be approved at this time. Several other employees submitted leave requests before you did, so approving yours would leave us seriously short-handed.

You're really needed right now, so your request for vacation cannot be granted. With all the new accounts in your department, your management skills are critical.

Paragraph 2

Submit another request in three weeks.

Your request can be reconsidered when Jane and Hal return from vacation.

Next month, we should be back on schedule. Your request will be reconsidered then.

EMPLOYEE BENEFITS: SPELLING THEM OUT

To:
From:
Date:
Subject: Employee Benefit Package

As a new employee, you need to know details about the generous benefits program offered by our company. You are entitled to the following benefits:

- Sick Leave—Accrued at 1.5 days per month.
- Vacation Leave—Accrued at 1.5 days every other month for the first five years; 2.5 days every other month for 5–20 years' service; 2.5 days every month for more than 10 years' service.
- Personal Leave—Three (3) days per calendar year. NOTE: Personal leave may only be taken with your supervisor's approval.
- Health Insurance—Your choice of one of three major medical plans. Costs vary, so contact the Personnel Department for details.
- Dental Plan—Optional coverage is available. See the Personnel Administrator for details.

Best wishes for many long years of service.

MEMO WRITER TIPS

1. List benefits and provide a brief explanation of each. Be sure to include information about where employees can obtain more specific information.

PHRASING ALTERNATIVES

Paragraph 1

Here is a list of benefits provided to our employees. Read the list carefully and contact a personnel representative for specific details.

Welcome to Aims Manufacturing. A list of the benefits included in our comprehensive employee welfare package follows:

Use the following list of company-sponsored benefits wisely and well.

EXPLAINING COMPENSATORY LEAVE

To:
From:
Date:
Subject: Compensatory Leave

Compensatory leave is provided for all classified employees, in lieu of overtime pay. All compensatory leave must be approved by the department manager. Leave is accrued at the rate of 1.5 hours compensatory leave for documented time worked past eight (8) hours per day, Monday through Friday. For approved work done on Saturday and Sunday, 2.0 hours of compensatory leave are earned for every 1.0 hour worked.

All approved compensatory leave must be recorded in your department's leave log and can be taken as approved by your manager. In no case is compensatory leave to be used without prior approval of your department manager.

MEMO WRITER TIPS

1. Spell out who is entitled to accrue compensatory leave, as well as specific details about compensatory leave.

2. Include information about special restrictions on this leave.

PHRASING ALTERNATIVES

Paragraph 1

Professional, Technical, and Managerial groups are entitled to accrue compensatory leave. This benefit is offered instead of overtime pay. Compensatory leave is accrued at the following rates:

- 1.5 hours compensatory leave per 1.0 hours worked (above eight (8) hours) on weekdays.
- 2.0 hours compensatory leave per 1.0 hour worked on weekends.

Since supervisory employees are not paid overtime, they may be compensated for work above and beyond the standard 40-hour work week at the following rates:

Paragraph 2

Only beyond-duty-hour work assignments approved by your supervisor are eligible for compensatory leave accrual. Supervisors must therefore monitor and approve any requests for compensatory leave benefits.

Supervisors must approve all requests for compensatory leave, as well as overtime work requests.

EXPLAINING CHILD-LEAVE BENEFITS

To:
From:
Date:
Subject: Child-Leave Benefits

In our continuing effort to create an associate-friendly environment, the company now provides generous benefits for employees with children.

When an associate gives birth to or adopts a child, the company provides one month of paid leave. In addition, associates may use as much as 60 days of their annual leave in these instances (in addition to the one month of paid leave).

Unpaid leave can be taken after the birth or adoption of a child for a period of up to six months (including the one month of paid leave and any annual leave taken). Child-leave cannot exceed six months' total.

If associates take a child-leave (paid and/or unpaid), they will be reinstated to the same or similar position when they return to work.

Arrangements can also be made to telecommute and/or reduce work hours following the birth or adoption of a child. To do this, discuss possible arrangements with your manager.

If you have questions about your specific situation, contact your Human Resources Technician.

MEMO WRITER TIPS

1. Discuss your company's leave benefits.
2. Refer employees to company policy or other sources for more specific information.

EXPLAINING FAMILY-LEAVE BENEFITS

To:
From:
Date:
Subject: Family-Leave Policy

The family-leave policy is designed to provide staff with leave options in the event of a serious family emergency.

If a serious family emergency occurs, employees can use *earned* sick-leave, up to a maximum of 30 days and *earned* annual leave, up to a maximum of 30 days. If an employee needs more than 60 days to resolve the family crisis, he/she can apply for short-term disability leave by contacting the Personnel Office.

Family emergencies do occur, and we like to accommodate staff whenever possible. If you have specific questions, contact the Personnel Office or refer to your *Associates' Handbook.*

MEMO WRITER TIPS

1. Discuss the intent of the leave policy.
2. Include any constraints or restrictions.

EXPLAINING MEDICAL AND DENTAL COVERAGE

To:
From:
Date:
Subject: Medical and Dental Coverage

The enclosed brochures describe your medical and dental options. Read them carefully before you choose a health plan for you and/or your family.

If you have any questions, I'll be happy to answer them for you. Just call me at EXT. 233.

enclosure

MEMO WRITER TIPS

1. Let employees know where they can find out about medical/dental options.
2. Enclose any brochures or charts that explain these benefits.
3. Tell them where they can get additional information.

PHRASING ALTERNATIVES

Paragraph 1

The attached chart compares/contrasts the three health plans offered by our company.

Schedule an appointment with me so I can explain your medical and dental benefits to you.

Your medical and dental benefits are described in the attached pamphlet.

Paragraph 2

Call me at ext. 101 if you need more information.

Let me know if I can answer any questions you have.

Read this information carefully and decide which plan you'd like to have. When you come to sign your medical/dental forms, I'll be glad to answer any of your questions.

GRANTING BEREAVEMENT LEAVE

To:
From:
Date:
Subject: Bereavement Leave

Accept the approval of your request for bereavement leave, along with my most sincere condolences on the loss of your mother. This is, no doubt, a very difficult time for you and your family, so if I may help in any way, please do not hesitate to let me know.

MEMO WRITER TIPS

1. Offer sympathy along with this approval and extend an offer of assistance to the employee.

PHRASING ALTERNATIVES

Paragraph 1

Your request for bereavement leave has, of course, been approved. On behalf of the company, allow me to extend our sincere sympathy to you and your loved ones in this time of sorrow. Let us know if we can help in any way.

Bereavement leave has been granted. In your time of loss, know that I, along with our entire staff, support you in this time of grief. Our assistance is available for the asking.

GRANTING A LEAVE REQUEST

To:
From:
Date:
Subject: Leave Approval

Your request for two weeks' vacation leave, effective Monday, June 1 has been approved. Enjoy a well-deserved vacation. See you in two weeks.

MEMO WRITER TIPS

1. Say that leave has been approved and include the effective date.
2. Add a friendly note, wishing the employee well, if you wish.

PHRASING ALTERNATIVES

Paragraph 1

Enjoy a hard-earned vacation beginning next week. See you when you return in two weeks.

Your leave request has been granted for the period June 1 to June 14.

HIGHLIGHTING HOLIDAYS

To:
From:
Date:
Subject: Holiday

In celebration of Memorial Day, all offices will be closed on Monday, May 31, 19_____. Enjoy the day and drive safely. See you on Tuesday.

MEMO WRITER TIPS

1. Name the holiday in the first sentence and state which offices will be closed.

PHRASING ALTERNATIVES

Paragraph 1

May 31, 19_____, Memorial Day, is a paid holiday. Therefore, all offices will be closed. Have a safe and enjoyable weekend.

A day off with pay. In commemoration of Memorial Day, we will not work on Monday, May 31, 19_____. Whatever your plans, make them safe.

LEAVE: USE IT OR LOSE IT*

To:
From:
Date:
Subject: Leave: Use It or Lose It

Only 60 days of annual leave can be carried over from one fiscal year to the next. Currently, you have accrued 90 days of annual leave, and you will accrue an additional 16 hours of leave time by September 1.

If you do not want to forfeit annual leave, you must take 46 hours of vacation time between now and August 31.

---

*This memorandum was written by a Public Affairs Specialist employed by the federal government.

MEMO WRITER TIPS

1. Explain the policy regarding leave accrual.

2. Tell the employees how much leave she/he currently has, how much will be accrued before the beginning of the fiscal year, and how much leave must be taken.

3. Remind the employee that unused leave will be lost.

PHRASING ALTERNATIVES

Paragraph 1

If you fail to take 46 hours of annual leave between now and July 1, you will lose this leave time. Only 60 days' leave can be transferred from one fiscal year to the next.

Since you will have accumulated 92 days of annual leave by the end of this fiscal year, you are required to take 32 days' leave or forfeit this time. Only 60 days annual leave can be carried over to the new fiscal year. Please make arrangements to use your valuable leave time, no later than June 30.

OUTLINING PENSION PLAN IMPROVEMENTS

To:

From:

Date:

Subject: Pension Plan Improvements

Effective July 1, the following improvements will be made to our pension plan. Employer contributions will be increased by 5 percent per month, and employees with five or more years of service will be eligible to receive 10 percent of employer contributions, should they resign from the company between their 5th and 10th years of service.

We are happy to be able to provide these enhancements to your benefits package. A brochure describing the plan's new features should be available by May 1.

MEMO WRITER TIPS

1. Use the first sentence to say that improvements are being made to the pension plan and be sure to include the effective date.

2. Briefly explain what the changes will be, and tell employees how they can find out additional details.

PHRASING ALTERNATIVES

Paragraph 1

Beginning July 1, several enhancements will be made to the company pension plan.

The pension plan has been upgraded, and these changes will take effect July 1.

You'll be happy to know that a number of changes have improved your pension plan.

Paragraph 2

These enhancements are well deserved. Contact your personnel representative for additional details.

Improving your pension benefits should serve to make your retirement picture even more secure. We're pleased to be able to offer them to you. Call Ext. 560 for more information.

OUTLINING SEVERANCE PAY AND TERMINATION BENEFITS

To:
From:
Date:
Subject: Severance Pay

You are entitled to two weeks' severance pay, in the event of a lay-off. The Personnel Department can also provide you with information about filing for unemployment compensation.

MEMO WRITER TIPS

1. List severance or termination benefits.

2. If your company offers outplacement or retraining services, include information about these services, as well.

3. Let employees know where they can get additional details about these benefits.

PHRASING ALTERNATIVES

Paragraph 1

Under company policy, no severance pay can be provided. If you resign, you will be paid for unused annual leave. You cannot receive payment for unused sick leave.

You are entitled to one month's severance pay if you are laid off because of lack of work. The company's outplacement office will also provide you with information about resume writing, interviewing, and effective job search strategies. Call Extension 178 for more information.

You can find information about severance pay and termination benefits in your employee handbook, pages 26–28.

PUBLICIZING A HOLIDAY/VACATION
WORK SCHEDULE*

To:
From:
Date:
Subject: Holiday Work Schedule

The following schedule will provide adequate coverage during the holiday season:

	DAYS OFF	11/24	12/24	12/26	12/31	1/2
Mark Matthews		X			X	
Joan Strong			X			X
Lillie Morgan		X		X		
George Halliburton				X		X
Marjorie Owens			X		X	

---

*This memorandum was written by a nursing supervisor.

MEMO WRITER TIPS

1. Diagram the schedule, if possible. This will make the schedule easier to read.
2. Use dates or times as headings for a chart of your vacation or holiday schedule.

PHRASING ALTERNATIVES

Paragraph 1

Here's the holiday work schedule:

The vacation schedule is as follows:

This chart outlines the holiday schedule for employees in the marketing department:

REFERRING BENEFIT INQUIRIES TO PERSONNEL

To:
From:
Date:
Subject: Benefit Inquiries

Please direct your questions about benefits to the Personnel Office (Ext. 443). They can give you the information you need.

PHRASING ALTERNATIVES

Paragraph 1

The Personnel Manager will be pleased to answer the questions you have about your benefits. Please call her at EXT. 741 to schedule an appointment.

Your questions about benefits can best be answered by personnel representatives. If you stop by their office in Room 341, I'm sure they'll be able to explain your benefits in detail.

I'm unable to answer your questions about dental benefits and am, therefore, referring you to Mr. Dave Martin in the Personnel Department. I'm sure he'll be able to clear up any confusion.

REPORTING BENEFIT STATUS TO A SUBORDINATE

To:
From:
Date:
Subject: Leave Status

According to my records, you have 36 hours of annual leave and 189 hours of sick leave. If you have questions, call me at Ext. 199.

PHRASING ALTERNATIVES

Paragraph 1

You currently have the following unused leave:

> Vacation Time—180 hours
> Sick Time—94 hours
> Personal Leave—16 hours

If these numbers do not match your calculations, stop by my office as soon as possible.

Your leave balance is as follows: 36 hours annual; 48 hours sick. Please see your supervisor immediately if you question these figures.

REPORTING BENEFIT STATUS TO THE BOSS

To:
From:
Date:
Subject: Benefit Status

As of November 15th, I have 42 hours of annual leave and 120 hours of sick leave. I trust this information will clear up any questions you may have about my benefit status.

MEMO WRITER TIPS

1. Since this message is for your boss, keep it short and direct.

PHRASING ALTERNATIVES

Paragraph 1

You requested information about my leave status. My leave balance is as follows:

> 42 hours annual leave
> 120 hours sick leave

If you need additional information, let me know.

Here is the information you wanted about my leave balance:

> Annual Leave—42 hours
> Sick Leave—120 hours

Just let me know if you need more information.

REQUESTING FORMS
FOR BENEFIT CLAIMS

To:
From:
Date:
Subject: Request for Claim Form

Please send a copy of the dental insurance claim form to my office, Suite 304. Thank you.

MEMO WRITER TIPS

1. Put the name of the claim form you need in the first sentence.
2. Include your office, building number, etc. in order to keep your reader from having to look it up. This will expedite matters.

PHRASING ALTERNATIVES

Paragraph 1

I need a copy of the insurance claim form for MediHealth Limited. Let me know if there is any special procedure I need to follow. My office is Room 304, Annex A. Thanks.

Send a copy of Form 2213, Claim Request, to my office—Room 1214. Thank you.

REQUESTING BUY-BACK OF EXCESS LEAVE

To:
From:
Date:
Subject: Buy-Back of Excess Leave

Since I will be unable to use 36 hours of excess annual leave by June 30, I am requesting the company to buy this leave back and include the refund in my June 30 paycheck.

If you have questions, call me at EXT. 114.

MEMO WRITER TIPS

1. Be sure to include specifics about the number of hours and type of leave you want bought back.

2. Provide the reader with your phone extension, in case there are any additional questions.

PHRASING ALTERNATIVES

Paragraph 1

I am unable to take vacation time between now and the end of the fiscal year. This means that I will have 18 hours more than the 60 hours that can be carried forward into the next fiscal year. Therefore, I would like to sell this leave back to the company, so that I will not lose this accrued time.

Company policy only permits 60 hours of accrued vacation leave to be brought forward from one fiscal year to the next. Since I currently have a leave balance of 84 hours, but will be unable to use this time before September 30, I'm requesting a leave buy-back.

Paragraph 2

Please send any necessary forms to my office and call me at Extension 2356 if you need additional information. Thank you.

Call me (ext. 601) if there are any problems with my request.

REQUESTING LEAVE WITH PAY*

To:
From:
Date:
Subject: Request for Leave with Pay

I need annual leave with pay for November 20–22. My family is having a reunion in Connecticut over the Thanksgiving holiday, and I would like to be able to join them for this occasion.

    Thank you.

MEMO WRITER TIPS

1. Say what kind of leave you need, when.
2. Provide a brief explanation of why you need the leave.

PHRASING ALTERNATIVES

Paragraph 1

    I am requesting 80 hours of vacation leave, July 15 through August 1. My leave balance will adequately cover this vacation. Thanks.

    May I have 24 hours of paid annual leave for the period 1/14–1/17? My grandmother died last night, and I want to attend her funeral.

    Please approve 40 hours of vacation leave for me: March 12–March 16. I am having some family problems that I need this time to resolve.

REQUESTING LEAVE WITHOUT PAY

To:
From:
Date:
Subject: Request for Leave without Pay

A family emergency requires my immediate attention. Therefore, I am requesting 60 days of leave without pay.

---

*An elementary school teacher wrote this memorandum.

I will make sure my work assignments have been brought up to date so my section can continue to function efficiently in my absence.

Your consideration in this matter is greatly appreciated.

MEMO WRITER TIPS

1. Begin by explaining why you need the leave without pay. Give as much detail as you think appropriate.

2. Then ask for the leave, specifying how long you will need to be away.

3. Provide the reader with assurances that your work can be managed effectively while you are away.

PHRASING ALTERNATIVES

Paragraph 1

As you know, I have applied for the doctoral program at the University of Camden. Recently, I learned I have been accepted for the next school year. This intensive program will require more time and commitment than would be possible with a full-time work commitment. For this reason, I am requesting 12 months of leave without pay in order to complete my doctoral studies.

Paragraph 2

This doctorate will help to make me a greater asset to the company, and I have every intention of doing whatever is required to make sure my duties are taken care of while I am on leave.

Paragraph 3

I would be happy to discuss this matter with you in person, should you feel that necessary.

COMMUNICATING ABOUT
A CLASSIFICATION STUDY*

To:
From:
Date:
Subject: Compensation/Classification Study

As you know, a study of our job classification system for exempt positions was completed in December 19_____ . Thirty (30) exempt positions, including those of several department heads and division managers, were audited during this study. The study, conducted by J. J. Franklin, Inc., resulted in recommendations that our company adopt a new, more relevant job classification program and a salary structure that eliminates the different job families.

We concur with these recommendations and will be conducting, in conjunction with the Franklin consultants, a comprehensive review of all salaried positions in 19_____ . Jack Curtis of Employee Relations will act as project manager.

The outcome of the project will be an updated compensation system, including revised classifications, salary ranges and salary administration procedures for exempt and non-exempt salaried positions. This new compensation system is to be implemented in January of 19_____ .

Meetings will be scheduled soon between groups of salaried employees and the consultant to explain the project. The meetings are expected to occur in April and should clarify any questions you might have.

Your cooperation and involvement will be appreciated and crucial to the success of the project.

MEMO WRITER TIPS

1. Give background information on the classification study, what prompted the study, what positions are involved, who will be involved in the study.

2. Outline how the classification study will take place.

3. Say when the study should be completed and what the outcomes of the classification study are likely to be.

---

*A transportation manager, the administrator for five departments, wrote this memorandum.

CORRECTING A PAY ERROR

To:
From:
Date:
Subject: Pay Calculation Error

An error was made in your paycheck, period ending March 31, 19____ . You were paid 3.5 hours overtime when you should have been paid 7.5 hours overtime.

The difference, $92.85, will be included on your next paycheck. I apologize for this error and hope it did not cause you any financial difficulty. If you have any questions, call me at Ext. 246.

MEMO WRITER TIPS

1. Begin by saying that an error was made and indicate on which paycheck the error appeared.

2. Explain the error in detail.

3. Close by discussing how and when the error will be corrected and apologize for the mistake.

PHRASING ALTERNATIVES

Paragraph 1

You probably noticed that your March 31 paycheck was short by $45.67. On your timecard, 5.0 hours was misread as 3.0 hours. The balance due you will appear on your April 15 check.

You were inadvertently overpaid $93.84 on your March 31 check. You were paid 7.5 hours at double time when you should have been paid time-and-one-half.

Paragraph 2

The overage will be deducted from your April 15 paycheck. If you have any questions about this error, call me at Ext. 4212.

Sorry for any inconvenience this may have caused you. Thank you for your patience.

INFORMING AN EMPLOYEE
OF A CHANGE IN PAY STATUS

To:
From:
Date:
Subject: Pay Status Change

Your promotion from Grade 5 to Grade 6 becomes effective July 1. Therefore, your pay rate of $7.49 will be increased to $8.67 and will be reflected on your July 15 paycheck.

Congratulations. If you have any questions, call me at Ext. 1104.

MEMO WRITER TIPS

1. Explain the reason for the change in pay status in the first sentence.

2. Detail what the pay change will be and tell the employee when he/she can expect to see this change reflected in his/her paycheck.

PHRASING ALTERNATIVES

Paragraph 1

Since you will be Acting Department Manager effective July 1, your pay will be adjusted to reflect the new monthly salary of $2459.67. This increase will appear on your July 15 paycheck and will continue as long as you are serving in this acting capacity.

Effective October 1, your shift from hourly to salaried pay status will result in an increase of $123.45 per pay period. This change also means you will be paid bi-weekly rather than weekly and that you will receive the same salary each pay period, less deductions for unpaid leave, etc., should those occur. Your October 15 paycheck will reflect these changes.

Paragraph 2

If you have questions or problems, please call me.

INFORMING A SUBORDINATE PAY CALCULATIONS ARE CORRECT

To:
From:
Date:
Subject: Pay Calculations

The pay calculations you questioned on your November 1 paycheck are correct. Here's why:

40.0 regular hours @ $ 8.20/hour	= $328.00
5.0 overtime hours @ $12.30/hour	= 61.50
2.0 overtime hours @ $16.50/hour	= 32.80
	= $422.30

These were the hours that appeared on your time card for this pay period. If you worked additional overtime hours, please see your supervisor immediately.

MEMO WRITER TIPS

1. Don't keep the reader in suspense. Say in the first sentence that pay calculations were correct.

2. Then detail upon what information these pay calculations were based.

3. Tell the reader how she/he should handle any discrepancy.

PHRASING ALTERNATIVES

Paragraph 1

According to payroll computations, you were paid for 40 hours of regular time and 5.0 hours of overtime (at time-and-one-half). This totals $678.54, the amount paid you on December 1.

The $754.32 paid you on October 15 is correct, according to our calculations. This amount reflects your $600.00 base salary plus your $154.32 commission for that month.

Paragraph 2

If you still have questions, call me at Ext. 401 or stop by my office.

Come by my office if you feel you should have been paid for additional hours.

LISTING HOURLY EMPLOYEE WAGES

To:
From:
Date:
Subject: Hourly Employee Wages

Below is a list of hourly employees and their salaries:

1.	Sue Singleton	$10.56
2.	Joseph Atwater	$10.49
3.	Matthew Caison	$10.49
4.	Susan Stanton	$ 9.47
5.	Martin Barnes	$ 9.23
6.	Francis Jones	$ 8.78

If you need additional information, let me know.

MEMO WRITER TIPS

1. Open with a sentence explaining what you are doing and then list names of employees and their wages.

PHRASING ALTERNATIVES

Paragraph 1

Thirty-six hourly employees work in the Personnel Department. Their names and salaries are listed on the attached printout.

The Data Systems department employs five hourly employees. They are Dan Jones, $11.56 per hour; Sandra Mason, $11.10; Judith Wilson, $10.46; Mark Haversham, $9.52; and Sandra Matlock, $9.04.

MAKING A MERIT PAY INCREASE*

To:
From:
Date:
Subject: Merit Increase

Congratulations. In recognition of your outstanding performance for the past year, you are receiving a merit increase of $1200 per year. This increase will become effective pay period ending January 24.

Keep up the good work!

MEMO WRITER TIPS

1. Tell the employee that the merit pay increase has been approved and reiterate what the increase is for.

2. Let the employee know how much the merit increase will be and when it will take effect.

PHRASING ALTERNATIVES

Paragraph 1

Your merit pay increase to the next step on the salary schedule has been approved. Your 2/26 paycheck should reflect this raise.

Your merit pay increase has been approved and processed. Expect to receive this increase on the paycheck you receive November 3.

You are an outstanding employee and have been awarded a merit pay increase, as a result. This increase, $82.00 per month, will be paid to you effective April 17. Congratulations on a job well done.

---

*This memorandum was written by an administrative assistant for an insurance firm.

OVERTIME PAY GUIDELINES

To:
From:
Date:
Subject: Overtime Pay Guidelines

Hourly employees are paid overtime for all approved hours worked beyond the standard 40-hour, Monday through Friday, work week.

Employees who work more than eight (8) hours Monday through Friday are paid time-and-one-half for their services, provided the total number of hours worked per week is more than 40.

Employees who work approved overtime on Saturday, Sunday, or holidays are paid double time.

All overtime must be pre-approved by the employee's supervisor before pay for these hours can be authorized.

MEMO WRITER TIPS

1. In the first sentence, define what constitutes overtime.

2. Explain what constitutes time-and-one-half and what constitutes double time.

3. Include any special conditions or restrictions that apply.

4. Be sure to include specific information, as this will preclude questions that may arise about overtime in the future.

PHRASING ALTERNATIVES

Paragraph 1

Overtime pay is defined as hours worked beyond eight (8) per day, Monday through Friday, as well as work performed (beyond 40 hours) on weekends and/or holidays.

Paragraph 2

Pay guidelines are as follows:

Time worked over eight (8) hours = hourly rate + one-half
Time worked (beyond 40 hours) on weekends/holidays =
    hourly rate + one-half

Paragraph 3

No overtime pay will be granted unless a supervisor approves it before it is worked. Approval will not be given for overtime after the fact.

APPROVING OVERTIME PAY

To:
From:
Date:
Subject: Overtime Approval

Your request to work 16 hours of overtime during the week of April 5, 19____, is approved. If you find you need more time to complete this project, let me know.

MEMO WRITER TIPS

1. In the first sentence, say how much overtime has been approved and during what period of time the overtime must be worked.

PHRASING ALTERNATIVES

Paragraph 1

Twenty-four hours of overtime has been approved for this week. Hopefully, this will get the job done. Call me if you think it will not.

You may work overtime to complete the Lansing Project, up to a maximum of 32 overtime hours. Good luck.

DENYING OVERTIME PAY

To:
From:
Date:
Subject: Overtime Pay Denial

Overtime pay cannot be authorized until next fiscal year. While I realize this may really take a toll on your department, cost overruns have eliminated my ability to approve overtime pay.

If you have alternatives, I'd be happy to discuss them with you.

MEMO WRITER TIPS

1. Say overtime has not been approved in the first sentence.
2. Explain why this overtime has been denied.
3. Close on a positive note by suggesting other ways to handle the situation.

PHRASING ALTERNATIVES

Paragraph 1

Unfortunately, all requests for overtime must be denied at this time. We really took a beating this year, one that has depleted our overtime budget.

Your request for overtime pay cannot be approved at this time. Lack of funds this close to the end of the fiscal year simply will not permit it.

Paragraph 2

Any suggestions???

Let's discuss how the work can get done in spite of this situation.

ELIMINATING EXCESSIVE OVERTIME PAY

To:
From:
Date:
Subject: Excessive Overtime

For the past 60 days, overtime pay costs have exceeded projected costs by 43 percent. At this rate, we'll be out of overtime funds when our busiest season hits next month.

Until further notice, no overtime is to be approved. We'll take this matter up at next week's staff meeting. Voice your concerns then.

MEMO WRITER TIPS

1. Since this is generally an unpopular though necessary decision, state the reason for discontinuing overtime at the beginning of the memorandum.
2. Then say that overtime has been curtailed and indicate how long this situation is likely to last.

PHRASING ALTERNATIVES

Paragraph 1

Our peak season starts in three weeks, and already we're way over what we paid in overtime costs last year. In order for us to have enough overtime money left to get us through our peak period, I will approve overtime only on a case-by-case basis and only when such overtime appears to be absolutely necessary.

Paragraph 2

If you have serious situations you feel warrant overtime costs, talk to me, and we'll see what might be done.

HANDLING UNAUTHORIZED OVERTIME PAY*

To:
From:
Date:
Subject: Unauthorized Overtime Pay—Leo Thompson

Both the Labor Agreement and the Fair Labor Standard Act authorize overtime payment only when such overtime has been approved by a supervisor. Since Mr. Thompson's supervisor had not approved the six (6) hours of overtime worked on October 11, no additional payment can be made.

MEMO WRITER TIPS

1. Explain under what conditions overtime can be paid.
2. Outline why the current request for overtime pay does not conform with approved guidelines.

PHRASING ALTERNATIVES

Paragraph 1

Personnel policies clearly specify that overtime must be pre-approved by an employee's immediate supervisor before payment for overtime can be authorized.

---

*This memorandum was written by a payroll department administrator.

Ms. Jones did not have this pre-approval when she worked two hours of overtime on February 27. Therefore, she cannot be paid overtime for these hours.

Overtime pay can only be paid when an employee has been directed to work overtime by his/her immediate supervisor. Overtime cannot be paid to Oliva Henry, therefore, because her supervisor did not direct Ms. Henry to work four (4) hours of overtime on May 17.

RECOMMENDING A RAISE
FOR A SUBORDINATE

To:
From:
Date:
Subject: Salary Raise Recommendation

Let's give Jan Carruthers a raise. Why? Because she has demonstrated exemplary performance for the past year. She singlehandedly established 22 new accounts. She operated her department 24 percent under projections. She has tirelessly worked long hours, weekends, and even holidays to give this company performance well beyond that for which she is currently being compensated.

I recommend a $100 per month increase, which is well within budget allocations. Jan is an outstanding employee, and I think her dedication and drive warrant a higher salary.

MEMO WRITER TIPS

1. Tell who should get the raise and why.
2. Include as many specifics as possible.
3. Include a recommended salary, if that is appropriate.

PHRASING ALTERNATIVES

Paragraph 1

Accept this as my recommendation for a salary increase for Bill Jones, Finance Department. Bill has made significant contributions to the company this year, among them

- designing a new procedure for tracking expenditures
- developing a computer program to automate this tracking

- cost savings in excess of $76,000
- successfully training two new accounting technicians.

Paragraph 2

Bill has worked hard and has my whole-hearted endorsement for a raise. If any employee deserves one, he does. Say an 8 percent increase?

REJECTING A SUBORDINATE'S RAISE REQUEST

To:
From:
Date:
Subject: Raise Request

Your positive contributions to our company have not gone unnoticed. Thank you for calling them to my attention. Your efforts to train new employees both in and outside your department are to be commended. You are a pivotal employee in your section, and your efforts keep things running smoothly.

As you know, however, our sales have declined markedly this year. This has produced a budget shortfall that has left us able to fund anticipated expenses, but no additional encumbrances.

When our financial condition improves, request for salary increases can be explored. Your admirable efforts are greatly appreciated and are to be commended. Keep up the good work!

MEMO WRITER TIPS

1. Begin by affirming the positives. Praise the employee for his/her contributions to the company or department.

2. Then explain why the raise cannot be granted.

3. Close by discussing when the raise request may be reconsidered. Phrase the denial in a positive way: Instead of saying, "Your request for a raise has been denied," say, "When funds permit, your request for a raise may be reconsidered."

PHRASING ALTERNATIVES

Paragraph 1

Your work performance is commendable. Developing that new system for tracking bookkeeping errors has improved operations in the accounts receivable department. Productive employees like you are what keep our company strong.

Your work is, without question, acceptable. Your attendance record is excellent, and you carry your weight in your section. Thank you for bringing your efforts to my attention.

Paragraph 2

Your department requested funds for upgrading the micro-computers and software. This conversion was seen as top priority and seems to be going quite well. When a major expenditure like this is made, however, other areas must remain at their current funding levels, in order to make a purchase of this magnitude possible.

We expect all our employees to meet or exceed standards, but we can only reward workers who put forth effort that goes beyond that called for by their job descriptions. Meeting standards is our goal.

Paragraph 3

Next fiscal year, we will again review our funding priorities, and your raise request may be reconsidered at that time. Until then, you can rest assured that your efforts are a valuable part of our team, even though our budget priorities do not allow us to reward you for those efforts in a monetary way.

Exceeding standards remains a goal for which you can strive. Once you have reached this plateau, we can reconsider your request for a raise. Until then, we hope you will continue to make positive contributions to your section.

TELECOMMUTING GUIDELINES

To:
From:
Date:
Subject: Guidelines for Telecommuting

The company encourages staff to telecommute, when appropriate (See Policy #32-8). Here are some guidelines for telecommuting:

1. Make sure your manager and secretary/assistant know you will be working off-site/telecommuting by 8:00 a.m. that day. If you will be telecommuting for more than one day, make sure your manager and secretary/assistant know how to locate you in an emergency.
2. Make sure your voicemail message indicates when you will return telephone messages or calls.
3. Schedule time on telecommute days to reply to and/or send e-mail messages.
4. Make arrangements with your System Administrator if you need to access the company network while you are telecommuting.
5. If possible, prepare a telecommuting schedule for staff in your section. This way, colleagues will know, ahead of time, what days team members will be off-site.
6. Be sure to change your voicemail message when you return to your office.
7. Have a productive telecommute.

MEMO WRITER TIPS

1. Telecommuting is becoming more and more common. Prepare guidelines consistent with your organization's policies.
2. Be as specific as possible.

3

Model Memos for Work Assignments and Duties

Work is the primary business of your agency or organization. Who does what, when? Who got the job? Who was transferred? Who was promoted? Who retired? Few things in an organization are more important than knowing what, when, how, and by whom work gets done.

The memoranda in Chapter 3 do just that: tell personnel in your organization who's doing what work. Sometimes, you'll want to assign someone to a task force or a committee to solve a special problem or challenge. You may want to give someone a special project, alert workers that an especially heavy workload is headed their way, distribute a work schedule, or assign someone to a temporary or acting position. Work assignments must be given, monitored, or changed. And information about these work details must be communicated to those who have a need to know.

Sometimes you'll have a need to know. You may think your work has outstripped your salary. Then you'll want your position audited or your own job duties changed. Memos in this chapter can help you frame questions or get information about your own work as well.

The job of managing business is work. The memoranda in this chapter work to clarify job assignments and duties. Use them to do this work, so you can spend more time doing business.

ANNOUNCING A NEW APPOINTMENT*

To:
From:
Date:
Subject: Typing/Clerical Support

I would like you all to help me welcome Jane Anderson, our new secretary, to the LTC team. Jane is located in the Learning Resources Center, and is doing some great work for us. Her hours are 9:00 a.m. to 3:30 p.m., Monday through Thursday, and 8:00 a.m. to 4:00 p.m. on Fridays.

If you have typing, photocopying, and other projects, please complete a "Work Request" Form (sample attached). Submit your completed request form to me, and I will see that your work is done as quickly as possible. Please DO NOT LEAVE requests on Jane's desk, since there is no security in the LRC when she is not there, and items may get lost or picked up by students. Blank request forms can be found on top of the mailboxes in the faculty lounge.

Be sure to fill out the top portion of the form and make sure you include the date and time you need the project back, so I can prioritize work requests. Please try to allow at least 24 hours of lead time on any project. If you have any questions about work requests, please see me.

I am really excited to have Jane here, and I am sure you will be pleased with the work she does. Help make her feel welcome.

MEMO WRITER TIPS

1. Tell who the new employee is and where they are located.

2. Describe, briefly, what the new employee will be doing, and explain new procedures that may result from this employee's hiring.

PHRASING ALTERNATIVES

Paragraph 1

Max Devereau has been hired as the new computer programmer in the Data Systems Division. Max has 15 years' experience in the computer field, and we are pleased we could persuade him to join our company.

---

*This memorandum was written by the office manager of a private school.

The new face in the bank manager's office belongs to Jan Currant. She is Mr. Richmond's new Executive Assistant, and we're pleased to have her on staff.

Paragraph 2

Mr. Devereau will be handling programming for Units 5 and 6, as well as providing us with guidance on how to hone our new Management Information System software.

Stop by her desk and make her feel welcome. We all look forward to working with you, Jan.

Paragraph 3

Welcome aboard, Max.

ANNOUNCING AN EMPLOYEE TRANSFER

To:
From:
Date:
Subject: Employee Transfer

Barbara Wallace is being transferred to the Compliance Section, beginning January 1. Her analytical skills will definitely help to tackle the complexities of the new compliance standards and procedures.

She'll certainly be missed in our division.

MEMO WRITER TIPS

1. Say who's being transferred where in the opening sentence.

2. Give a brief explanation of why the transfer is being made, in order to head off the rumor mill.

PHRASING ALTERNATIVES

Paragraph 1

Risk management welcomes Will Shrooeder, a recent transfer from the Casualty Group. Their loss is now our gain. Welcome, Will.

We are losing one of our brightest stars. Cindy McNernty is being transferred to the home office in February. Cindy has really made a difference in our operations, and we'll be sorry to see her go.

Paragraph 2

Best of luck in Cincinnati, Cindy.

ANNOUNCING A PROMOTION

To:
From:
Date:
Subject: Employee Promotion

Will Lansing is being promoted to Chief Analyst, effective October 1. Will's talents in the company are legendary, and we're sure he'll be just as effective in his new position.

Congratulations, Will!

MEMO WRITER TIPS

1. Include the name of the promotee and the title of the new position.
2. Include at least one sentence that stresses why the promotion has occurred.
3. Close on an upbeat note. Keep the tone light and congratulatory.

PHRASING ALTERNATIVES

Paragraph 1

Please take a moment to congratulate Will Lansing on his recent promotion to Chief Analyst. Will has been an invaluable asset to the Prevention and Loss Section, and we all wish him well on his new assignment.

I'm sure you'll be pleased to learn that Will Lansing has been promoted to Chief Analyst, beginning January 1. While Will's skills and talents will be missed, I know he's excited about this chance to move up.

Paragraph 2

Best wishes, Will.

ANNOUNCING A RETIREMENT

To:
From:
Date:
Subject: Jane Woodward's Retirement

After more than 20 years of dedicated service, Jane Woodward is retiring from the company December 31, 19____ . Jane joined the company in 19____ as a mail clerk and through hard work and outstanding talents worked her way up to Operations Chief.

Jane and her family plan to travel to the Northwest after she retires for a much-deserved rest. Join us in the staff lounge at 3:00 p.m. on Friday, December 31, to wish Jane farewell.

MEMO WRITER TIPS

1. Spell out who is retiring when.

2. Include a bit of history about the employee's contributions and progress in the company, as an incentive to others.

3. Close by announcing any plans for a retirement party or other activities.

PHRASING ALTERNATIVES

Paragraph 1

Both sadness and joy accompany my announcement of Jane Woodward's retirement from our company on December 31. Jane has provided us with her services for more than 20 years, and it goes without saying that she will be missed.

Join me in wishing the best to Jane Woodward, who is retiring from the company on December 31. When Jane joined our company more than 30 years ago, we had only 16 employees and occupied a small office in our old building. With efforts from employees like Jane, we have come a long way.

Paragraph 2

A retirement dinner will be held on Friday evening, December 31 at Luigi's Restaurant. Bud Bates, Ext. 240, is handling the details.

Contact Mia Parsons for information about Jane's retirement tribute. Jane, all our wishes for a happy, healthy future go with you.

APPOINTING SOMEONE
TO A NEW POSITION

To:
From:
Date:
Subject: New Financial Analyst Appointee

Effective Monday, January 10, Ms. Susan Landess will assume the duties of Financial Analyst, a new position in the Accounting Department. For the past two years, Susan has contributed a great deal by interpreting financial information and making accurate forecasts and projections. This assistance has become such a valuable part of our financial operations that we decided to create a full-time position. As we continue to grow, we are convinced this new job will save us money and a great deal of time.

Please join us in congratulating Susan on her new position.

MEMO WRITER TIPS

1. Put the name of the individual and the title of the new position right up front.

2. Briefly describe why this position has been created, why the individual was placed in this position, and what the company hopes to gain by adding the new job.

PHRASING ALTERNATIVES

Paragraph 1

Beginning January 1, a Technical Writer position will be added to the marketing unit. Will Lathrop has been appointed to this new position. Will has unofficially been performing technical writing duties for the past year. With the increased tech writing workload, I decided it was time to create a full-time job to meet this need. Will's journalism and advertising background, along with his computer expertise, make him an exceptional candidate for this job.

Jan Avery has recently been appointed Payroll Clerk, a new position in the Personnel Department. As you know, we had been contracting with an outside agency for payroll support. However, our growth over the past two years now supports an in-house payroll position. As payroll liaison with our former contractor, Jan has been doing this work for a number of years and was, therefore, a perfect choice for this new role.

Paragraph 2

Congratulations, Will.

Doing our payroll in-house will help the process run more smoothly, save us money, and provide faster turn-around time on payroll questions and/or concerns. Jan will, doubtless, continue to do an able job of taking care of our payroll needs.

APPOINTING A WORKER TO A TASK FORCE OR COMMITTEE

To:
From:
Date:
Subject: Task Force Appointment

As you know, I have recently formed a task force to study the issue of company-sponsored daycare. Because of your problem-solving and communication skills, I thought you'd add a valuable perspective to this task force.

The first meeting of the task force is slated for Monday, March 3, 19_____ , at 2:00 p.m., Board Conference Room. Contact Alice Delio for additional details. As always, I know you will help this group make valuable recommendations on this important issue. Thank you for your service.

MEMO WRITER TIPS

1. Discuss what the task force is to study in the first sentence.

2. Briefly explain what the goal of the task force is and why you think this individual should serve on this particular task force.

3. Include any pertinent information about contacts, meetings, etc.

4. Thank the employee for serving on the task force or committee.

PHRASING ALTERNATIVES

Paragraph 1

A Benefit Policy Task Force has been formed to survey the various benefit packages available and make recommendations about those that will serve our needs best. Your interest in benefit issues, along with your expertise in insurance, make you a logical person to serve on this committee.

Congratulations on your appointment to this year's Budget Committee. Your expertise in finance and your participation in the budget process for the past few years will make you an invaluable asset to this group.

Paragraph 2

Hal Majors, Beth Stewart, and Franklin Austin have also been appointed to serve on this task force. Franklin has been tasked with setting up the task force's first meeting. Contact him for additional details. Thank you for giving your time and energy to this important work.

Marge Hodgkiss is in the process of setting up the committee's first meeting. Call her at Ext. 203. I'm confident this group will hammer out a workable budget for next year. Thanks.

APPOINTING SOMEONE TO A TEMPORARY OR ACTING POSITION*

To:
From:
Date:
Subject: Temporary Appointment

Effective Monday, May 14, 19____ , you are temporarily appointed to the position of Acting Chief of Police. You will be responsible for the overall management of the department until the screening process for a new police chief has been completed and a new chief of police has been hired.

I am confident you will serve the citizens well while we search for a new department head. Congratulations on your appointment.

MEMO WRITER TIPS

1. Say what the temporary or acting position is.
2. Include when this appointment will begin, and indicate how long it will last.
3. Provide a brief description of what the interim appointee's responsibilities will be.
4. Close by adding your vote of confidence.

---

*This memorandum was written by a city manager.

PHRASING ALTERNATIVES

Paragraph 1

Until a new crew chief can be found, I want you to serve as Acting Crew Chief. Your appointment to this position will begin on Monday, June 14 and last until a new crew chief can be selected.

Congratulations on your appointment to the post of Acting Real Estate Manager. Stan Reynolds will be resigning on October 1, and it will probably take several months to get someone to fill the position.

I am pleased to appoint you as temporary Payroll Supervisor. The vacancy was announced last Thursday, and the closing date for the position is October 1. Until a new supervisor can be hired, you will be responsible for managing payroll operations.

Paragraph 2

I know you'll do a fine job.

Thanks for agreeing to take on this interim post. Your leadership skills will be needed more than ever now.

Accept my best wishes for a successful temporary appointment.

ASSIGNING A PROJECT WITH DEADLINES

To:
From:
Date:
Subject: Wilbourne Project

I need you to do a feasibility study on the Wilbourne Project and will need information about your progress by the following dates:

2/6	Drilling reports for the past six months
2/14	Analysis of Wilbourne's annual report
2/21	Cost estimates
2/28	Personnel projections
3/15	Final report with recommendations

This is an important project, and your timely updates will help me make decisions about this acquisition.

MEMO WRITER TIPS

1. Tell the reader what information you need, when. If the work can be divided into parts, list or bullet the deadlines for each part.

2. Explain why the deadlines are necessary.

PHRASING ALTERNATIVES

Paragraph 1

Please prepare your annual report and submit it to me no later than Wednesday, April 3. This will give me enough time to prepare the entire report for the division and get it to the vice president by May 1.

The supply inventory you're currently doing needs to be finished by July 15. Meeting this deadline will give us enough time to stock up on supplies we need before the end of this fiscal year.

This month's newsletter must be written and in camera-ready form no later than October 12. Unless we get it to the printer by October 15, we'll miss our distribution date.

CHANGING A SUBORDINATE'S JOB TITLE*

To:

From:

Date:

Subject: Job Title Change

Your new job title will be Director, Public Relations. This change will take effect on February 1. This job title more accurately reflects your current duties and responsibilities.

MEMO WRITER TIPS

1. In the first sentence, name the new job title.

2. Include the date when the change will take place.

3. Tell why this change in title has been made.

---

*This memorandum was written by the owner of a communications consulting firm.

PHRASING ALTERNATIVES

Paragraph 1

Effective April 18, your title will be changed from Director of Community Relations to Assistant Dean, Community Services. The new title describes what you do much better.

As we discussed, your job title will be changed to Supervisor of Volunteers on August 1. You'll have a lot more credibility in the eyes of the prospective volunteers you're recruiting.

Executive Assistant describes your role much more adequately. So, effective immediately, your job title is being changed. Thanks for the hard work you do.

CHANGING A WORK ASSIGNMENT

To:
From:
Date:
Subject: Change in Work Assignment

On Monday, January 3, you will be assigned to microfiche quality control for the next 30 days. In our efforts to familiarize everyone with all aspects of microfiche production, you will be moved to this position temporarily in order for you to experience the other end of production.

During this time, Cynthia Connover will be your immediate supervisor. Report to her at 8:00 Monday morning. Good luck on your new detail.

MEMO WRITER TIPS

1. Tell the employee what/where the new work assignment will be and what date this change will take place.

2. Briefly explain why the change has occurred.

3. Include information about who the new supervisor or manager will be and where/when the employee should contact this person.

PHRASING ALTERNATIVES

Paragraph 1

Your work assignment has been changed from shipping to delivery, effective Monday, March 4. This change was necessary to cover Phil's two-week vacation. When he returns, you will be reassigned to your regular duties.

Effective tomorrow, you will begin your new assignment in the message center, Room 304. They are currently short-handed and since this is our peak season, we need some extra help in this area. This new assignment will last approximately 30 days, at which time you will return to your present duties.

Paragraph 2

See Joe Lingo at 6:30 Monday morning. He will train you and get you started. Thanks for helping out in Phil's absence.

Margaret Levine will be your new supervisor. Report to her office at 1:00 p.m. today. She will spend this afternoon orienting you to your new duties.

CONFIRMING A RELOCATION

To:
From:
Date:
Subject: Relocation Confirmation

Your relocation to the regional office in Spokane, Washington, has been confirmed. Your reassignment there becomes effective Monday, July 10, 19____ .

A list of relocation benefits is attached. Contact the Personnel Office for additional details.

MEMO WRITER TIPS

1. Announce the confirmation of the move, to where, and the date the employee is to report to the new assignment.

2. Direct the employee to where he/she can find out about benefits available for relocation.

PHRASING ALTERNATIVES

Paragraph 1

This memo confirms your relocation to the home office, beginning Monday, August 21. This should provide you with ample time to make your arrangements here, visit the new city, and make the move.

Paragraph 2

Jan Addles in the Personnel Office can put you in contact with realtors both here and there and fill you in on the particulars. Your talents will be missed. I wish you well in your new home.

CROSS-TRAINING EMPLOYEES

To:
From:
Date:
Subject: Cross-Training

On Monday, November 1, 19_____ , you and John Smith will begin cross-training on each other's job. It is important for each employee in the unit to know the job of every other employee. This way, we can adequately cover the section when an employee is out and also get a better feel for how the process works all the way along the line.

Your supervisor, Kay Donalds, will meet with both of you first thing Monday morning. I'm sure you will find this cross-training beneficial and productive.

MEMO WRITER TIPS

1. Identify when and why cross-training is to begin.
2. Give the employees instructions on how to proceed.

PHRASING ALTERNATIVES

Paragraph 1

Your cross-training will begin on Monday, December 12, 19_____ . Having a work team totally versed in the functions of each person's job creates a more efficient, knowledgeable work unit.

Cross-training is an important element of keeping a work unit efficient. Therefore, you will start cross-training on Friday, October 10, 19_____ .

Paragraph 2

See Sue Givens at 8:00 on Monday. She will explain how the process is to work and will be a resource while you are learning each other's jobs.

Your supervisor will begin by conducting a four-hour block of instruction on both your jobs. Then you will begin hands-on training that afternoon. I know you will enjoy this added dimension of your work.

DISBANDING A TASK FORCE OR COMMITTEE

To:
From:
Date:
Subject: Disbanding a Task Force/Committee

The recommendations your committee submitted for company-sponsored daycare will be studied thoroughly. Thank you for your diligent work on this committee.

After your suggestions have been reviewed, each of you will receive a copy of my response.

MEMO WRITER TIPS

1. Tell the committee members what the outcome of their efforts will be and thank them for working on the committee.

2. Tell them when they might expect to hear from you about the recommendations they have made.

PHRASING ALTERNATIVES

Paragraph 1

The Benefits Policy Task Force has now completed its work. Your suggestions seem thorough and evidence a great deal of hard work and effort.

Your service on the New Accounts Task Force is now complete. Your recommendations will be considered, and a summary of final decisions will be distributed to each of you.

Paragraph 2

These suggestions will now be presented to the Board at its next meeting. Each of you can expect to receive a summary of the Board's decisions with regard to your recommendations.

Thanks for all your hard work.

DISCUSSING THE CREATION OF A NEW DEPARTMENT*

To:
From:
Date:
Subject: Special Services Division

A new department, the Special Services Division, has been created, effective July 1. Dr. Arlen Hayes will direct this division.

Special Services will more adequately serve the advising and counseling needs of students. Our rapid growth has made this change necessary, if we are to keep pace with the growing demand for student services.

A revised organizational chart is attached.

MEMO WRITER TIPS

1. Discuss what the new department is.
2. Briefly outline its services and why the department was created.

PHRASING ALTERNATIVES

Paragraph 1

A Facilities Management Department has been created. Since we canceled our contract with Ajax Janitorial Services, we must take care of our own facilities needs. Madge Hamilton has agreed to supervise this department.

The attached organizational chart updates our structure: a new division, Computer Repair, has been included. John Peck will direct the operations of our newest division.

Paragraph 2

This new department will handle room assignments, security, cleaning and maintenance.

Performing our repairs in-house will save us considerable money and downtime.

---

*This memorandum was written by a college president.

DISTRIBUTING A WORK SCHEDULE*

To:
From:
Date:
Subject: Work Schedule

Here's the work schedule for October 1 to October 30:

	MON	TUES	WEDS	THURS	FRI	SAT	SUN
7:00 a.m.– 3:30 p.m.	Baker————————————————————Jones———
3:00 p.m.–11:30 p.m.	Jones————————————Lucas————————————
7:30 p.m.– 4:00 a.m.	xxxxxxxxxxxxxx Bridges————————————————xxx
11:00 p.m.– 7:30 a.m.	Lucas—Harris————————————————Bridges

MEMO WRITER TIPS

1. Present the schedule in as simple a form as possible.
2. If you can chart or graph it, the schedule will be easier to follow.

PHRASING ALTERNATIVES

Paragraph 1

The schedule for the month of April is as follows:

Here is the schedule of your work hours for the next month.

These are work schedule hours for the next 60 days.

EXTENDING A TEMPORARY APPOINTMENT†

To:
From:
Date:
Subject: Use of Temporary Employee beyond 90 Days

This is confirmation of my approval of your extended use of the temporary employee who is doing traffic reporting for the commuter traffic network. It is my

---

*This memorandum was drafted by a police department watch commander.
† The Director of Administration for a metropolitan transit district prepared this memorandum.

understanding that it is important to have the individual continue in this function beyond the 90-day limit called for in our Temporary Pool Guidelines. I encourage you to recommend a part-time position if you plan to continue this activity beyond the end of the current contract period.

MEMO WRITER TIPS

1. Name the temporary appointment, and tell how long it has been extended/approved for.
2. Thank the appointee for continued good service.

PHRASING ALTERNATIVES

Paragraph 1

An extension has been granted on your temporary contract. You will be retained for an additional 30 days in this capacity. As per company policy, no extensions can be granted beyond 30 days, unless a full-time permanent position can be justified. We do not anticipate announcing such a vacancy.

Your temporary contract as Data Systems Operator has been renewed for another 90 days. You have worked diligently to help us eliminate our work backlog, and we are confident we should be up-to-date, with your help, by the end of the 90 days.

Paragraph 2

Please sign the attached contract and return it to the Personnel Office. If, for some reason, you will be unable to accept this extension, please let me know today.

GIVING A SUBORDINATE ADDITIONAL DUTIES

To:
From:
Date:
Subject: Additional Duties

As you know, Lee Atwater will be taking a year-long leave of absence, beginning June 1. You expressed an interest in assuming some of his duties until he returns July 1 next year. Of the ones we discussed, you seemed most interested in and have the skills to do the following:

- Schedule training seminars
- Conduct management training, as needed
- Develop requests for proposals (RFP's) for contractual services
- Conduct training needs assessments

These duties seem to mesh well with your current activities, so I would like to assign them to you. I am recommending an increase of $3,537.00 to compensate you for these additional responsibilities. Understand that you will be doing these functions only until Lee returns, at which time we will have to reevaluate the situation and make reassignments, as necessary.

If these additional duties meet your approval, call me so we can make the necessary arrangements with the personnel office. Taking on these duties would both help the company and develop your skills as well.

MEMO WRITER TIPS

1. Explain why the additional duties are being given to the employee.

2. In most cases, this issue would have been discussed with the subordinate in person, so the memorandum serves as notice of your final decision and confirmation of the specifics entailed.

3. Spell out, specifically, what the additional duties will be and how/if the employee will be compensated for carrying them out.

4. Let the employee know what the next step in the process should be.

5. Close by affirming your hope that the employee will accept these additional duties.

PHRASING ALTERNATIVES

Paragraph 1

Last week, we discussed the possibility of your taking on additional assignments, in order to balance out the effects of our recent early retirement policy. A number of employees in your department have chosen the early retirement option, which means their work duties must be redistributed among the remaining members of the department.

Until a new security technician can be hired, please check the third and fourth floors, in addition to your regular duties. Your hourly rate will be increased by $.40 per hour in order to compensate you for these extra duties.

Paragraph 2

The responsibilities that most closely match your experience and expertise include (1) developing a prospect list, (2) following up on cold sales calls, and (3) assuming responsibility for our Bush/Hannon Service Area.

Please see me immediately if you have any questions. We will try to hire an additional person as soon as possible.

Paragraph 3

Since no monetary compensation can be offered to you, with the exception of additional commission incentives, I am willing to discuss how your current duties might be adjusted in order for you to take on these new assignments.

Paragraph 4

Let's meet this week to discuss this in more detail.

MAKING A SPECIAL PROJECTS ASSIGNMENT

To:
From:
Date:
Subject: Special Project Assignment

You have been assigned the following special project, in order to help collect sufficient data for our annual report, due June 30.

1. Contact each department and collect the annual budget analyses.
2. See finance for budget forecasts for the coming year.
3. Get a list of goals/accomplishments from each department head.
4. Write a brief narrative outlining the achievements of each department.
5. Prepare a summary of the organization's operations for the past year.

Mark Whitten is available to help you. I need all this information no later than June 1. I know you'll get the job done.

MEMO WRITER TIPS

1. Tell the employee he/she has been given a special project.

2. Include why the special project is needed and how long the subordinate will need to work on this task.

3. Be specific about what you want the employee to do.

4. Let him/her know whether additional assistance is available.

PHRASING ALTERNATIVES

Paragraph 1

We have decided to bid on the Caldwell Construction Project. April 30, 19____ , marks the bid deadline, so someone will have to devote full time to this special project until then.

The new Production Planning Software Project is underway. I need someone to assume responsibility for software design and, naturally, thought of you. I realize this will add additional duties to your present assignments, but I think we'd be able to adjust your duties in such a way that you could devote full time to this special project, at least through the debugging stage.

Paragraph 2

Since your proposal helped us win the Carstead Project last year, I'd like you to assume responsibility for developing this proposal, as well.

I've scheduled a meeting in my office on Wednesday, September 3 at 1:00 p.m. to discuss the Project. Join me then.

Paragraph 3

Let me know what kind of help you'll need, and I'll see what can be arranged. This is an important project, one I'm confident you'll handle in your usual efficient way.

NOTIFYING SUBORDINATES ABOUT AN UPCOMING PEAK WORKLOAD

To:
From:
Date:
Subject: Upcoming Peak Period

Our peak period of activity will begin in the next two weeks. If last year is any example, we can expect our call volume to increase by about 200 percent during this time.

Please have your equipment double-checked this week to make sure it's in proper working order. Check your supplies and order any additional forms or other supplies you will need. Review your training manual so that you're thoroughly familiar with codes and procedures.

Remember, each new call represents the possibility of additional income for us all. Your past performance has been admirable, and I'm sure we'll tackle this year's peak with the same energy and efficiency.

MEMO WRITER TIPS

1. Announce when the peak period will occur and what workers can expect in the way of increased workload.

2. Discuss whatever steps they should take to prepare themselves for this increase in work.

3. Let employees know you are confident they'll be able to handle the increased volume.

PHRASING ALTERNATIVES

Paragraph 1

Let's gear up for the season rush likely to hit July 1. Make sure all displays look their best. Sales prices should be prominently displayed at marked locations. Each salesclerk should review checkout and refund procedures. Floor managers should inspect their departments for cleanliness and to ensure adequate inventory is available.

Claims traditionally increase about 45 percent each spring. As this busy season approaches, make sure your equipment and supplies are at peak levels and that you are ready to handle the increased workload.

Paragraph 2

This is our busiest time of the year, folks. So sell, sell, sell! Remember service and customer satisfaction are our trademarks.

I'm counting on each of you to once again get us through this harried season. When it's over, we'll celebrate in the usual fashion.

READJUSTING A SUBORDINATE'S DUTIES

To:
From:
Date:
Subject: Change in Work Assignments

Some adjustments seem necessary, in order to better manage the increasing workload in secretarial support services. Since the various divisions have increased the number of personnel needing secretarial support, the following adjustments are being made:

Current Work Assignments	
Real Estate/Commercial	B. Peck
Accounting/Data Processing	N. Jones
Research/Budget	F. Scott
Contracts	J. Smith
New Accounts	L. Troup
Old Accounts	B. Metacamp

New Assignments	
New/Old Accounts	B. Metacamp
Accounting/Budget	F. Scott
Contracts	J. Smith
Research	N. Jones
Data Processing	L. Troup
Real Estate/Commercial	B. Peck

This new arrangement should more evenly distribute the workload. After 60 days, we'll discuss the reorganization to see how effectively it seems to be working. Thank you for your cooperation during this change.

MEMO WRITER TIPS

1. Explain why the change is being made and specifically outline what duties will be readjusted and what personnel will be affected.

2. Include information about any other special arrangements, such as trial periods, outlets for grievances, etc.

PHRASING ALTERNATIVES

Paragraph 1

Currently, your major responsibilities include answering the switchboard, screening and forwarding incoming calls, taking and routing messages, and processing incoming mail.

Up until now, your routes have included the southern and eastern sections of our delivery area. With the addition of a new driver and an additional vehicle, you will now be responsible for the southern section only. The new driver will service the eastern delivery area.

Paragraph 2

With the installation of our new Generations Switchboard, the number of incoming lines will double. For this reason, your duties are being adjusted so that your primary responsibility will be answering calls for marketing, real estate, and claims. The relief switchboard operator will be assigned to answer calls for purchasing, personnel, data entry, and administration.

This division will give you both approximately the same number of customers and will enable me to reduce overtime costs and costs related to vehicle repair.

Paragraph 3

Hopefully, this will effect an equitable division of duties. If you have questions, let me know.

REJECTING A REQUEST
FOR POSITION AUDIT

To:
From:
Date:
Subject: Position Audit

As a result of annual performance appraisals, certain positions are slated for audits during the upcoming fiscal year. While I discussed the increasing complexity of your job, I did not target your position for audit next year. Therefore, your request for a desk audit must be denied at this time.

At appraisal time next year, let's examine your duties closely, and I'll decide whether a position audit might be justified then.

MEMO WRITER TIPS

1. Explain what the procedure is for position audit and how positions for such audits are identified.

2. In this instance, give the reasons first, then tell the subordinate that the audit has not been approved.

3. Explain what future actions might be taken.

PHRASING ALTERNATIVES

Paragraph 1

An analysis of your current duties indicates they parallel those outlined in your job description. Position audits are conducted when an employee's duties and/or responsibilities clearly call for higher skill, educational, or experience levels than those for which the employee is currently being paid.

Current funding levels have necessitated a freeze on hiring and promotion for the rest of this fiscal year. Therefore, your request for position audit cannot be approved.

Paragraph 2

Since this does not appear to be the case in this instance, I cannot approve an audit of your position as it is currently structured.

I appreciate your desire to move up in the agency, and I will reexamine your request at the proper time.

Paragraph 3

Should this change in the future, I will reevaluate your case.

RELIEVING A SUBORDINATE
OF A TEMPORARY/ACTING POSITION

To:
From:
Date:
Subject: Change in Temporary Assignment

A new Operations Manager, Maude Sommerset, will begin work on August 1, 19_____. You will then return to your former duties as Assistant Manager of Operations.

Ms. Sommerset, who has 15 years of experience and impeccable credentials, will have a fine assistant upon whom to rely. Your efforts as Acting Operations Manager have helped us get through a very difficult period, and they are very much appreciated.

I'm sure you'll help your new manager in any way possible. Thanks again for your hard work over the past three (3) months.

MEMO WRITER TIPS

1. In the case where someone else has been hired to fill the position permanently, tell the employee who that person is and mention something about what makes that individual qualified for the position.

2. Thank the employee for serving in the acting capacity.

PHRASING ALTERNATIVES

Paragraph 1

Effective July 1, you will resume your duties as Assistant Branch Chief. A new Branch Chief will begin work on that date. I understand Stan Whittlefield, a manager with 17 years' service with the company, got the job. Stan and I worked together years ago when we were just starting out. He is an able manager and a good man.

You have done an admirable job as temporary Payroll Supervisor for the past three (3) weeks. After extensive interviews with a number of qualified applicants, I have chosen someone with 15 years' supervisory experience for this position.

Paragraph 2

I want to commend you for supervising operations for the past two (2) months.

I'm sure she'll have many questions, and I hope you'll welcome her to our company and help her make the transition as quickly and smoothly as possible.

Paragraph 3

Thank you for a job well done.

Accept my sincere appreciation for your efforts to meet payroll demands until a permanent supervisor could be found.

REQUESTING A POSITION AUDIT*

To:
From:
Date:
Subject: Request for Position Audit

When I accepted this position, I was told that the job would be audited for a possible salary upgrade. I would like to know when such an audit might occur, as my responsibilities seem to warrant a higher salary.

MEMO WRITER TIPS

1. Ask for the position audit.
2. Explain why you think an audit is warranted.

PHRASING ALTERNATIVES

Paragraph 1

Since I agreed to take on additional responsibilities when the other receptionist in my office resigned, I am requesting an audit of my current job. I am now answering twice as many incoming phone lines, as well as taking messages for four additional departments.

The work assignments and job responsibilities of my job seem to match those of an associate editor, rather than an editorial assistant. Would you audit my job, to determine whether my position should be upgraded? Documentation for this audit request is attached.

---

*A paralegal in a law firm wrote this memorandum.

RESPONDING TO A SUBORDINATE'S TRANSFER REQUEST

To:
From:
Date:
Subject: Transfer Request

I have received your request for a transfer and am forwarding it to the Personnel Department for further action. From what they tell me, transfer requests are currently taking between two and four weeks to process.

I will let you know the status of your request as soon as Personnel informs me.

MEMO WRITER TIPS

1. Acknowledge that you have received the request for transfer.
2. Advise the employee of what the next steps will be and when you might get back to him/her with a response.

PHRASING ALTERNATIVES

Paragraph 1

Your request for a transfer has been received.

Your transfer request has been received.

Paragraph 2

The Human Development Office handles all such requests, based on available openings, seniority rights, and performance ratings.

Approval of transfers is based on a number of factors: number of requests, seniority, available openings, and reason for request.

Paragraph 3

These requests normally take two to four weeks to process. I should have a notification of action within 30 days.

I will contact you within the next 30 days to let you know the status of your request.

Model Memos about Work Performance Issues

Once everyone knows what work gets done by whom, HOW that work gets done becomes the critical factor. If employees work hard and well, a memorandum can applaud their efforts. When workers are doing their jobs, but could be doing more, a memorandum might motivate them to put forth extra effort. When employee performance is substandard, the talk you have with the employee about improving work habits can be followed up by a memorandum that outlines corrective action.

Exemplary work performance needs attention. Who won an award or a contest? Who met production or sales goals? Who satisfactorily completed probation with the company? Who's the employee of the month? Who's marking another anniversary date with your agency?

Routine work performance issues must be communicated: time for performance appraisals, time to resign and move on, time to follow up on work that has deadlines.

Unsatisfactory work performance issues demand attention as well. Use the memoranda in this chapter to warn an employee whose "moonlighting" has begun to affect job performance. Document a counseling session with an employee or document your counseling session with your boss. Follow up on a customer complaint and explain, in writing, why discourteous treatment and inefficient service can't be tolerated. Address problems of excessive absenteeism or tardiness. When you need a written record of poor job performance, use one of the model memoranda in this chapter to help you make your case.

The model memoranda in Chapter 4 can help you make it clear HOW the work in your organization should be or has been done.

ACCEPTING A SUBORDINATE'S RESIGNATION

To:
From:
Date:
Subject: Acceptance of Resignation

With regret, I accept your resignation from your position as Marketing Manager. You leave behind an impressive record with the company.

I know I speak for all of us when I wish you continued success with your new position. If I can ever be of any service in the future, please don't hesitate to contact me.

MEMO WRITER TIPS

1. In the first sentence, accept the resignation and name the position from which the employee is resigning.
2. Include at least one sentence commending the employee for his/her contributions to the company.
3. Wish the employee well in future endeavors.

PHRASING ALTERNATIVES

Paragraph 1

Your resignation from your Radiology Technician position is accepted.

I am sorry to see you go, but realize your need to move on. Your resignation is accepted, effective March 14.

Paragraph 2

You will be difficult to replace, and your hard work will be missed.

I applaud your exceptional contributions to the organization for the past three (3) years.

Paragraph 3

On behalf of all of us, good luck and best wishes. Congratulations on your appointment at Radion Corporation.

I wish you continued success in your career.

ANNOUNCING A
PERFORMANCE REVIEW

To:

From:

Date:

Subject: Annual Performance Review

I have scheduled the following appointments for annual performance reviews:

Jan Slokam	Monday, December 3, 8:00 a.m.
Phil Tolbert	Monday, December 3, 9:30 a.m.
Michele Jones	Monday, December 3, 11:00 a.m.
Leslie Richard	Tuesday, December 4, 8:00 a.m.
Arthur Hammond	Tuesday, December 4, 9:30 a.m.
Annette Osborn	Tuesday, December 4, 11:00 a.m.

I have to complete all performance reviews by December 10 and submit them to the personnel office. I look forward to discussing your work performance for the past year with you, to identify your strengths and areas that may need improvement.

We will meet in my office.

MEMO WRITER TIPS

1. Tell employees when and where their performance reviews will be conducted.

2. Outline a schedule if you have several employees to review.

3. Add a positive comment about the purpose for the performance review process.

PHRASING ALTERNATIVES

Paragraph 1

Please plan to meet with me on Friday, June 1, to review your performance for the past year. Meet me at 9:00 a.m., my office.

Performance review time is once again upon us. The evaluation process is an important one, as salary increases and promotions are based upon the results of annual performance appraisals. Your review will take place Tuesday, January 14, 10:30 a.m., in my office.

Annual performance reviews will begin next week. Yours has been scheduled for Thursday, May 24 at 11:00 a.m. We will meet in my office.

Paragraph 2

Come prepared to discuss the contributions you've made during the past year. I am anxious to discuss how well you've performed since your last appraisal.

Annual performance reviews are an important part of our continuing efforts to upgrade performance and create a solid work team. I look forward to discussing your production efforts with you.

We will have the opportunity to determine whether or not the goals we set last year have been met. Getting feedback about performance helps us all do a better job.

ANNOUNCING AN AWARD

To:
From:
Date:
Subject: Top Producer Award

Harry Beckman has been chosen to receive the Top Producer Award for fiscal year 19_____ . As lead salesperson in his department, Harry established 52 new accounts and exceeded sales goals by 43 percent.

Harry will receive his award at this Friday's recognition banquet. Join me in congratulating Mr. Beckman on his fine work and outstanding sales record.

MEMO WRITER TIPS

1. Put the names of the recipient and the award in the first sentence.
2. Briefly explain why the award has been given.
3. Include information about presentation ceremonies.
4. Close by congratulating the recipient and encouraging others to do the same.

PHRASING ALTERNATIVES

Paragraph 1

This year's Faculty Member of the Year is Janice Calgood, Social Sciences Professor.

I am pleased to announce this year's Management Excellence award winner: Mr. Avery Smith.

John Jones, Chief of Research and Development, is this year's Outstanding Employee award recipient.

Paragraph 2

Mr. Beckman's software design has earned the company well over $5.6 million dollars.

Mark's unit consistently exceeded production goals by 35 percent.

Marsha Menton's efforts have positively affected employee relations and have improved communication throughout the organization.

Paragraph 3

Congratulations, Harry, on your outstanding performance. I know your colleagues will personally take the time to congratulate you, as well.

Stop by Jane's office and congratulate her on receiving this prestigious award.

This honor, in small part, symbolizes our recognition of your excellence, and we all send special congratulations to mark this significant achievement.

ANNOUNCING A CONTEST WINNER

To:
From:
Date:
Subject: "Sky's the Limit" Contest Winner

Ms. Margaret Slokam has won the "Sky's the Limit" sales contest. Along with topping the charts with $51,000 in monthly sales, Margaret also designed an effective sales logo and slogan.

Margaret will receive a $500.00 cash bonus and a weekend stay for two at the Retreat Inn in Vail.

Congratulations, Margaret, on a job well done.

MEMO WRITER TIPS

1. Name the contest and the contest winner.
2. Spell out why the winner won.
3. Tell what the reward will be, as an incentive to others in the department.
4. Congratulate the winner.

PHRASING ALTERNATIVES

Paragraph 1

Our monthly promotion contest has been won by Mr. Martin Coil.

The winner of our Hawaiian Luau contest is Harry Phillips.

I am pleased to announce the winner of the Trailblazer Contest: Ms. Margaret Slokam.

Paragraph 2

Martin sold more than $45,000 worth of goods last month.

As contest winner, Harry sold 65 new policies last quarter.

More than 35 new accounts were opened by Margaret during the past 60 days.

Paragraph 3

For his outstanding performance, Martin will receive an all-expenses-paid trip for two to Oahu.

Harry will get a $1,000 cash bonus.

In addition to a weekend for two at the Kinnerly Lodge, Margaret will receive a $50.00 per month salary increase.

Paragraph 4

Join me in congratulating Martin on this significant accomplishment.

On behalf of the company, congratulations on your contest win.

Congratulations are certainly in order. You've done an outstanding job!

ASKING AN EMPLOYEE TO COMPLETE A SELF-APPRAISAL*

To:
From:
Date:
Subject: Annual Work Plan

Call Lisa sometime during the next two weeks to schedule an appointment to review your annual work plan. Use the attached form to discuss your (1) accomplishments for 19_____ , (2) goals for 19_____ , (3) goals for personal/professional career development, and (4) concerns or recommendations for improvement.

---

*This memorandum was written by the Dean of Instruction of a college.

MEMO WRITER TIPS

1. Let the employee know when the performance appraisal will be scheduled. Include where it will take place.

2. Include instructions for completing the self-appraisal form.

PHRASING ALTERNATIVES

Paragraph 1

Please complete the attached self-appraisal form and bring it with you to our appraisal conference: Monday, June 2, 3:00 p.m., room 202.

In preparation for your annual performance review, you need to fill out the attached self-appraisal form. I will schedule a review conference for you in the next few weeks.

A complete performance review process includes an employee's assessment of his/her performance as well as that of the supervisor. An appraisal form is attached. Please bring your completed form to my office on Monday, May 18, 1:00 p.m. We'll have the opportunity to compare assessments of your performance then. I look forward to a constructive, profitable discussion.

COMMENDING AN EMPLOYEE FOR A JOB WELL DONE*

To:
From:
Date:
Subject: Job Classification Study

One of the most important projects that employees can be involved in is to have input into a job classification system. I have been very pleased with the work that has been done by your group and know that the quality of our system will be much better as a result of your efforts. We expect to have the revised system in place in early 19____ .

For all of your hard work, I extend to you a heartfelt thank you.

---

*This memorandum was written by a Human Resources Specialist for a municipal government agency.

MEMO WRITER TIPS

1. Outline what job the employee(s) has(ve) done and why it is important to your organization.

2. Thank the employee for doing a good job.

PHRASING ALTERNATIVES

Paragraph 1

I want to commend you for taking the initiative to track the flow of paperwork in our department. Your work will save us a lot of duplication of effort.

Our supply system has needed to be revised for quite some time. The new system will make it much easier for people to get the supplies they need, when they need them.

Paragraph 2

Please accept my sincerest congratulations on a job well done.

Your efforts, above and beyond the call of duty, are commendable. I thank you.

COMMUNICATING ABOUT SUBSTANDARD PRODUCT QUALITY

To:

From:

Date:

Subject: Defective Brackets

Brackets in Lot #40 are defective. They should be able to withstand 40 pounds of pressure, but quality control has informed me these brackets barely handle 30 pounds of pressure.

These brackets will have to be melted and reforged, in order for them to meet specifications. I want someone assigned to check samples from each 100 brackets off the line.

Costly errors like this cannot be tolerated. Discuss the problem with your personnel and make sure we don't have this problem again.

MEMO WRITER TIPS

1. Be specific about what the product is and why it is defective.
2. Discuss what corrective action is to be taken, and remind the subordinate you don't expect this problem in the future.

PHRASING ALTERNATIVES

Paragraph 1

Quality Control has reported a 32 percent error rate in data entered in your section.

The switches produced on Friday, January 4 are not firing properly.

Page 3 of the newsletters printed last week for the Marketing Department are blurred.

Paragraph 2

Take the following corrective action today:

- Inspect the remaining computers in that shipment.
- Return any found to be defective to the line.
- Supervise, personally, any reworking required.

Ship the customer a new batch, Express Mail, no later than 5:00 p.m. today.

Pick up the defective chairs and deliver new ones.

Paragraph 3

Our customers expect quality products from us, and I intend to deliver. Let's see to it this doesn't happen again.

We are known for our quality manufacturing, and such substandard production costs us money, time, and reputation. Monitor production carefully so that this does not happen again.

We can't afford such costly mistakes, and I expect this problem will be corrected immediately.

COMMUNICATING ABOUT INEFFICIENT SERVICE

To:
From:
Date:
Subject: Late Delivery

Magnusson Office Supplies called yesterday to complain that the order they were promised for January 14 was not delivered until February 3. Magnusson is one of our best customers and has been doing business with us for more than 10 years.

I assured them this problem would not reoccur and gave them a 2 percent discount on the order. Follow up with a letter of apology and make sure this doesn't happen again.

MEMO WRITER TIPS

1. Describe, specifically, what the inefficiency was and, if possible, when it occurred.

2. Affirm the customer's right to receive efficient service.

3. Close by spelling out what corrective action is necessary, and reaffirm your position that incidents of inefficiency must be corrected.

PHRASING ALTERNATIVES

Paragraph 1

Neimeyer Company ordered 50 boxes of photocopy paper on February 12, but received 50 boxes of stationery instead.

Why were Mr. George Olman's (Case #44567) laboratory test results lost?

Hamilton and Associates called for price quotations three days ago, but no one has yet returned their call.

Paragraph 2

All customers are entitled to receive their orders—per their specifications—on time, and in good condition.

When orders aren't filled correctly and quickly, we lose money—and the respect of our clients. When respect is lost, we don't get their orders.

In a highly competitive field like ours, clients choose us because they have come to expect our efficient service. They expect it, and I expect we'll give it to them.

Paragraph 3

Call them and offer our sincere apologies for the mix-up. Let them know this was a one-time mistake, one they can expect will not happen again.

Enroll in the January 31 Customer Relations course offered by the training department. Call Jan Rutledge at EXT. 431 for additional details.

You normally function so efficiently; this complaint took me completely by surprise. I know this problem won't surface again.

COMMUNICATING ABOUT DISCOURTEOUS TREATMENT OF A CLIENT*

To:
From:
Date:
Subject: Citizen Complaint

Last Wednesday, Councilwoman Johnson called to find out why two patrol cars were parked side-by-side and why the officers sat in their cars, talking for 10 minutes. Dispatcher Lori Hood took this call.

Lori told the councilwoman, "I don't know; I'm not out there." The conversation lasted for more than 15 minutes, when the dispatcher finally turned the call over to the Watch Commander.

It was clear from listening to the recording that Dispatcher Hood was very rude to Ms. Johnson. I discussed this incident with Lori at length, and she has promised that it will not happen again. Since Lori is an excellent employee, and this is the first incident of this kind, no further action seems warranted.

---

*A Communications Supervisor for a police department wrote this memo.

MEMO WRITER TIPS

1. Describe the incident involving discourteous treatment in detail. Make sure your explanation focuses on facts, rather than speculations.

2. Affirm how important it is to maintain positive relationships with customers and clients.

3. If you are writing to your superior, tell what action has been taken, and reassure your boss that such an incident will not happen again.

4. If you are writing to a subordinate, use this memorandum as a follow-up to your verbal reprimand, reiterating what action has been/will be taken. Make it clear that discourtesy will not be tolerated.

PHRASING ALTERNATIVES

Paragraph 1

An irate customer called yesterday to complain that she was put on "hold" five times, transferred to three different departments, and then finally "hung up on" by the last person to whom she spoke.

Yesterday, I received a letter from a Mr. George Hagelthorpe, regarding discourteous treatment he received while shopping in our menswear department on November 15, 19____ .

Ms. Selma Jordan called yesterday to complain about the treatment she received on May 22, as she was trying to get current values on her stock portfolio.

Paragraph 2

I have discussed this matter with the employee in question, and he says the caller became verbally abusive, prompting him to terminate the call. While this in no way excuses his discourtesy, it does, in part, make his case that he was not wholly at fault.

Maintaining the positive regard of our customers is our number one priority. Without them, none of us would be employed. You might consider this fact the next time you are tempted to act rudely to a customer.

Rudeness to clients cannot be tolerated under any circumstances. In future, let your supervisor handle the call if you feel you cannot manage the client in a friendly, courteous way.

Paragraph 3

Because of the serious nature of this infraction and the fact that this is not the first time customers have complained about Ms. X's treatment, Ms. X is being suspended for three days without pay. I have informed her of her suspension and warned her that any future maltreatment of customers will result in her termination.

The employee has written a letter of apology to the client, and a letter of reprimand has been placed in her personnel file.

I expect we will have no further episodes of discourteous treatment of clients. Such acts can never be rationalized, under any circumstances. See to it that this never happens again.

CONGRATULATING A PEER ON A PROMOTION

To:
From:
Date:
Subject: Congratulations

Congratulations on your recent promotion to Retail Services Manager. You've really worked hard this past year, and no one deserves the promotion more than you.

Accept my best wishes for your continued success.

MEMO WRITER TIPS

1. Extend your congratulations, including the name of the new position.
2. Include at least one sentence that covers why you think the person deserved the promotion.

PHRASING ALTERNATIVES

Paragraph 1

Way to go, Jim. I just heard about your upcoming promotion to Regional Vice-president.

No one could be more pleased about your promotion to National Sales Rep.

Accept my heartiest best wishes on your promotion to Executive Assistant.

Paragraph 2

Keep up the good work!

On behalf of all my staff, we wish you the best.

Good luck in your new position; I know you'll do well.

CURBING MOONLIGHTING

To:
From:
Date:
Subject: Off-Duty Work Policy

Guidelines for work during off-duty hours are included in the employee handbook. Generally, the "moonlighting" policy does not restrict such work, unless the off-duty work affects on-the-job performance.

In the past 30 days, you have been tardy for work three times and have called in sick twice. While you assured me that your part-time job would not interfere with your work here, it would seem that your moonlighting is, indeed, beginning to affect your performance.

This is your primary job, and you are expected to be here every day, on time, and ready to work. If your attendance problems persist, we will need to review the issue of your off-duty work.

MEMO WRITER TIPS

1. Explain, specifically, why you are addressing the issue of moonlighting with the employee.

2. Refer to any policies or guidelines that may exist about this issue.

3. Tell the employee what action you expect him/her to take and how you may handle the situation if the problem(s) persists.

PHRASING ALTERNATIVES

Paragraph 1

The Employee Handbook outlines specific policies regarding moonlighting.

The policy about off-duty work is clear.

Are you familiar with the policy regarding moonlighting?

Paragraph 2

Moonlighting is acceptable as long as it does not have a negative impact on your work here.

Working off-duty jobs is strictly prohibited.

In most instances, employees can work other jobs, as long as they maintain acceptable performance here.

Paragraph 3

Recently, you have been so exhausted that you almost fell asleep on the job on at least two occasions.

Your moonlighting seems to have made it difficult for you to get here daily and promptly.

Your production has fallen well below standards since you began work on your part-time job.

Paragraph 4

I'm sure you realize how important it is for you to give this job your primary focus. Let's discuss the problems you've been having and resolve this issue once and for all.

Obviously, you cannot give optimal effort to both jobs. If you do not curb your moonlighting, you are in danger of having to choose which job you prefer.

Your moonlighting has begun to jeopardize your employment here. Unless you can resolve these problems, you will need to decide whether the benefits derived from your part-time employment warrant the problems you are currently experiencing on your primary job.

DEVELOPING CO-WORKER COOPERATION

To:
From:
Date:
Subject: Co-Worker Cooperation

During the past several months, several conflicts have emerged among management team members.

Our company is interested in maximizing *all* managers' potential. I would be happy to mediate a meeting to resolve any issues you and colleagues may have in this regard.

MEMO WRITER TIPS

1. Communicate about this issue in person, if possible.

2. If you write a memo, suggest a plan of action or agree to play a mediator role in order to promote co-worker cooperation.

DOCUMENTATION FOR TERMINATION ACTION

To: File
From:
Date:
Subject: Work Record—Harold Sanford

3/8/__	Mr. Sanford was 15 minutes late for work. Did not call in. (9:10 a.m.)
3/11/__	Harold called in sick; said he overslept. (9:18 a.m.)
3/19/__	Harold asked to leave work one hour early; said he had a family emergency. (4:18 p.m.)
3/20/__	Counseled Harold. Told him he needed to report for work each day, on time. Harold said he "had some personal problems," but would "get my act together."
3/22/__	Harold called in sick; said his car wouldn't start. (9:00 a.m.)
3/26/__	Harold took two hours for lunch without asking for annual leave. When I asked him why he'd taken so long for lunch, he said he "got caught in traffic." (2:30 p.m.)

MEMO WRITER TIPS

1. In the event you must terminate an employee, you will need documentation of the poor performance that led to the termination.

2. Record each incident as it occurs. Complete sentences are not necessary.

3. Include dates and times.

4. Provide as much specific information about what occurred as you can.

DOCUMENTING AN EMPLOYEE COUNSELING SESSION

To: File
From:
Date:
Subject: Counseling Session—Janice Owens

ITEMS DISCUSSED

    I had a counseling session with Janice Owens on Tuesday, July 3, 19____ , at 2:00 p.m. The following items were discussed:

1. Janice's frequent absences from work (five days in the past month).
2. Janice's missed deadlines on the Woodward and Keystone reports.
3. Janice's confrontational communication style. She has had arguments with three other employees in the department during the past two weeks.

EMPLOYEE RESPONSE

1. Janice said her child has been ill, and she has had to miss work because of this. She assured me she would make every effort to get to work every day, on time.
2. Janice said she could not get the figures from the research department, and she could not finish the reports without them.
3. Janice said she has been under considerable pressure lately and that this had probably contributed to her "short fuse."

SUPERVISOR REPLY

1. I suggested Janice make arrangements for childcare so she would not have to miss work again. She said such arrangements have been made.
2. I told Janice to let me know when she found herself unable to meet a deadline. I suggested I might be able to help her get the information she needed. She agreed.
3. I directed Janice to speak to each of the three workers, apologize to them, and explain why she had lost her temper.
4. I referred Janice to the Employee Assistance Program.

MEMO WRITER TIPS

1. Outline what topics were covered in the counseling session, as well as when the session took place.

2. Record the employee's responses.

3. Include any suggestions you made, and record what the employee said in response to these suggestions.

4. Be as specific as possible.

DRAFTING A RESIGNATION

To:
From:
Date:
Subject: Resignation

With regret, I will be resigning my position as Medical Technologist, effective Friday, February 24, 19_____ . I have accepted a position as Laboratory Chief at Montview Community Hospital.

Thank you for your assistance and support during the past four (4) years. If I can help you find a suitable replacement, let me know.

MEMO WRITER TIPS

1. State what position you are resigning from and the effective date of your resignation.

2. Give a reason for your resignation and keep it positive. Now is not the time, regardless of the circumstances, to "burn bridges."

3. Thank your present employer for assistance and support and offer to help with screening applicants or training a replacement, if you are inclined to do so.

PHRASING ALTERNATIVES

Paragraph 1

Please accept this memorandum as my resignation from my position as Manager III. Friday, June 22, 19_____ , will be my last day of work.

Regrettably, I must resign from my job as Mailroom Supervisor, effective Friday, January 17, 19_____ .

As of Friday, August 6, 19_____ , I am resigning as Policy Analyst.

Paragraph 2

While I have enjoyed my employment at XYZ Corporation, I feel now is the time to pursue other career goals.

My spouse is being relocated to Spartan, Tennessee.

Barton Electronics has offered me an excellent position with their company.

Paragraph 3

You have helped make my tenure here a successful, productive one, and I thank you for your assistance over the years.

The support and encouragement you have given me for the past two years have been greatly appreciated.

I appreciate the help you've given me during my employment with XYZ International.

HANDLING EXCESSIVE ABSENTEEISM

To:
From:
Date:
Subject: Frequent Absences

Each member of our work unit is an important part of the team. That's why even a single absence affects the overall functioning of the work unit.

During the past 30 days, you have been absent eight (8) times. This seems to me a bit excessive. We have spoken about your attendance problem in the past, and while you assured me you would correct the problem, your excessive absenteeism persists.

Expecting others to continually make up for your absences is unfair and cannot be tolerated. Accept this as notice that if you are absent again, disciplinary action will be taken, and termination proceedings may begin.

Feel free to call me or come by my office if you wish to discuss this matter further.

MEMO WRITER TIPS

1. Some positive statement about the necessity of being at work may start the memo off on a positive note.

2. You should then give specifics about the number of absences the employee has had.

3. If this has not been a persistent problem, warn the employee about the attendance problem; set up a time to discuss the situation face-to-face.

4. If this is a recurring problem, a more severe tone is warranted, and you should tell the employee what disciplinary action you plan to take.

PHRASING ALTERNATIVES

Paragraph 1

You are an essential part of our work group, and your absence makes things difficult for us all.

Regular attendance, except for legitimate absence, is required of all personnel.

Each employee must do his/her job efficiently if the work group is to perform successfully.

Paragraph 2

You have been absent 14 times in the past 30 days; this is not acceptable.

You have developed a pattern of absenteeism, by missing work 10 times in the past 20 days.

Your excessive absenteeism—9 of the past 20 days—cannot be tolerated.

Paragraph 3

After our original discussion, you agreed to change this pattern. Still, the problem exists. If you cannot get to work regularly—every day—you will be fired.

When I spoke to you about this problem initially, you made a commitment to report for work every day. Since you have not kept your part of the bargain, I must begin termination action.

You said you would not be absent again when we discussed this issue, but your excessive absenteeism has continued. You are suspended without pay for five (5) days.

HANDLING EXCESSIVE TARDINESS

To:
From:
Date:
Subject: Excessive Tardiness

Productive employees make reporting for work on time a habit. You, on the other hand, seem to have made tardiness a regular occurrence. You have been late for work six (6) times in the past two (2) weeks, an unacceptable record of tardiness.

If you are having specific problems that make it impossible for you to get to work on time, I want to know about them. In any event, your September 15 paycheck will be docked for the time you were late.

MEMO WRITER TIPS

1. If you like, begin the memo with a statement about how important it is to get to work on time.

2. Outline, specifically, how many times the employee has been tardy.

3. Ask the employee to make you aware of any extenuating circumstances that may be causing these difficulties.

4. Close by telling the employee what corrective action you expect to be taken and what the result of failure to do so will be.

PHRASING ALTERNATIVES

Paragraph 1

Each employee is responsible for getting to work every day—ON TIME. Attendance records show you've been late for work three (3) times this week.

Reporting for work promptly each day underscores an employee's commitment to his job and his co-workers. Why have you been tardy for work four (4) times in the past twenty days?

If a job is important, then coming to work on time is important, as well. Your excessive tardiness—six times in the past two weeks—has not gone unnoticed.

Paragraph 2

You can either get here on time or look for another job.

This excessive tardiness will not be tolerated, and unless your attendance pattern improves, you will be suspended without pay for at least five (5) days.

If you continue this pattern of excessive tardiness, dismissal will be the result.

IMPROVING PRODUCTIVITY

To:
From:
Date:
Subject: Productivity

For the past three (3) years, your work record has been one of the best in our department. Lately, however, some of the letters you have typed have been sent out with errors, phone messages have either not been taken or have been misplaced, and several key contracts have yet to be prepared for signature.

This substandard performance is certainly not representative of the work you are capable of doing. If you have some personal or work-related problems that are affecting your work habits, I'd be only too happy to discuss these with you.

Your work record has been one of the best in the department, and I trust you will take whatever steps are necessary to correct any deficiencies in your performance right away.

MEMO WRITER TIPS

1. Begin the memo on a positive note, by saying something positive about the employee's past performance.

2. Outline examples of the employee's substandard performance.

3. Offer to discuss why productivity has not been the best.

4. Close by encouraging the employee to take appropriate corrective action, and discuss what you expect the employee to do.

PHRASING ALTERNATIVES

Paragraph 1

I have always been able to count on the fact that you would do your work and do it well. However, in the past month, some problems with productivity have surfaced.

You are a valuable and productive employee in this division. Is there some reason your recent performance has not been up to standards?

Anytime a job needs to be done well, Travis Smith is the one who gets it. Recently, however, your work has not been handled as quickly or efficiently as it might have been.

Paragraph 2

The McKenney Project is now behind schedule. There must be some reason for this recent change in your performance. I'd like to know what it is.

Several payments to vendors are 90 days past due. I am always available to talk to you about problems you might be having.

The budget forecasts were due two (2) weeks ago, and this seriously delays the preparation of next year's projections. Let's discuss the situation and work out a way to resolve it.

Paragraph 3

I know you'll get back on schedule and bring your performance up to standards.

You know what production standards are, and I'm sure you'll work hard to meet them once again.

I'm confident your productivity will improve right away.

INITIATING COMPLAINT FOLLOW-UP

To:
From:
Date:
Subject: Complaint Follow-Up

Just this morning, Ralph Netcam of Randolph Enterprises called my office to complain that the shipment promised him for January 1 has not yet been delivered.

Find out what is causing the delay and notify Netcam when he can expect his shipment. Be sure to offer our apologies for this foul-up.

MEMO WRITER TIPS

1. Outline what the complaint is, when it was received, and from whom.

2. Direct the appropriate employee to take whatever action is necessary to resolve the matter.

PHRASING ALTERNATIVES

Paragraph 1

Attached is a complaint from Mrs. Teresa Richmond, Delbert Industries. Apparently, there was a mix-up made in her order.

I just spent a half-hour on the telephone apologizing to a Mr. Hank Simms for the rude treatment he says he received from one of our operators.

Justin Cruz of Network Corporation claims they were overcharged $591.00 on last month's bill.

Paragraph 2

Follow up on this problem and resolve it today. A letter of apology would be an appropriate response.

Research the complaint and let me know what actually happened. I want to get back to the client by 5:00 p.m. today.

Can you determine what actually took place and call the customer to smooth things over?

INCREASING SALES PERFORMANCE

To:
From:
Date:
Subject: Sales Performance

Your sales goals, based on the size of your territory and the past purchases of your clients, were fixed at $42,000.00 per quarter. Actual sales for the past quarter were only $34,000.00. This represents the third quarter this year where your sales goals were not met.

We all know the market fluctuates, and there are a number of reasons why sales drop from time to time. I'd like to know why your sales performance has fallen off in recent months and what we might both do to turn this situation around. You're an able sales rep, and I trust your figures for next quarter will improve.

MEMO WRITER TIPS

1. Your memo will have more "teeth" in it, if you can state specifically how much sales performance has lagged.

2. Offer to provide assistance and close by telling the sales person you expect improvement.

PHRASING ALTERNATIVES

Paragraph 1

Your sales performance has been less than optimal for the past three months. Sales in your region have decreased 14 percent.

You're one of our finest sales personnel, which makes me wonder why you haven't made sales quota for two months. Sales volume on your route was $4,000 less than projections.

You're obviously putting forth the effort, but not making the sales. During the past 90 days, your sales have declined to 22 percent below quota.

Paragraph 2

Let's sit down and discuss why sales have been so difficult to generate in your region. I'm confident this temporary lull will be corrected within the next 60 days.

I've asked your Sales Manager to work with you for the next 30 days. I look forward to figures that either meet or exceed goals next month.

If additional training would help, let me know and I'll schedule you for the next training session. As an experienced sales rep, you know how to get the sales; go do it.

INFORMING AN EMPLOYEE ABOUT DISCIPLINARY ACTION

To:
From:
Date:
Subject: Disciplinary Action

Efforts to improve your performance and correct your poor attendance record have failed. Accept this memorandum as official notice that your case has been submitted to the Discipline Review Board for further action.

Their next meeting is scheduled for Monday, August 11, 19____. Following this meeting, you will be notified about what disciplinary action will be taken. Until that time, you are to report to work as scheduled.

MEMO WRITER TIPS

1. Inform the employee why disciplinary action is being taken, what the process will be, and when the employee can expect to know what action will be taken.

PHRASING ALTERNATIVES

Paragraph 1

The following disciplinary action is being taken. Effective June 15, 19____, you are suspended without pay for one week.

You were officially warned that if your production did not improve, disciplinary action would be taken. You are being demoted to Technician II, beginning Monday, July 11, 19____.

Since you have chosen to ignore previous warnings about your deficient performance, disciplinary action is now in order. You will be suspended with pay, beginning immediately, until a thorough investigation has been done. At that time, you will be informed of your status.

MEETING PRODUCTION QUOTAS

To:
From:
Date:
Subject: Production Quotas

Congratulations on once again achieving assigned production quotas. Turning out both quality and quantity is no easy task. It doubtless took extraordinary effort on each team member's part.

Thanks for a job well done.

MEMO WRITER TIPS

1. Congratulate the reader for meeting production quotas.
2. Affirm the hard work you're sure went into this effort.

PHRASING ALTERNATIVES

Paragraph 1

You again exceeded production quotas this month. Making these goals took considerable time and effort.

Please accept my sincere thanks for meeting your production quota. I'm certain this could not have been achieved without hard work and maximum output.

Your diligent work and effort have paid off in fulfilled production goals. This accomplishment could not have been made without concerted effort on your part.

Paragraph 2

I applaud your achievements.

Accept my sincere thanks for an outstanding job.

Pass my congratulations along to each member of your section.

MEETING SALES GOALS

To:
From:
Date:
Subject: Sales Goals

Congratulations on putting forth the effort needed to meet your sales goals this quarter. Such consistent achievement did not go unnoticed. You're a valuable member of our sales team, and I'm confident you'll continue to meet or exceed sales goals in the months ahead. Way to go!

MEMO WRITER TIPS

1. Congratulate the subordinate for making sales goals.
2. Add a sentence that affirms the hard work needed to achieve this goal.
3. Thank the employee and encourage him/her to continue to meet these standards.

PHRASING ALTERNATIVES

Paragraph 1

You've made sales goals this quarter—OUTSTANDING. Without top sales skills, this would not have been possible. Keep up the good work in the weeks and months to come.

I just wanted to applaud your making sales goals this month. Consistently meeting sales goals is a sure mark of sales ability. You've done an excellent job. Thank you.

Allow me to congratulate you for making sales goals this quarter. Thanks for a job well done. Meeting sales goals month after month keeps us in business.

MOTIVATING A PROCRASTINATOR

To:
From:
Date:
Subject: Meeting Deadlines

Why put off until tomorrow what needs to be accomplished today? I expected your report on the Lofton Project last Wednesday.

I know you've done some of the work on it, and I also recognize how busy you've been these past few weeks. You just need to make the time to finish the Lofton report.

Have it on my desk by the end of the week. If you can't, let me know why today.

MEMO WRITER TIPS

1. Procrastinators often put things off to defy established guidelines. Threatening them, therefore, is only likely to produce more procrastination.

2. Take a light approach. Specify what work needs to be done and when you expect it. Use an encouraging tone.

PHRASING ALTERNATIVES

Paragraph 1

The figures on the Abbingdale venture were due on my desk last week, but for some strange reason, I've yet to receive them. Make some time this week to complete the project.

Where are the statistics you promised me last Thursday? This task is easy for you and should not take long to finish, once you've made the time to get at it.

The old procrastination "bug" must have bitten again, just when I desperately need those forecasts for Mr. Waterman. I'll expect them by Friday, along with an explanation today if you don't think you can get this done.

MOTIVATING SUBORDINATES UNDER PRESSURE

To:
From:
Date:
Subject: Bid Submissions

The deadline for bid submissions is rapidly approaching, and I know you must be feeling the pressure. Thanks for all the hard work you've done so far. I'm confident you'll meet this deadline, and I appreciate your efforts.

MEMO WRITER TIPS

1. Acknowledge that you know the employee is under pressure and reiterate why.

2. Encourage the subordinate by expressing your confidence in his/her ability to finish the task, and thank the employee for his/her diligence.

PHRASING ALTERNATIVES

Paragraph 1

As the deadline for end-of-year reports approaches, I know you must be feeling the pressure. Be assured your hard work is appreciated. I know you'll finish this project on schedule.

The auditor arrives next week, so I know your department is under a great deal of pressure right now. I'm confident all accounts are in order.

Don't let the deadline on the Forbes account get you down. You were given this task because you always make deadlines in time, on time, every time.

Paragraph 2

Know that your hard work is greatly appreciated.

Please accept my thanks for your diligent efforts. Keep working at it; I know you'll complete the project on schedule.

RECOGNIZING EMPLOYEE ANNIVERSARY DATES WITH THE COMPANY

To:
From:
Date:
Subject: Anniversary Date

Congratulations on the completion of your third year with the company. You are a valued employee, whose diligent efforts have made you an invaluable asset to our firm.

Here's hoping you'll celebrate many more anniversary dates with Langley Associates.

MEMO WRITER TIPS

1. Congratulate the employee on the anniversary, specifying how many years the employee has been with the company.

2. Include a positive statement about the employee's work, and close by letting the employee know you expect him/her to be around for years to come.

PHRASING ALTERNATIVES

Paragraph 1

Please accept my sincere congratulations on your 5th anniversary date with Jetts Enterprises. Productive employees like you make us a successful company.

Ten years have passed quickly; congratulations. Your contributions to this organization during that time have been exemplary.

On behalf of the company, I extend my best wishes to you for the completion of eight years of service. I'm certain you'll celebrate many more productive years here.

Paragraph 2

Thank you for years of dedicated service.

RECOGNIZING SUCCESSFUL COMPLETION OF PROBATION*

To:
From:
Date:
Subject: Certification of Six Months' Service

I would like to take this opportunity on behalf of the Mayor and City Council, City Manager and the Career Service Board to congratulate you on the satisfactory completion of your probationary period. The Career Service Board will certify you in your current position and bring you under the protection of the Career Service system at the Board's next meeting on July 5.

Satisfactory completion of your probationary period will be, I hope, the first of many accomplishments in your career with the City.

MEMO WRITER TIPS

1. If formal approval was required, tell when and how this occurred.
2. Congratulate the employee for completing the probationary period.
3. Add a sentence that wishes the employee a successful tenure with the organization.

PHRASING ALTERNATIVES

Paragraph 1

Congratulations on the successful completion of your probationary period with the city of Galveston.

Accept my best wishes on the successful completion of your probationary period with McKnaughton, Inc.

You have successfully completed your probationary period at Lebold Corporation. Let me be the first to congratulate you.

Paragraph 2

I hope this will be the beginning of a rewarding, successful career with this agency.

Let this be the first in a series of successful accomplishments with our organization.

---

*The Personnel Manager for a municipality authored this memorandum.

As a full-time, permanent member of our team, may you have many more successes in the years to come. Again, congratulations.

RECOMMENDING A PROBATIONARY EMPLOYEE FOR FULL-TIME EMPLOYMENT

To:

From:

Date:

Subject: Full-Time Employment Recommendation

Ms. Janice Hanover is hereby recommended for full-time, permanent status as Medical Technician I. She has successfully completed her probationary period.

I recommend she be certified effective January 1, 19_____.

MEMO WRITER TIPS

1. Recommend the employee for permanent status, naming the position.

2. Include any effective dates and/or information about salary increases.

PHRASING ALTERNATIVES

Paragraph 1

I hereby recommend Mr. Harvey Smith for full-time, exempt status. Mr. Smith has successfully met the requirements for Telemarketing Representative.

I certify the successful completion of probationary period for Ms. Sharon Boyd and recommend full-time, permanent status, effective Monday, January 10, 19_____. Successful performance has been documented.

Accept this as official recommendation for the granting of career status to Mr. Michael Overstreet, effective at the end of his six months' probationary period, February 14, 19_____. Mr. Overstreet has passed probationary requirements and will make a valuable addition to our housekeeping staff.

Paragraph 2

His probation ends March 3, 19_____, and I recommend full-time status be granted the following working day.

Please initiate a $.50/hour increase, effective pay period ending August 1.

Draft necessary paperwork for presentation at the Personnel Board's next meeting, October 15.

RECOMMENDING THE DISMISSAL
OF A PROBATIONARY EMPLOYEE

To:
From:
Date:
Subject: Dismissal Recommendation—Lawrence Green

I recommend Lawrence Green (Janitor I) be dismissed immediately. He is a probationary employee hired on August 3. After three months on the job, he is still unable to perform even basic tasks. I have provided additional training, but Mr. Green just doesn't seem to have the skills we need.

A record of his work performance to date is attached.

MEMO WRITER TIPS

1. Say you want the probationary employee dismissed.
2. Briefly discuss why and include documentation.

PHRASING ALTERNATIVES

Paragraph 1

Lois Markham, a probationary Community Relations Specialist, should be terminated, effective Friday, March 15. Seven community residents have made complaints about Ms. Markham. Each of these complaints has been researched, and the citizens were found to have legitimate complaints in each case.

I am recommending that Mr. Everett Hawkins, a probationary telemarketing representative, be dismissed at once. Mr. Hawkins has admitted he falsified his call records.

Paragraph 2

I have counseled Ms. Markham four times, but there has been no improvement in her job performance. In our last counseling session, I told Lois that any further complaints from citizens would result in her immediate dismissal.

Since falsifying call records is grounds for immediate termination, Everett Hawkins's final check should be prepared today.

RECOMMENDING A SUBORDINATE FOR EMPLOYEE OF THE MONTH*

To:

From:

Date:

Subject: Employee of the Month Nomination

We would like to nominate David Hawthorne, Communications Supervisor, for the November Employee-of-the-Month Award, in recognition of his achievements and contributions to the city and the police department.

David has been instrumental in developing and carrying out various projects that have resulted in more efficient operations within the department. He has also shared his expertise in communication skills through workshops conducted for supervisors and managers of various city departments.

Through his direction, guidance and managerial skills, he has enhanced the role of the Communication Specialists. He has also developed a positive rapport between the operations and communications units of the department.

Mr. Hawthorne is a highly respected, dedicated employee and a definite asset to both the city and this department.

MEMO WRITER TIPS

1. In the first paragraph, name the employee and the award for which he/she is being nominated.

2. In paragraph two, outline why the employee deserves the award.

3. Conclude by affirming the employee's value to the organization.

PHRASING ALTERNATIVES

Paragraph 1

With pleasure, I nominate Gladys Stackhouse for the October Employee-of-the-Month award.

Mr. Frank Overton is my recommendation for the July Employee-of-the-Month.

Please accept this memorandum as my nomination for Ms. Julie Hampstead for the September Crew Member-of-the-Week.

---

*Two police department administrators wrote this memorandum.

Paragraph 2

Gladys has designed a new record-keeping system that will save the company approximately $12,900 per year. In addition, she has worked tirelessly to revamp data entry procedures.

Four customers wrote letters last month commending Frank for his courteous, prompt service. He is a real team player who gets along well with both his superiors and peers. Such great customer relations skills cannot go unrecognized.

Julie operated her department $15,000 under budget for the fiscal year. Her management expertise has created an effective working group in her unit. Her group has consistently met or exceeded quotas for the last quarter.

Paragraph 3

Gladys's exemplary service makes her an ideal candidate for this award. Her work reflects well on her and on the company.

Mr. Overton is a model employee who is deserving of this award without a doubt.

Such a valuable member of our organization deserves this kind of recognition. I hope you will give this nomination every consideration.

RECOMMENDING TERMINATION

To:
From:
Date:
Subject: Termination Recommendation—Judy Block

I am recommending termination of Judy Block, copywriter trainee. Ms. Block's work has been consistently unoriginal. In addition, every piece of copy she has written has had to be revised by another copywriter. Her work contains glaring grammatical and spelling errors. Judy Block does not have the writing skills necessary to perform her job satisfactorily.

Her work performance record, including documentation from counseling sessions, is attached.

MEMO WRITER TIPS

1. Say you want the employee terminated.
2. Briefly explain why.
3. Include documentation.

PHRASING ALTERNATIVES

Paragraph 1

I recommend Art Jones, Draftsman II, be terminated immediately. The errors he made on the Gilchrist blueprints cost us a major construction project. This makes the second major job we have lost because of Jones's inaccurate drawings.

Please initiate termination action for Alonzo Weathers. Mr. Weathers has proven he is not dependable. During the past month, he has been late for work nine (9) times and has called in sick seven (7) days (documentation attached).

REPRIMANDING A SUBORDINATE FOR MISSING A DEADLINE*

To:
From:
Date:
Subject: Performance Review

You have been requested on several occasions to return your performance review to my office. The last request was June 22, at which time you stated that it was at your home because you were making comments on it. I directed you at that time to return it. To date, you have not returned it and have not indicated a reason for not doing so.

I am directing you to bring your review to your weekly meeting with me on Tuesday, June 28, 19_____ .

MEMO WRITER TIPS

1. Stick with the facts on this one, so the reprimand doesn't end up sounding like an attack on the person involved. Outline what deadline was missed and any other pertinent facts in the case.

2. Spell out clearly what the employee is to do to rectify the situation. Be sure to include specific dates, times, etc.

---

*The Director of Administration for a metropolitan transportation district prepared this reprimand.

PHRASING ALTERNATIVES

Paragraph 1

The deadline for submitting input on next year's budget proposal was last Friday. I have yet to receive yours.

Your department newsletter should have gone to the printer's no later than August 15. Why didn't it?

I expected the report you were asked to prepare by June 15 and was disappointed when I did not receive it.

Paragraph 2

Projection schedules are important deadlines and must be met. Failure to do so results in significant setbacks for not only your department, but the company as a whole.

Surely you realize how important deadlines are.

You explained why you could not prepare the report by the target date and were granted an extension. So why the continued delay?

Paragraph 3

You are directed to finish the report and have it on my desk no later than Friday, August 15 at 3:00 p.m.

Delays such as this prevent progress and cannot be tolerated. Get your work to me by this afternoon.

I will expect that analysis by 2:00 p.m., January 4. Don't disappoint me again.

WARNING AN EMPLOYEE ABOUT SLEEPING ON THE JOB

To:
From:
Date:
Subject: Sleeping on Duty

Sleeping on the job will not be tolerated—period. You are being paid to perform a service, one I'm sure you cannot do while you are asleep.

Any further reports like this will result in your dismissal.

MEMO WRITER TIPS

1. Since sleeping on the job is a serious infraction, come right to the point in this memo.

2. Be sure to let the employee know what consequences will result if he/she continues to sleep on the job.

PHRASING ALTERNATIVES

Paragraph 1

On July 22, you were found asleep on duty. Sleeping on the job carries severe penalties, including suspension and/or dismissal.

Sleeping on the job is a serious violation of company rules. Though this is a warning, another violation will result in immediate termination.

I received a report that you were discovered asleep on your June 14 watch. You will be fired on the spot the next time you are found sleeping on the job.

WARNING AN EMPLOYEE ABOUT UNSATISFACTORY PERFORMANCE

To:
From:
Date:
Subject: Warning an Employee about Unsatisfactory Performance

Certain problems with your performance have arisen, including the following:

1/3/96	Reporting for work 30 minutes late without calling
1/6/96	Errors in balance sheet detected and returned for correction
1/15/96	Mid-month budget report submitted late
1/17/96	Insubordination noted in counseling session with supervisor

These incidents represent serious problems with your performance, and counseling does not seem to have corrected them. If your efforts do not improve significantly by your next quarterly review, termination action will be initiated.

MEMO WRITER TIPS

1. Problems with performance are generally a very ticklish situation. Be sure to keep adequate documentation, including dates and times when an employee was advised about problems.

2. In this memo, list the specific performance problems.

3. Inform the employee what corrective action, if any, is to be taken and what the consequences will be if performance does not improve.

PHRASING ALTERNATIVES

Paragraph 1

Deficiencies in your performance have been noted in the following areas:

Your work is below standards in the following ways:

Your work has not been satisfactory for these reasons:

Paragraph 2

A corrective action plan has been outlined for you, and your work will be reviewed each week for the next 30 days. If improvements are not noted, I will be forced to terminate you.

Suspension without pay is the next step, should these problems go uncorrected.

You will continue to be employed here as long as satisfactory progress is made toward improving these deficiencies.

5

Model Memos for Meetings

Plans get made, goals get set, problems get solved, ideas get discussed—in meetings. The model memoranda in Chapter 5 will help you set up the meetings you need to get the results you want.

Use these memos to:

- Announce a meeting
- Cancel a meeting
- Confirm a meeting
- Reschedule a meeting

This chapter also has models that show you (1) how to write a meeting agenda, (2) how to ask someone else to conduct a meeting in your absence, (3) how to prepare meeting minutes, and (4) how to communicate with others about what happened in a meeting.

All you have to do is add the day, date, time, and place of your meeting to one of the models in this chapter. Send the memo to the people in your organization who should attend the meeting, and your meeting is set.

ANNOUNCING A DEPARTMENTAL MEETING, OPEN FORUM

To:
From:
Date:
Subject: Departmental Meeting, Open Forum

A departmental, open-forum meeting has been scheduled for Monday, July 11, 19____. No agenda has been prepared, and you should come prepared to discuss whatever concerns, issues, problems, or questions you may have.

MEMO WRITER TIPS

1. Let employees know that this is a meeting to discuss whatever it is that may be on their minds.

2. Include information about the date, time, and location in the first sentence of the memorandum.

PHRASING ALTERNATIVES

Paragraph 1

We will meet on Friday, March 3, 19_____ , at 2:00 p.m. in Conference Room 2A. This will be an open meeting where ideas may be exchanged freely.

A general discussion meeting will be held on Thursday, February 1, 19_____ , at 1:00 p.m. in the staff lounge. Your input is always valuable, so come prepared to give it.

Join the other members of your department for a roundtable discussion on Monday, May 12, 19_____ . It will begin at 4:00 p.m. in my office. This meeting will give us the opportunity to discuss general issues, problems, questions, and concerns.

ANNOUNCING A DEPARTMENTAL MEETING, SPECIFIC AGENDA*

To:
From:
Date:
Subject: Staff Meeting: Thursday, November 3, 2:00 p.m., R401

Please join us for a general staff meeting this Thursday, November 3.

Agenda
1. Space Needs
2. Staff Retreat
3. Security
4. Joint Programs with Pickens Center: An Update
5. New Building Report

---

*This memorandum was written by a community college Dean of Instruction.

6. Faculty Communications, Mailboxes at Sites
7. Courier Mail
8. Student Evaluation of Faculty
9. Other

MEMO WRITER TIPS

1. Include all pertinent information: day of week, date, time, and place. As in this memo, you might opt to include this information right up front in the "subject" line.

2. List the agenda items, beginning with those items that will require the most discussion.

PHRASING ALTERNATIVES

Paragraph 1

Our departmental meeting will be held on Friday, August 2, 1:00 p.m. Conference Room A. The agenda is attached.

Plan to attend our staff meeting this Wednesday, September 4, 19____, at 8:00 a.m. in room 307. Agenda items submitted thus far are listed below.

Mark your calendars for the next department meeting: Thursday, August 5, 8:30 a.m., Room 311A. Come prepared to discuss the following items.

ANNOUNCING A ROUTINE MEETING*

To:
From:
Date:
Subject: Monthly Dispatch Meeting

Our monthly dispatch meeting will be held on Tuesday, June 5, 19____, at 1700 hours in the conference room.

MEMO WRITER TIPS

1. Keep this memo short and to the point: say what day, date, time, and place the meeting will be held.

---

*This memorandum was written by a records and communications supervisor.

PHRASING ALTERNATIVES

Paragraph 1

This month's account update meeting will be held on Wednesday, August 1, 19____ , at 3:00 p.m. We'll meet in the Director's office.

Please plan to attend the March staff meeting on the 4th. The meeting will begin at 8:00 a.m. in Room 304. Coffee and carbohydrates will be provided.

This week's staff meeting has been scheduled for Friday, May 4, 19____ , 8:00 a.m., Conference Room B.

ANNOUNCING A SPECIAL MEETING

To:
From:
Date:
Subject: Budget Allocations Meeting

A special meeting, to discuss this year's budget allocations, has been scheduled for Friday, April 1, 19____ , at 3:00 p.m., Taft Conference Room. Avery Bell, Budget Director, will join us.

Bring your budget requests and last year's budget printouts, as well as any questions or concerns you may have. See you there.

MEMO WRITER TIPS

1. Announce the special meeting, along with the day, date, time, and place. Explain the purpose of the meeting so attendees will know what to expect.

2. Let people know whether they should bring specific materials or information with them.

PHRASING ALTERNATIVES

Paragraph 1

Please plan to attend a special meeting on Monday, September 4, 19____ , at 8:30 a.m., Room 701. Jan Talbot will review the revised purchasing procedure.

Jack Letterman, Human Resources Manager, will explain the new benefits package at a special meeting on Tuesday, November 4, 19____ . We will meet at 9:00 a.m. in the 3rd floor conference room. Don't miss this informative session.

A policy review session will be held on Friday, January 4, 19____ , at 10:00 a.m., Main Conference Room. All supervisory personnel are required to attend. Light refreshments will be served.

ANNOUNCING A MANDATORY MEETING*

To:
From:
Date:
Subject: Mandatory Meeting

On Wednesday, November 7, 19____ , from 3:00 p.m. to 5:00 p.m., we will have a mandatory staff meeting for all supervisory and management personnel. It will be held in the City Hall Conference Room.

We will briefly review last year's goals and accomplishments. The majority of our time will be spent outlining next year's goals. Management philosophy and procedures will also be discussed.

See you on November 7.

MEMO WRITER TIPS

1. In the "subject" line, state that this is a mandatory meeting. Mention this fact again in the first paragraph.

2. Be sure to include all essential information: day of week, date, time, and location.

3. Include at least a one-sentence description of what will take place at the meeting.

PHRASING ALTERNATIVES

Paragraph 1

A mandatory meeting of all auditors has been scheduled for Monday, August 3, 19____ , 1:00 p.m., Conference Room J. Last year's audit results will be discussed.

Plan to attend a mandatory meeting for account executives this Friday, January 16 at 2:30 p.m. The meeting will be held in my conference room. I'd like to discuss last quarter's sales figures.

All clerical personnel will meet on Wednesday, February 4, 19____ , at 8:00 a.m. SHARP. This is a mandatory meeting: no excuses, no exceptions! A representative from human resources will preview the new performance appraisal process.

---

*This memorandum was written by a Chief of Police.

ASKING A SUBORDINATE
TO CONDUCT A MEETING

To:

From:

Date:

Subject: Chairing Friday's Staff Meeting

Jan, please chair the staff meeting scheduled for Friday, October 3, 19____ , at 2:00 p.m., 1st floor boardroom. I'll be making site visits that afternoon and won't be able to attend.

The meeting agenda is attached. If you have any questions, let me know. Thanks.

MEMO WRITER TIPS

1. Ask the person to take over the meeting and be sure to provide the pertinent details: day, date, time, and place of meeting.

2. Explain why you won't be there and offer to fill him/her in on what is to be discussed.

PHRASING ALTERNATIVES

Paragraph 1

I've been called to the San Francisco plant on Friday and won't be able to attend the 9:00 a.m. meeting (staff lounge) scheduled for that date. Would you take over for me?

I need you to conduct the department meeting on Monday, October 4, 19____ , 3:30 p.m., Room 111. I have to brief Mr. Jansen on new accounts and will, therefore, be unavailable.

Paragraph 2

These are the items on the agenda: . . . I really appreciate this.

My secretary can furnish you with the agenda. Call me if you have any questions.

I'd planned to get an update from each department head. Field what you can and make a list of those things I'll need to handle when I return. Thank you.

CANCELLING A MEETING

To:
From:
Date:
Subject: Meeting Cancellation

The board meeting scheduled for Monday, February 14, 19____, at 2:00 p.m. has been canceled. Agenda items will be discussed at the next meeting.

MEMO WRITER TIPS

1. Announce that the meeting—with day, date, time—has been called off. Include a reason if you think it pertinent or necessary.

2. Add a brief note about when the items scheduled for discussion will be addressed, if you wish.

PHRASING ALTERNATIVES

Paragraph 1

I have canceled the Monday, March 3, 19____, meeting scheduled for 2:00 p.m. I will reschedule as soon as possible.

We will not meet on Friday, April 14, 19____, as planned. I've been asked to make a presentation at the district office and won't be available on that date. If you need to discuss any pressing problems, give me a call.

Please note that the March 5, 19____, 3:00 p.m. meeting has been canceled. Several people had schedule conflicts, so I'll arrange another meeting within the next two weeks.

CONFIRMING A MEETING

To:
From:
Date:
Subject: Meeting Confirmation

I just wanted to confirm our August 14, 19____, 3:00 p.m. meeting. I'm eager to discuss my proposal with you and look forward to seeing you on Monday.

If your plans have changed, let me know.

MEMO WRITER TIPS

1. Mention the date and time you are confirming. A reminder about the purpose of the meeting should also be included.

PHRASING ALTERNATIVES

Paragraph 1

This memorandum confirms our performance review conference scheduled for Friday, November 18, 19____, at 2:00 p.m. I trust this time is still convenient for you. See you then.

Unless I hear otherwise, I assume we still plan to meet on Wednesday, August 4, 19____, at 8:00 a.m. I've compiled all the information you wanted and look forward to discussing it with you then.

PREPARING MEETING MINUTES*

AUGUSTINE COMMUNITY COLLEGE
INTEGRATED THINKING SKILLS PROJECT
ADVISORY COMMITTEE
MINUTES
Monday, March 14, 19____, 3:00 p.m.

Members Present: Blanche Dobbins, Carla Edwards, James Gardner, Mitch Harper, Harold Mitchell, Frank Wilson
Members Absent: Laurie Pfiefer, Grant Young

Draft of ACC Model

Draft of ACC Model was discussed. Consensus was that the model provides a common language and that it is a good beginning. The Project Director will prepare a matrix that identifies most useful skills for courses and present this matrix to Academic Council.

Thinking Skills Course

A course in thinking skills, possibly to be offered this fall, was discussed. Thinking skills identified in ACC Model would form basis for this course. The course would then help students apply these skills to a variety of disciplines.

---

*These minutes were prepared by a Special Projects Director at a community college.

Recognition for Project Participants

Consensus was that participants should be recognized. Suggestions included (1) certificates of completion/appreciation, (2) acknowledgment at commencement exercises, (3) mention in the staff newsletter, (4) press release with photograph, (5) recognition luncheon.

Adjournment

Meeting adjourned at 5:00 p.m.
Minutes prepared by Linda C. Wright

MEMO WRITER TIPS

1. Center the name of the organization and the name of the committee at the top of the page.

2. Include the date and time of the meeting.

3. List those members present and those members absent.

4. Construct categories for each of the major areas discussed. Briefly describe the discussion related to each of these categories.

5. Say when the meeting was adjourned and who prepared the minutes.

REPORTING THE PROGRESS OF QUALITY CIRCLES

To:
From:
Date:
Subject: Quality Circle—Update

The quality circle for technical training met on Friday, August 4, 19____ , and discussed the following issues:

CONCERNS

1. Lack of in-house training
2. No release time to pursue outside training
3. Bugs in the new PC network

RECOMMENDATIONS

1. Conduct a needs assessment of employees to determine what training people want.
2. Solicit volunteers to develop and conduct identified training needs.
3. Hold off on any decisions about outside training until we determine what needs we have and whether we have capability to do it in-house.
4. Schedule an additional training session of the PC network, to be conducted by the vendor at no cost to us.

Your comments and suggestions are always welcome. If you have input on these or other issues, contact your QC representative before our next meeting: Monday, September 4, 19____ . A list of QC members is attached.

MEMO WRITER TIPS

1. Structure your memo to list the problems/recommendations made by quality circle participants.

2. Invite the input of others. Let them know whom they should contact and when the next meeting of the group will be.

PHRASING ALTERNATIVES

Paragraph 1

As always, I like to keep you informed about the progress our quality circles are making. At the July 14 meeting, these issues were addressed:

Problems . . .

Recommendations . . .

The quality circle representing your department met on November 11 and made the following recommendations: . . .

Here's an update on the July 6 quality circle meeting.

Paragraph 2

If you'd like to see other issues addressed, contact _____ at Ext. _____ . The QC group will meet again on Friday, August 9, 19____ .

I'm sure QC participants welcome your opinions. Let your representative know what you think before Friday, October 11.

Your feedback can help QC groups operate more effectively. Talk with the QC member in your section. The group meets on the second Wednesday of each month.

RESCHEDULING A MEETING

To:
From:
Date:
Subject: Rescheduling 8/14 Meeting

The August 14 staff meeting has been rescheduled for Monday, August 22, 19____, at 10:00 a.m. in Room 817. See you then.

MEMO WRITER TIPS

1. Mention the date of the original meeting and then give the day, date, time, and place of the new meeting.

PHRASING ALTERNATIVES

Paragraph 1

Instead of meeting on Friday, April 12, we will meet on Monday, April 15, 19____. The meeting will start at 2:00 p.m. in Room 200.

Our May 21, 8:00 a.m. meeting date has been changed to Tuesday, June 2, 8:30 a.m., my office.

Please mark your calendars for the following change in our January 3 meeting date and time:

WHEN: January 19, 19____, 9:00 a.m.
WHERE: Second Floor Conference Room
WHY: Discussion of new computer software.

See you on the 19th.

6

Model Memos about Organizational Change

Change remains the one constant in your organization today. As today's leader or manager, you can't know all the answers. But if you are to be successful, you'll need to ask and collaboratively find answers to the "right" questions. If your organization is to survive and thrive in the times ahead, you and the people who work with you in it must adapt to change more readily than ever before.

You can access, change, and analyze information with the click of a mouse. You can automate functions as never before. Global competition from within and without dogs your every decision. You have far too many people to manage. You have far too many underprepared workers. There are many quick-fixes, but very few long-range solutions to the constant barrage of forces that affect your company's bottom line.

To survive the challenges currently facing your business, your companies and agencies must learn to collaborate, not compete. You must stop merely training employees and, instead, help staff learn and develop. Notions that companies are well-oiled machines will increasingly be replaced by horizontal views of organizations as living, dynamic systems. Employees will move around, rather than move up or down. Organizational managers and leaders will have to solve problems more proactively than reactively. Managers will spend more and more of their time creating new markets, new niches, new ways of delivering consistent, quality service to customers.

Communication in these change-driven markets will have to change as well. Information will become power as never before. As staff-centered managers and leaders, you will soon recognize, if you haven't already, that information—as power—must be shared. Those in the organization who control the information will have the power. And since front-line, supervisory, and managerial personnel control your business's interaction with your customers, they must have the information and power they need to do business effectively.

In your fast-paced environment, there'll be little time or reason for the grapevine or rumor mill to mangle your business's power. All members of your business's system will need you to communicate with them, honestly and candidly, about subjects once reserved for executive ears only, such as reorganization, downsizing, rightsizing, or reengineering plans. Straight talk, not rumor and conjecture, will preserve your agency's morale, productivity, and its most valuable asset—empowered people.

The memoranda in Chapter 6 can help. Use them to communicate about changes in your organization:

- Total-quality initiatives
- Reengineering
- Reorganization
- Organizational vision
- Mentor programs
- Restructuring
- The change process itself

The model memos in this chapter can help you write about change. And in the years to come, change will likely be the hallmark of your trade.

COMMUNICATING ABOUT ORGANIZATIONAL VISION

To:
From:
Date:
Subject: Organizational Vision

"Where there is no vision, the people perish." Vision is an integral part of defining not only who we are, but who we hope to become. That's why we must develop and adhere to a collective vision. Unless we know where we're going, we'll have no idea how to get there, nor will we know when we've arrived.

As I see it, our vision must include the following elements:

1. We must strive to provide exemplary service to all our clients.
2. We must learn to view each other as clients, as well. We cannot provide good service to our clients unless we can also provide good service to one another.

3. Whenever possible, those closest to the source of a problem should be empowered to solve it.

4. Information must be shared freely. The more we know, the more efficiently we can all operate.

I know it's easy to get bogged down in the day-to-day challenges we face. Still, we must keep our vision in mind if we are to succeed.

MEMO WRITER TIPS

1. Affirm the importance of organizational vision.
2. Specify any key elements you think your company needs to consider.

PHRASING ALTERNATIVES

Paragraph 1

Some people talk a lot about organizational vision and values. I expect we'll not only talk about, but act on it and out of it. We have turned quite a few corners in the past year, and no doubt, there'll be more to turn in the years to come. As we gear up to meet these challenges, we will need something stable to help us through. That's where our organization's vision comes in. Each of us is responsible for creating the kind of company for which we can all be proud to work. In order to reach this goal, however, we must have a clear picture of what that organization will look like.

Vision. Values. Where are we going? How will we get there? How will we know when we've arrived? We must have a vision, a picture of what we'd like to be, to tell us "why" we work here. We must have values; those things we think are most important, to tell us "how" to work here. If we cannot adequately describe what we aspire to be, we cannot reach the heights for which we are all aiming. More than a statement to be posted on area bulletin boards, our vision statement must become a way of life in our corporation.

Paragraph 2

Our vision should include the following principles.

The organizational vision of ABC Pharmaceuticals affirms the following:

Paragraph 3

Your continued support and hard work is necessary if we are to actualize our vision. Keep up the good work.

I know we often get sidetracked by the challenges we face each day, but we must keep our vision at the forefront if we hope to grow and expand.

COLLECTING FEEDBACK FROM STAFF ABOUT VISION STATEMENTS

To:
From:
Date:
Subject: Request for Input—Vision Statement

As you know, we are doing our strategic plan for next year. I asked each department to submit vision statements you thought best conveyed what our company's image should be. The vision statement is an important part of reaching company goals. It gives all of us a common aim, a common vision of what we can become.

The following vision statements have been submitted so far:

1. APEX—Taking you to new heights in electronics manufacturing.
2. Climb with APEX to success in electronics.
3. Improving electronics through better products and service—the APEX.
4. APEX—Frequencies above the competition.
5. APEX strives to give you the best in electronics products.
6. Why buy from them when you can get the best from APEX?
7. At APEX, our vision is to meet your electronics needs, on time, in time, every time.
8. APEX—New standards for tomorrow's electronics, today.

Please take a few moments to let me know which of these vision statements you think is best and why. You can either write down your thoughts and send them to me, Rm. A203, or leave a message on my voicemail, Box 1809, by Friday, February 1. Thanks for your input.

MEMO WRITER TIPS

1. Explain the importance of vision statements in your first paragraph.
2. List the statements under consideration (or attach a list).
3. Ask staff for their input and give them a deadline, if appropriate.

PHRASING ALTERNATIVES

Paragraph 1

For the past several months, the company has been involved in generating a corporate vision. Our vision statement will guide our operations in the coming years. Each of you has suggested vision statements. After careful review, the following statements have been selected for further consideration.

I could write a vision statement and distribute copies to all staff. That would get the job done, but it would not make you an integral part of the process. Because we need a collective vision, I have asked managers to have staff draft possible vision statements. Your ideas have been very insightful and creative.

Paragraph 2

Here are the vision statements I'd like you to review and comment on:

I'd like your feedback on the attached vision statements:

Paragraph 3

Review each statement carefully and indicate the one you like best by circling it and returning this memo to Daniel Cordova in HR by Monday, March 12. I look forward to choosing a vision statement that expresses our best.

Check the vision statement you like best and return the sheet to Mary Ontero, Suite 304, by Wednesday, November 14. Or fax your response to (333) 333-4567 by the same date. Take a few moments to explain why you prefer your selection. This information will help in final decision making. Your assistance has been greatly appreciated, and I'm confident we'll come up with a vision statement of which we can all be proud.

STRESSING ORGANIZATIONAL VALUES

To:
From:
Date:
Subject: Company Values

Aaron Technologies operates with five values in mind: resourcefulness, collaboration, exemplary service, responsiveness, and professionalism. These values should underlie all operations and guide day-to-day functioning. Both individuals and departments should collaborate when possible and operate systemically; none of us can be successful without the success of all others.

Providing our customers with exemplary service on time, every time is our main focus. Without satisfied customers, we have no reason for existence. I hope that everyone will be responsive to the needs of both internal and external clients. This means, at the very least, that we'll return telephone calls within 24 hours and resolve customer complaints within 72 hours. In all that we do, we will respond professionally, resolve conflict positively, and promote excellence.

We have spent a great deal of time developing these company values. Now let's all work together to make them a daily reality.

MEMO WRITER TIPS

1. Identify what your company/corporate values are.
2. Give staff specific examples of what these values mean in terms of day-to-day work.
3. Close by stressing the importance of actualizing company values.

PHRASING ALTERNATIVES

Paragraph 1

We spent a good part of the past year developing organizational values: Excellence—doing the very best each of us can in every situation; Respectfulness—respecting different points of view and different perspectives, treating customers and each other with respect; Creativity—solving problems in creative ways, using all the resources at our disposal; Honesty—speaking the truth (as we see it) in the organization; and Empowerment—each individual taking responsibility for solving problems and making suggestions to make his/her job, department, and ultimately the company better—these are the values we developed.

Three values are the trademarks of the way we do business: Effort, Excellence, and Efficiency. Teams are expected to produce well-crafted products. Each person on the production line assumes responsibility for the quality of the completed automobile. Excellence means taking no short-cuts that will cause defects in our cars. We want our products known for their mechanical soundness and beautiful appearance. Efficiency means finding ways to do things right the first time. Faster is not always better, however. We strive to do things well, not just to do them quickly.

Paragraph 2

Each of us should practice these values each day. Only then we will become the company we all want to become.

When every associate makes these values live through their work, we'll design an automobile that can't be matched.

COMMUNICATING ABOUT AN ANNUAL PLAN

To:
From:
Date:
Subject: Annual Plans For 19_____

It's again time for management personnel to prepare next year's annual plans. Your annual plan should contain four key elements:

1. **Departmental Achievements.** Be as specific as possible. Use measurable results when available.
2. **Departmental Objectives for next year.** Based on your unit plan, these are your department's objectives for next year. They may also include additional training and career management strategies for staff.
3. **Personal and/or Professional Accomplishments this year.**
4. **Areas for Departmental Improvement.** Be as specific as possible.

Submit your completed plans to me by Friday, May 1. I look forward to meeting with each of you to discuss your annual plans.

MEMO WRITER TIPS

1. Specify the elements each plan should include.
2. Include the deadline for submitting annual plans.

PHRASING ALTERNATIVES

Paragraph 1

Our annual evaluation process has begun. In order to complete evaluations by the target date, prepare your annual plans and include the following headings:

You should have already begun to prepare your annual plans. In order to construct a realistic strategic plan for next year, you will need to complete your annual plans as soon as possible. Make sure you include the following in your plans:

Paragraph 2

Completed annual plans should be delivered to my office no later than Friday, April 30. Thank you.

I'll expect to receive your annual plans by Friday, April 30. I look forward to evaluating them during our annual appraisal session. Thanks.

EXPLAINING THE CHANGE PROCESS

To:
From:
Date:
Subject: Coping with Change

Right now I think we are all suffering from what might be called "change overload." I thought this would be a good time to share some insights on coping with change. Some of these notions are taken from the work of Virginia Satir and others.

As we go about any process of change, we experience at least five stages:

Honeymoon Stage

Initially, there is a period of calm after a major change. This is called the "honeymoon stage." Since most people have not yet felt any real effects of change, staff generally seem to think, "Oh, this isn't so bad." This period rarely lasts very long, however.

Resistance Stage

The "honeymoon stage" quickly gives way to resistance to change. Once staff members realize that change is indeed going to occur and, worse yet, that *they* may have to change what they've done in the past, they begin to resist change. People generally feel things were much better "in the old days" or "the way they used to be" during this stage. Resistance is a natural part of ultimately accepting the change. It allows staff to grieve the perceived loss of the old before they can begin to accept the new.

Acceptance Stage

Once employees have had a chance to grieve the old, they gradually move into the acceptance stage. They become aware that change is imminent and that perhaps it won't be as bad as they had previously thought. The acceptance stage appears as staff members become more comfortable with the change and develop coping skills to deal with it.

Practice Stage

In the practice stage, employees begin to practice the change actively. If there's been a change in procedure, they practice the new procedure. If there's been a policy change, they actively begin enforcing the new policy. If there's been a reorganization, employees begin to interact more frequently with their new boss and/or their new peers. This is the stage where staff gain comfort with the change through the application of new skills.

Discovery Stage

Once staff members have acquired a level of comfort with the change as well as the skills necessary to operate successfully in the changed environment, they discover that the change has actually occurred and that they have been part of making the change successful. They discover that the new isn't so bad after all.

Hopefully, this discussion of the change process will help us all as we go about adapting to new circumstances and situations. Each part of the process is key to moving on to the next stage. In most cases, change will ultimately occur, if we can be patient with the process itself.

MEMO WRITER TIPS

1. Change is a difficult process for most people, both inside and outside the workplace.

2. This or other change models, when shared with other staff, can help people recognize the various stages of change.

3. Use a light tone in your memo and reassure staff as much as possible that the change will, ultimately, be something with which they can live.

HANDLING CHANGE PROBLEMS

To:
From:
Date:
Subject: Problems with the New Voicemail System

Two months ago, we installed the new voicemail system. It has gotten rave reviews from some staff members and groans and curses from others. Apparently, people are still having problems using the system, specifically with changing voicemail messages when staff members are out of the office for extended periods of time.

Please update voicemail messages when necessary. This cuts down on the time customers wait to have their calls returned. To update your voicemail message, do this:

1. Dial into your voicemail box.
2. Press * 9 and you will hear a menu.
3. Press 1 at this point to update your voicemail message.

4. Press 5 to rerecord your message.

5. Record a new message, informing callers about your current day's schedule, including when you can be reached and/or when you will return their calls.

   For example, you could leave this message: "You've reached the voicemail box of Hans Schmidt. Today is November 4. I'll be in meetings most of the day and on the road November 5 and 6. If you leave a message, I'll return your call when I return to the office on November 7. Thank you for calling."

6. Once you have recorded your new message, press the * key.

7. You will hear a menu; press 1 if your message is acceptable. If you want to record your message again, press 5 and rerecord; repeat steps 6 and 7.

Additional voicemail training sessions have been scheduled for Tuesday, November 19; Thursday, November 21; and Friday, November 22. Plan to attend one of these sessions to familiarize yourself with voicemail operations. If you have specific voicemail problems or questions, call Pedro Rojas, Communications Specialist, ext. 222.

MEMO WRITER TIPS

1. Address the nature of the change problem in your first paragraph.
2. Explain the result(s) of the failed change.
3. Reiterate the new process, procedure, method, or policy.
4. Provide the reader with information about resources for help with the change.
5. Reaffirm that the change will work in time.

PHRASING ALTERNATIVES

Paragraph 1

The switchboard has been overwhelmed with calls from irate customers this past week. Customers have not received return calls in our prescribed 24-hour window. Some of this may be due to unfamiliarity with the new voicemail system.

Several users are not checking their voicemail boxes each day. This creates an overload on the system and breaks down communication among departments. Voicemail messages are only stored for seven days. After this time, they are deleted from your mailbox.

Paragraph 2

The new policy requires you to do the following:

Please check your voicemail box each day and save only those messages that cannot be answered immediately. Realize they will only be stored for seven days. Allowing yourself a specific time each day to answer voicemail messages may help resolve this problem.

Paragraph 3

Don Wright can provide you with additional training on the new policy. Call him at ext. 4789 or stop by his office in Rm. 419. He'll be happy to help.

The computer support department provides individualized assistance for voicemail users. Contact Beverly Johnson, ext. 2390, for information about training.

OVERCOMING RESISTANCE TO CHANGE

To:
From:
Date:
Subject: Resistance to Change

I am concerned about your department's waning morale and productivity, since Lao Chang's recent promotion to director.

Though you were also one of the applicants for the director's position, I believe that, in time, you'll come to agree he was the best person for the job.

You have always been known for your professionalism and dedication to the company. Change is often difficult, but I am confident you and Lao can make your department stronger than ever before. I'm counting on you.

MEMO WRITER TIPS

1. Discuss the exact nature of the resistance to change.
2. Appeal to the reader's sense of fair play and loyalty to company goals.
3. Spell out specifically what action you'd like the reader to take.
4. Close on a positive note.

PHRASING ALTERNATIVES

Paragraphs 1 and 2

I had expected your usual strong support of our new product line. Though the benefits of the new Model T47 have been proven fully, I am troubled at how long it has taken for your staff to implement Policy #24-89.

Paragraph 3

Customers are getting conflicting information from your department and Finance. If you need additional support to make this policy go, let me know. I really need your help.

STAFF REDUCTIONS THROUGH ATTRITION

To:
From:
Date:
Subject: Hiring Freeze

Uncertainty about next year's budget requires me to implement a six-month hiring freeze effective immediately. This means no new staff will be hired, even when current staff resign, retire, or are terminated. Managers will work with staff to arrange adequate coverage in the meantime. Hopefully, this freeze will reduce personnel costs through attrition and avert lay-offs in the immediate future.

I appreciate everyone's support as we weather this employment freeze.

MEMO WRITER TIPS

1. Explain how attrition will be realized—through a hiring freeze, lay-offs, early retirement, and so on.

2. Give a reason for the action.

3. Close by calling for the assistance of staff members.

PHRASING ALTERNATIVES

Paragraph 1

In our ongoing efforts to reduce personnel costs through attrition, I am announcing an employment freeze. The freeze will began Monday, February 4, and continue indefinitely. The positions of personnel who resign, retire, or are terminated will remain vacant until further notice.

Managers with 20 or more years of service, between the ages of 50 and 55, can take early retirement, effective January 1. This early-retirement option will remain in effect for 90 days. It includes generous benefits, including healthcare options and service credits. We are hoping that eligible managers will take advantage of this package so that attrition will avert downsizing at a later date.

Paragraph 2

This means that all staff will be asked to carry additional responsibilities. I know you are up to the task and appreciate your support through these difficult times.

Interested managers should contact their human resources technician on or after January 1 for more details. Your loyal, productive service continues to be appreciated.

DOWNSIZING/RIGHTSIZING NOTIFICATION

To:
From:
Date:
Subject: Downsizing/Rightsizing

As I told you in yesterday's meeting, last year's revenues were at an all-time low. This represents the third year in a row that profits have fallen to unacceptable levels. If we hope to survive, drastic measures must be taken to cut costs.

Unfortunately, this means we will need to downsize. Members of the actuarial and benefits departments will be hardest hit. Wherever possible, I will attempt to allow early retirement and attrition to help with the reduction in staff. Still, 200 associates will need to be let go by December 1.

Seniority and performance evaluations will be used to make the necessary cuts. Those affected will be notified by mail this week. Know that these reductions are absolutely essential. They are certainly no reflection on the exemplary service you have provided. Outplacement services will be made available to all associates who want to use them. If you have any questions, contact HR at ext. 456.

MEMO WRITER TIPS

1. This is one of those heretofore "executives only" issues. Executives don't like talking about downsizing, and employees don't like hearing about it. When a downsizing is imminent, the grapevine will work overtime unless you, as leader, communicate candidly with staff along the way. Productivity may suffer, as employees spend time spinning scenarios, unless you tell them at least what you know. Even though workers won't like getting the news any more than you'll like giving it, they'll respect your candor and honesty, in most cases.

2. Soften the blow by explaining why the downsizing is necessary.

3. Specify which employees will be affected and the date the downsizing will occur.

4. Describe any outplacement, early retirement, or other benefits that will be made available to affected staff.

5. If at all possible, downsizing news should be delivered face-to-face. A memo may be used to follow-up on these face-to-face meetings.

6. Commend workers on their service, if appropriate.

PHRASING ALTERNATIVES

Paragraph 1

I am sorry to announce that the downsizing we've all been predicting for months is soon to become a reality. Revenues have fallen consistently for the past five years, and though we have tried several strategies to save costs, our only alternative now is to decrease personnel costs by terminating some staff members.

As we discussed at last week's staff meeting, I have no choice but to right-size our staff. Costs continue to eat away at waning profits. If we are to stay afloat, our only course of action is to let some employees go. I wish this action could be averted, but we currently have no other option.

Paragraph 2

The entire engineering division will be eliminated. This involves 4,000 employees. Official termination notices will be mailed this Friday. Employees between 50 and 55 years of age with at least 18 years of service may be able to take advantage of our early-retirement option.

Ninety-eight terminal operators will receive their termination notices with next week's paychecks. Two weeks' severance pay will be included in these checks. The Human Resources Department will help employees locate other employment, as possible. All affected employees should investigate unemployment compensation.

Paragraph 3

This is an action I, and the Board of Directors, greatly regret. We wish all employees well in their searches for suitable employment. Thank you for your service to ABC Associates.

This downsizing has nothing to do with the loyal service you have provided over the years. We are ready to assist you in any way we can. Direct any other questions you may have to your immediate supervisor.

OUTPLACEMENT ASSISTANCE

To:
From:
Date:
Subject: Outplacement Services

Outplacement services will be provided for all members affected by the recent rightsizing. These services will be provided by Optimum Transition, a well-known outplacement firm. Optimum Transition will conduct workshops on resume writing, interview skills, networking, placement firms, and career development and search. Optimum Transition will also meet with members individually to help them develop a personalized job-search plan.

Workshops have been scheduled for the following dates and times. All workshops will be held in Conference Room C:

Resume Writing	Monday, January 5, 8:00 a.m.–5:00 p.m. Wednesday, January 7, 12:00 noon–9:00 p.m. Saturday, January 17, 9:00 a.m.–6:00 p.m.
Job Interview Skills	Tuesday, January 6, 8:00 a.m.–5:00 p.m. Thursday, January 8, 12:00 noon–9:00 p.m. Saturday, January 24, 9:00 a.m.–6:00 p.m.
Career Development	Monday, January 12, 8:30 a.m.–12:30 p.m. Tuesday, January 13, 1:00–5:00 p.m. Friday, January 16, 9:00 a.m.–1:00 p.m.

Optimum Transition will also hold group meetings for job-searchers between 12:00 noon and 1:30 p.m. each Monday, beginning January 19. Call Ibo Abdullah in HR, ext. 203, to set up individual appointments.

I hope you will all take full advantage of these services. The company wishes you well in your job search.

MEMO WRITER TIPS

1. Describe who will provide outplacement services and give information about their credentials.
2. Detail which services will be offered and when.
3. Encourage workers to take advantage of the services provided.
4. Let workers know whether there are fees or charges for services.

PHRASING ALTERNATIVES

Paragraph 1

Please take advantage of the outplacement services provided free of charge by the company. The Human Resources staff will work with each employee to develop a job-search plan. The HR staff has helped hundreds of former employees find suitable employment and/or training. Some former staff have also enrolled in college to enhance their employability.

Trevor Outplacement has been hired to help staff affected by the recent buy-out. Trevor has worked with several large corporations in the metro-area and has a 75 percent placement rate. In addition to seminars on job-search skills, Trevor will run a support group for staff. Employees may use these services through June 30. For a minimal charge of $125, staff can also register with Trevor's placement group.

Paragraph 2

Human Resources has scheduled the following outplacement meetings:

Call Dale Struthers, ext. 4520, for more information.

Trevor Outplacement will conduct seminars as follows:

Abdul Akar, suite 2406, can answer any other questions you may have.

Paragraph 3

We hope all affected staff members will use these outplacement services. Good luck as you put your talents to work in another organization.

I am pleased to provide these outplacement services for outgoing associates. I hope you will use them fully, and I wish you the best as you locate employment.

EXPANSION INTO INTERNATIONAL MARKETS

To:
From:
Date:
Subject: International Expansion

Changing global markets have produced new overseas business opportunities for our company. Beginning March 1, we will be expanding our operations into South Africa. An advance team has already visited South Africa several times over the past year, and the time is right for us to make our move.

Elliott Chapman has been selected to head up our overseas operation. Congratulate Elliott when you see him. He has already begun the process of locating an office site and has begun to select members of his team. We are excited about this new venture. It will provide us with vast potential for new markets.

MEMO WRITER TIPS

1. Discuss why and where international expansion will take place.

2. If known, take this opportunity to inform staff about who will oversee expansion efforts.

PHRASING ALTERNATIVES

Paragraph 1

As you know, I have been investigating international possibilities for our operations for some time. I am pleased to announce that we will soon begin operations in the Pacific. Our plans are to open offices in Tokyo by the end of this year. These new offices will allow us to capture as much as 15 percent of the market share for our products.

In order to expand our revenue sources, we will soon be expanding operations into Mexico and Canada. Since our product is virtually unknown in these regions, we will have a chance to vastly improve profits over the next few years. Our first stores are slated for openings in Mexico City and Toronto, Ontario. A great many people have been involved in these expansion efforts, and they are to be commended for all the hard work they've put in over the past two years. Special thanks go to Bob Arnot, Maria Lopez, Cynthia Andover, Jesus Santiago, Will Scott, and Steve Franklin.

Paragraph 2

I have not yet named a director for our new office. I am currently interviewing interested personnel and will make a selection within the next few weeks. An advance team—Li Hi Cho, Frederico Lomax, and Jennie Barker—will be responsible for site selection and other negotiations until a head of operations has been chosen. I hope you will all do whatever is necessary to ensure the success of our new international venture.

Nela Nakimoto has been named President of our new Asian division. She will be responsible, along with her staff, for setting up our new operations. I know you will all want to join me in congratulating Nela on her selection.

ANNOUNCING REORGANIZATION PLANS

To:
From:
Date:
Subject: Reorganization Plans

Over the past four years, we have experienced growth. You have worked hard to serve our customers well, despite our phenomenal growth. We have reached a point, however, where we can no longer continue our excellence within our existing structure. For this reason, we will reorganize on January 20.

Currently, we provide service through three divisions: Human Resources, Technical Services, and Product Services. To meet the growing demand for new products and improved service, we need two new divisions: Research and Development, headed by Kyle Lewis; and Customer Service, managed by Julie Benson.

Research and Development will help us keep pace with changes in technology, product lines, and potential markets. Customer Service will handle customer orders, questions, and complaints.

Vacancy announcements for positions in these new divisions will be posted within the next two weeks. If you qualify, apply. I know each of us will do what it takes to help our two new divisions succeed. Thank you for your continued support.

MEMO WRITER TIPS

1. Reorganization may have been "for executive ears only" in the past. To forestall rumors and maintain productivity, candidly explain the reason for the reorganization with staff who need to know. Since most employees will be concerned primarily with how the reorganization will affect them, spell this out in your memo. The grapevine will work overtime when a pending reorganization has not been discussed openly with staff.

2. Outline how the reorganization will look and, if you know, how and which current staff members will be affected.

3. Explain when the reorganization will take place and, if necessary, how it will be instituted.

PHRASING ALTERNATIVES

Paragraph 1

Recent changes in technology require us to reorganize. The introduction of a faster chip for the PC 4 microcomputer requires us to decentralize operations and make better use of existing staff while adding new staff, as necessary. Staff displaced by this reorganization will be retrained or reassigned, as possible. Current staff will develop a production plan for the faster chip. The requirements of this production plan will include staffing requirements as well. Though I cannot give you an exact date for reorganization, it is expected to occur no later than March 31.

As most of you know, Cassidy Jones, our VP of Operations, has resigned effective October 1. Cassidy's resignation has given us an opportunity to assess our current structure and has shown me how we might reorganize. This reorganization will allow us to provide the same level of service while decreasing overall personnel costs. The new organizational structure will be put in place on October 1.

Paragraph 2

It is anticipated that at least six members of the current production line will need to be reassigned to other tasks. Three technicians who have experience with the new technology will need to be hired as soon as possible. These technicians will train other production staff. Some classroom as well as on-the-job training will be required. All technicians will continue to report to Sherrie Bennett, the production supervisor.

The Operations and Customer Services divisions will be merged into one division, called Customer Operations. We will post a job description for a VP of this new division as soon as one can be developed. A specific plan for how the two departments will be merged along functional lines will be discussed at an upcoming staff meeting. A proposed organizational chart is attached.

Paragraph 3

Reorganization plans have been structured to create minimal disruptions for existing staff and operations. If you have questions, contact the human resources office at ext. 234.

I know that each of you will do all you can to help these reorganization plans go smoothly. I encourage any of you who are interested in applying for the VP's position to apply as soon as the vacancy announcement is posted. As is our policy, we will do all we can to fill the position from our pool of internal applicants.

CLARIFYING REORGANIZATION PURPOSE

To:
From:
Date:
Subject: Purpose of Reorganization

Many of you have had questions about the recent reorganization, so I'm writing this memo to clarify why it was necessary. Our new CEO has a proven track record of making troubled companies profitable. She has been so successful because she has developed high-performance management teams at her last two corporations.

She thought, and I concurred, that we needed such a team here at Mayflower. We needed to reorganize, to identify and begin to develop team members. That reorganization has taken place and has gone as smoothly as possible under the circumstances.

I hope you now understand why these changes had to be made and that you will continue to provide our new CEO with your support.

MEMO WRITER TIPS

1. Be as candid as possible about the reasons for the reorganization. Face-to-face communication may work best in these situations. Nevertheless, an organizational "grapevine" is a powerful communication tool. If you are less than candid about the reasons for the reorganization, the "grapevine" is likely to come up with reasons all its own.

2. Give enough detail to allay fears employees may have about adverse effects of the reorganization. Keep your memo short and to the point.

PHRASING ALTERNATIVES

Paragraph 1

Our industry's recent deregulation will allow us to expand operations. These new opportunities require us to assess current operations and organizational structure.

One of the results of our recent reengineering efforts has been the realization that we need to streamline and decentralize operations. In order to respond more quickly to changes in the field, we need to flatten our organizational structure.

Paragraph 2

The Parts and Service Department will be merged with Technical Services. Staff who fill service orders will work more closely with staff who repair equipment. As a result, all staff members will get a better view of how much their jobs are interrelated and interdependent.

The reengineering final report recommended that we empower staff closest to the customer to meet customer needs, when possible. To this end, management will soon discuss a reorganization proposal. Later, group meetings will be held with all other personnel.

Paragraph 3

Though this change will cause some stress initially, ultimately it will enable us to better serve our customers. Providing better service can help us meet the challenge of deregulation. Thank you for your continued support as we work through these changes.

The company plans to do whatever it can to foster a constructive change process. We will need your help to make this possible.

UNVEILING A RESTRUCTURING PROPOSAL

To:
From:
Date:
Subject: Proposed Restructuring

The Patient Accounts Department processes many of its accounts using manual or minimally electronic practices. These outdated processing functions created the need for three sections within the PA department: accounting, accounts payable, and collections. These staff have an untenable workload that includes cumbersome check and cross-check procedures.

Shortfalls in accounts receivable and a 7-percent error rate are just two of the major problems that have resulted from PA's current methods. In addition, the patient services representatives have been bombarded with calls about billing errors or discrepancies from both patients and insurance carriers.

The Patient Accounts department has spent the last several months auditing their procedures and has submitted a proposed restructuring plan. This new structure depends on the installation of a totally automated system, including an electronic data exchange. PA has monies in its budget to purchase the new equipment and train staff members in its operation.

The automated system PA plans to purchase is manufactured by International Health Services Technology. It will dramatically decrease manual work and will allow the current three sections to merge with patient and financial services. Some positions would be eliminated under the proposed plan. These employees would either be assigned to other positions within the hospital, if possible, or out-placed. A copy of the proposed department organizational chart is attached.

Before undertaking such a major overhaul, PA is soliciting input from users about potential pitfalls. Please send your input to Freida Archapago, PA Supervisor, by Monday, October 19.

MEMO WRITER TIPS

1. Review the current structure or organizational pattern at the beginning of the memo.
2. Explain the problems or challenges the current structure causes or precipitates.
3. Discuss which factors are prompting the proposed restructuring.
4. Outline what the proposed restructuring would look like. Use a chart, if necessary.
5. Discuss the benefits of the proposed restructuring.
6. Ask for any feedback or input needed and provide a due date for such feedback.

PHRASING ALTERNATIVES

Paragraph 1

More than 40 percent of our employees took advantage of the company's recent early-retirement offer. The purchasing, equipment services, inventory, and warehouse operations were hit hardest by these early retirements. In some sections, staffing has been reduced by 50 to 60 percent.

Paragraph 2

While these early retirements will help to shore up revenue shortfalls and decrease overall operating expenses, obviously this dramatic decrease in personnel has created strenuous workloads for those employees who remain. If we are to continue to supply customers with products within our established seven-day guideline, solutions to the problem of unmanageable workloads must be found.

Paragraph 3

Given these significant workload issues, I'm proposing a reorganization of the current Supply Services unit of the company. Under the proposed restructuring, at least four new warehouse handlers would be hired to fill orders. Warehousing, inventory, equipment services, and purchasing would then be absorbed by the Customer Service Division. A Director of Supply Services would be added to the staff to supervise the operations formerly housed in separate units.

Paragraph 4

These proposed changes would more evenly distribute workload while still reducing supervisory overhead. This restructuring would also enable customer-service technicians and supply staff to work more closely together in handling customer needs and problems.

Paragraph 5

I'd like your suggestions. Please plan to attend my next staff meeting, Wednesday, April 21, 10:00 a.m., Bolt Conference Room, to discuss any questions or concerns you might have.

REORGANIZATION STAFFING PATTERNS

To:
From:
Date:
Subject: New Staffing Pattern

As a result of reorganization, our new staffing pattern will look like this. Marge Walters will serve as Director of Customer/Technical Services. Don Phillips is the Assistant Director. Five customer service and five technical service reps will report directly to Don. The new organizational chart looks like this:

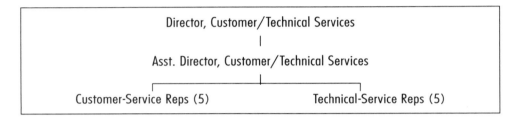

I hope this information clarifies the new staffing pattern.

MEMO WRITER TIPS

1. Reiterate what caused the staffing change.
2. Describe the new staffing pattern.
3. Use charts and/or graphics to clarify the staffing pattern.
4. Attach "before" and "after" charts if the change is a complicated one.

PHRASING ALTERNATIVES

Paragraph 1

Here is a copy of the current organization chart, as well as postreorganization staffing patterns. Since the reorganization is fairly complicated, I thought a visual look at the change would make it clearer.

In the recent reorganization, one additional VP and one Dean were added to the Strategic Planning Committee. Xan Phong has been named VP of Planning Services. Barbara Houston has been named Dean of Institutional Advancement.

Paragraph 2

If you still have questions, give me a call.

Under the new plan, the VP of Educational and Faculty Services will assume leadership for the Admissions, Financial Aid, and Faculty/Staff/Organizational Development Divisions, as well as the Learning Assistance Center. The Dean of Institutional Advancement will be responsible for Management Information Systems, Grants Development, and the College Foundation. A revised organizational chart is attached.

SUMMARIZING REORGANIZATION RESULTS

To:
From:
Date:
Subject: Reorganization Update

The reorganization that occurred several months ago seems to be going smoothly. Staff members are working hard to adjust to their new positions, and the reorganized divisions continue to be as productive as they were before.

I appreciate all the effort each of you has put forth to make this reorganization a success.

MEMO WRITER TIPS

1. Discuss positives of the reorganization at the beginning of the memo.
2. Cite any reorganization problems after the positives have been discussed.
3. Thank staff members for their cooperation.

PHRASING ALTERNATIVES

Paragraph 1

Our recent merger with Health-full Corporation has produced massive changes for our operations. Each of you has worked tirelessly over the past few months to ensure the success of this new venture. Operations now seem to be getting back to normal, with minimal disruptions because of the reorganization. Still, many staffing changes have occurred, including a complete change at the executive level.

The recent consolidation of the Compensation and Benefits and Employee/Labor Relations units has gone as well as could be expected. Your patience and support during this period have contributed to a fairly smooth reorganization. Time is now needed to adjust to changes in staffing and procedures.

Paragraph 2

As always, your support of these efforts has been greatly appreciated. It has made for a smoother transition for us and our patients.

I want to personally thank each of you, particularly the members of the new Human Relations unit for making this change as smooth as possible.

INTRODUCING AN ORGANIZATIONAL DEVELOPMENT CONSULTANT

To:
From:
Date:
Subject: Organization Development Consultant

Our agency has undergone constant changes in the past two years. In the last employee opinion survey, communication and interdepartmental relations were cited as serious challenges for us. In order to find out exactly what these problems are and how we might rectify them, I have contracted Mr. Javier Santiago, an experienced organizational development consultant, to work with us over the next few months. Mr. Santiago has worked as an organizational consultant for more than 10 years and holds Master's Degrees in both Industrial Psychology and Organizational Development. He has worked with many of the premiere firms in our field.

The organizational assessment survey you complete will be one of the tools Mr. Santiago uses to help us pinpoint our problem areas. As a follow-up to these surveys, Mr. Santiago will also schedule one-on-one interviews with some of you. Provide him with helpful information, and be as candid as you can. If we are to transform our current operations, we must accurately diagnose where our challenges lie. Please give Mr. Santiago your full support and assistance.

MEMO WRITER TIPS

1. Explain the need for an organizational development consultant.

2. Name the organizational development consultant and provide information about the consultant's credentials and client list as appropriate.

3. Let staff members know what they'll be asked to do.

4. Assure them that their responses will be confidential.

PHRASING ALTERNATIVES

Paragraph 1

Any time an organization goes through a major restructuring, problems and challenges emerge. In order to address your concerns and to find out, specifically, where our problems lie and how we can correct them, we will be working with Ms. Marlene Dotson, Organizational Development Consultant, over the next year. A graduate of the Harper School of Management, Ms. Dotson has worked with corporations like ABC, Trans-global Entities, Fairfax Associates, and Lyons Contracting. She is an experienced consultant whose strength is in meeting the needs of her clients.

Paragraph 2

Ms. Dotson will interview personnel, send out an opinion poll, and schedule focus groups with department staff members. I urge you to share your honest perceptions, problems, and concerns with her. You can be assured of strict confidentiality. If we are to enhance our corporation, we must work hard to uncover where our problems are. Thank you for your cooperation.

COVER MEMO FOR AN ORGANIZATIONAL ASSESSMENT INSTRUMENT

To:

From:

Date:

Subject: Employee Satisfaction Survey

This year's Employee Satisfaction Survey is attached. We learned a great deal from last year's survey and are proud to say that we have made a number of changes based on the information you provided.

This year's survey data will be used to continue those changes and to make others, as necessary. I hope you will complete the survey carefully and return it according to the instructions on the bottom of the form.

Results will be published on-line on the bulletin board update. As always, the information you provide will be held in the strictest confidence. Thank you for your prompt reply.

MEMO WRITER TIPS

1. Explain the purpose of the organizational assessment tool and how it will be used.
2. Assure associates that their survey data will be kept strictly confidential.
3. Provide instructions for completing and returning the form or tool.
4. Tell staff how and when results will be made known.

PHRASING ALTERNATIVES

Paragraph 1

Attached you will find an organization assessment tool. It has been designed to provide us with feedback about our operations, particularly in the areas of Communication, Teamwork, Customer Service, and Problem Solving.

Rogers, Barnes, and Hart will help us assess our organization. These consultants, widely known, have asked all line staff to complete the attached survey instrument. Information from this instrument will be used as part of our organizational diagnosis.

Paragraph 2

Human Resources personnel will tabulate the results, which will then be reported at our upcoming meeting. Your responses will be kept strictly confidential. I hope you will read each item carefully and respond honestly to each. Only through evaluating our agency in this way can we hope to improve.

This will help us learn what we are currently doing well and which areas we need to improve. Please complete the instrument as thoroughly and honestly as you possibly can. Results will be made public in a few months. Be assured that your responses will remain strictly confidential.

Paragraph 3

Return your completed forms to Dudley O'Brien, Room 301, by Monday, April 4. Your cooperation in providing us with this valuable information is greatly appreciated.

Follow the instructions on the back of the form when you have completed the survey. Thank you.

EXPLAINING TOTAL QUALITY

To:
From:
Date:
Subject: Total Quality Defined

W. Edwards Deming is the father of the quality movement. Total Quality (TQ) or Total Quality Management (TQM) advocates believe the best products and services can be given to customers when an organization uses all its brainpower to do so.

All of us know the expression, "If it 'ain't' broke, don't fix it." Well, TQM takes a radically different view: "The best time to fix something is when it 'ain't' broke." In other words, TQM promotes the proactive process of being involved constantly in improving products and services.

TQM also defies the laws of hierarchy. TQM challenges organizational leadership to find ways to engage every member of the organization in improving operations and solving problems. In addition, TQM stresses collaboration, rather than competition, and affirms the notion that shared information (not scarce information) can be an agency's most valuable tool.

TQM also uses concrete data, often in the form of charts and graphs, to track total quality efforts. Data shows us whether products and services have improved. Whether by improved test scores in schools, higher employee satisfaction indices in agencies, or higher ratings from customers, those involved in TQM find ways to ask customers whether, in fact, they received excellent service and/or products.

A continuous process, TQM is not a quick-fix. It takes a long time to change many of the organizational factors that sabotage continuous improvement. It may take years to provide all the organization's employees with needed training. It may take even longer for organization members to believe that management really wants and values their ideas. TQM embraces the notion of continuous service/product improvement. Each day provides a new opportunity to design systems and processes that produce products (or services) faster, more efficiently, and more cost-effectively.

> **MEMO WRITER TIPS**
>
> 1. Include specifics about what total quality means and how members of the entire organization will need to become involved.
> 2. Address ways in which TQM is likely to change your organization.
> 3. Stress the fact that TQM is an ongoing process, not a quick-fix.

ANNOUNCING A TOTAL QUALITY MANAGEMENT INITIATIVE

To:
From:
Date:
Subject: Total Quality Management

This year's strategic plan will focus on Total Quality Management (TQM). TQM helps organizations provide consistent, quality service for every customer. TQM also empowers staff closest to the source of the problem to solve it. This saves both time and money for our company and preserves revenue from repeat business.

Both we and our customers will regularly assess our progress toward providing quality service. Information from employee opinion surveys and customer satisfaction ratings will provide us with concrete data about how well we are doing.

In order to launch our efforts, Total Quality Teams, made up of staff from each department, will be formed over the next month. Teams will be comprised of staff at all levels of the organization: executive leadership, management, supervision, and front-line staff. Once teams have been formed, each team will select a team leader and a team coach. Each team's leader and coach will participate in in-depth Total Quality Management "training-for-trainers." They will then be responsible for training their own team members.

Total Quality Management training will be provided by TQM Enterprises, a nationally recognized consulting firm in the TQM field. They will be available for ongoing consultation as we undertake this important initiative.

Over the next two weeks, managers will meet with division staff to detail plans and to answer any questions you have. If you have questions in the interim, please contact Betty Arnold at ext. 7557. We are all excited about this opportunity to enhance our service to both internal and external customers.

MEMO WRITER TIPS

1. Explain why Total Quality Management is being initiated. Promote its positive aspects.

2. Briefly describe what Total Quality Management is and what it requires of staff.

3. Spell out the process for initiating TQM and let staff members know training will be provided and their questions will be answered.

PHRASING ALTERNATIVES

Paragraph 1

To continue to provide the best service possible for our valued customers, we will undertake an organization-wide Total Quality Management (TQM) initiative. Most of you have already heard about TQM at your regular staff meetings. TQM strives to continuously and quickly resolve customer problems and complaints. Front-line personnel, who most often encounter customer complaints, are given the training and authority to solve problems when they can. In the long term, this saves the company time and money and produces repeat customers.

In these times of diminishing resources, all of us focus on producing quality products for our customers. To remain competitive, we can distinguish our company through Total Quality Management (TQM). For the next few years, our organization will provide the best product we can, while maintaining or lowering production time and costs. We will resolve problems as quickly and completely as possible. We are excited about improving our already excellent products and services.

Paragraph 2

Monitoring staff and customer feedback lets us track our progress, using charts and graphs.

We will use the data collected from employees and customers to analyze our efforts, monitor our progress, and make changes where necessary.

Paragraph 3

Staff will do TQM for themselves and each other. Volunteers from each department will be chosen for Total Quality Management teams. These teams will promote TQM efforts throughout their areas. Each team will select a team leader and a team coach. They will be trained in TQM, and later, train other team members.

Groups of employees will promote TQM throughout the organization. Your supervisor will contact each of you to find out who wants to be on your department's team. Your team participation will be voluntary, and should not interfere with your current workload. Rather, it will provide team members with a tool for making departments and the company more efficient and effective. Training will be provided for team members.

Paragraph 4

TQM Associates will provide us with in-depth training. Many other companies in our industry have used this firm with excellent results.

Members of our Training Department who have had in-depth TQM training themselves will train TQM teams. Using in-house talent will provide good training and ongoing follow-up.

Paragraph 5

You'll have a chance to ask questions and air your concerns at our upcoming general meeting. If you have questions before the general meeting, call Pauline Ito at ext. 712.

We're very excited about this new initiative. Questions and concerns will be addressed at an upcoming meeting; more details will follow. In the meantime, if you have questions, stop by my office or call me at ext. 8843.

UPDATING TOTAL QUALITY PROGRESS

To:
From:
Date:
Subject: Update—Total Quality Initiative

On the one-year anniversary of the start of the company's Total Quality program, I thought it appropriate to update all employees on our progress. Though TQ certainly had its share of naysayers at the outset, the results we've achieved in just one short year have been startling.

- Purchasing has reduced its procurement budget by eight percent.
- Management Information Systems has improved its customer satisfaction rating by 2.3 points.
- Client complaints, over the past year, have been reduced by 38 percent.
- The average time spent resolving customer complaints has decreased from 2.7 hours to .9 hour.

Kudos to you all. TQ has proven to be one of the wisest investments we've made in a long time.

MEMO WRITER TIPS

1. Include the time-frame and any particular conditions of TQ's inception in your first paragraph.
2. List or bullet tangible results of the total quality initiative.
3. Enlist continued support by praising participants.

PHRASING ALTERNATIVES

Paragraph 1

Since we implemented TQM, we've seen astounding results. Our efforts took a lot of work, but they have paid off—by significant improvements in our bottom line.

The company operationalized Total Quality almost two years ago. Teams of staff in all areas of the corporation received training in TQ practices and met regularly during this time. Though they worked hard to make this project a success, the results thus far are less than noteworthy.

Paragraph 2

- Sales have increased 14 percent.
- Sales reps have been able to close a sale in 3.2 fewer hours.
- Twelve sales representatives have joined the Silver Million Club.
- The number of prospects who don't purchase homes has decreased by 3.4 percent.

The item return rate has been reduced by only .3 percent. Revenues during the last holiday sales season increased by only 1.2 percent. The advertising department spent 12 percent more dollars with no comparable increase in sales.

Paragraph 3

You can all be very proud of the progress and changes we've made so far. Continued TQ focus and team effort will, undoubtedly, have bigger pay-offs next year. Congratulations to you all!

As a result of the dismal showing of results thus far, the Total Quality project is being scrapped. TQ task forces will continue to meet less frequently to discuss alternative ways of improving sales and our bottom line. Thanks for giving TQ your best.

ANNOUNCING REENGINEERING EFFORTS

To:
From:
Date:
Subject: Reengineering

We're about to begin the major reengineering efforts we've discussed at length. Through reeingineering, we will fully assess what we are doing well and which areas need improvement. Reengineering will allow us to view our operations from new perspectives.

Reengineering details will be explained at next month's general staff meeting. This meeting, hosted by our organization effectiveness consultants, will familiarize staff with our reengineering project. Bring your questions to the meeting.

Reengineering will help us recreate our operations, maximize productivity, and preserve valuable resources. Creatively, we will use our collective brainpower to reconceive our workplace and workforce. I hope you will be as excited about reengineering as I am.

MEMO WRITER TIPS

1. Briefly explain what reengineering is and why it is being undertaken. Reassure employees by outlining its benefits.

2. Schedule a meeting to discuss reengineering face-to-face; inform employees when this meeting will take place.

3. Let employees know what reengineering will require of them.

4. If possible, include a flow chart or diagram of your reengineering process.

PHRASING ALTERNATIVES

Paragraph 1

To improve company efficiency and effectiveness, we will reengineer—look at our organization through new eyes. As you all know, we must remain competitive in order for our business to thrive. Reengineering should help us redesign processes, methods, and staffing patterns, to maximize our productivity and increase the bottom line.

"Business as usual" won't help us stay on top. To become more effective, we will initiate a reengineering plan over the coming year. Reengineering will let us look at what we do well and how we might improve. Through reengineering, we can design new ways of doing business, ways more compatible with the ever-changing demands of our market.

Paragraph 2

Each of you will play an important part in making reengineering a success. In teams facilitated by one of our internal organization development engineers, you will dream—dream about new products, delivered through new media, to new markets. You will also develop the competencies needed to design and implement reengineered systems. At your next staff meeting, come prepared to discuss how you think reengineering may affect your division.

An all-company meeting has been scheduled to discuss reengineering. Bring your ideas and/or suggestions to the meeting and come prepared for a lively presentation and discussion. The reengineering meeting will be held on Wednesday, November 11, at 10:00 a.m., in Loveland Conference Room.

Paragraph 3

Reengineering will help us recreate our company. Using the collective creativity and brainpower of our staff, we can develop new, more effective ways to make and sell even better products. Reengineering can benefit us all. I'll see you at the meeting.

We know best how to reconfigure ourselves and our operation. Reengineering will help us decide how we can make our company better. I hope all of you will commit yourselves to reengineering. In the end, all of us will benefit.

SUMMARIZING REENGINEERING RESULTS

To:
From:
Date:
Subject: Results of Reengineering Efforts

The results of our reengineering efforts are in. Our teams and internal organization development consultants made reengineering a success. The results are promising.

- Communication has been enhanced among divisions, particularly the technical and human-services branches. Employee satisfaction polls show a positive increase of 2.4 points over the past two years. Employees indicate significant improvements have been made in the areas of labor negotiations, grievance resolution, and interdepartmental responsiveness.

- The production department has refocused its efforts on the development of P94 silicon chips and teleconferencing products. Market studies indicate these are the best areas for revenue generation over the next five years. We will cut back our production of the P90-93 chips and enlarge our teleconferencing operations.

- Two divisions—corporate communications and marketing—have merged. The new Marketing and Promotions Division will develop promotional materials and handle both internal and external communication, including the corporate newsletters, product brochures, public relations, and public information.

- The Continuous Service Improvement Teams that have been in place during this process will continue to meet regularly and monitor our redesign and total quality efforts.

Additional changes will be made over the next few months. I personally want to thank each and every employee for their commitment to reengineering. We will all reap the benefits of streamlined and improved operations and new product development.

MEMO WRITER TIPS

1. Outline the major findings of the reengineering activity.
2. Thank staff members for their participation in the process.
3. If results are less positive than expected, be as candid as possible.

EMPLOYEE MENTOR
PROGRAM GUIDELINES

To:
From:
Date:
Subject: Mentor Program Guidelines

A mentor is defined as a wise and trusted teacher. The word comes from the Greek: Mentor was Odysseus' counselor. A mentor has an apprentice/mentee—"any beginner, a learner."

A mentor teaches skills or provides the information needed to perform an identifiable task. Mentoring is focused in the present. A mentor teaches what you need to know now. Ideally, a mentor's concern is to help others develop their own abilities and do their own work.

You have been selected to serve as a mentor. Your knowledge, skills, and abilities will not only familiarize your mentee with job skills, but also with how to be successful in our organization. As a mentor, you will be a valuable resource for your mentee. You can provide him/her with information about whom to contact, company resources, career management, and many other skills.

The mentor program has a number of objectives: (1) To help new associates have a smoother transition into our company; (2) To provide aspiring managers with the skills and contacts they need to prepare themselves for management positions as they arise; (3) To provide mentors with a chance to use their talents to help others and, ultimately, the company as a whole; (4) To reduce the cost of turnover by retaining more employees; (5) To expand the resources and networks of new employees or staff in new positions.

Here are guidelines for the Mentor Program:

1. Mentor and Apprentice Selection and Orientation

    A cadre of mentors is selected. Effective mentors must have all the qualities of successful managers as well as (a) a desire to participate in the program, (b) the time required to cultivate a mentor relationship, and (c) that rather elusive ability to garner confidence and respect and use these investitures to motivate, counsel, and influence the behavior of others.

    Once mentors have been selected, they participate in an orientation session designed to acquaint them with the philosophy and procedures of the program and the backgrounds of their assigned mentees. They are also given information about how to contact their mentees.

Mentee selection is based on amount of supervisory experience, familiarity with our corporate setting and, as near as can be judged, management ability. Mentees are then matched with suitable mentors. Ordinarily, mentor relationships arise out of associations, so matching is a difficult task. The match is based on interpersonal and skill factors.

Mentees are then notified about the program, including whom their mentors will be.

2. <u>Mentor/Mentee Meeting</u>

Mentors are then asked to contact their mentees and arrange a meeting at a mutually convenient time. During this meeting, mentor and mentee get to know each other better and develop an action plan for meeting both their needs.

3. <u>Mentor Shadowing Experience</u>

The mentor and mentee arrange a shadowing experience. During this experience, the mentee shadows the mentor, to see what the mentor does and how the mentor does it. After the shadowing experience, the mentor and mentee discuss the experience and what the mentee learned from it.

4. <u>Mentee Shadowing Experience</u>

Next, the mentee is shadowed by the mentor. This gives the mentor a chance to observe the mentee as he/she goes about his/her duties. Again, the two discuss the experience, and the mentor points out the mentee's strengths and areas for improvement.

5. <u>Ongoing Collaboration</u>

The mentor and mentee talk and/or meet as necessary throughout the year to discuss the mentee's progress and any questions or problems the mentee may have. The mentor also helps the mentee establish networks and identify other resources in the company. The mentor may also elect to discuss the mentee's performance with his/her current manager, in order to get an additional perspective on ways in which the mentor can be helpful.

6. <u>Mentor Summary</u>

The mentor submits a final summary of the mentor relationship and process by the end of the year. This summary should include the mentor's recommendations for program improvement.

7. <u>Mentee Summary</u>

Each mentee completes an evaluation form which outlines his/her assessment of the program's effectiveness.

8. <u>Review</u>

Desdemona Cole, project director, reviews all mentor and mentee summaries. Recommendations for program improvement are noted, and practicable suggestions are implemented subsequently. Any necessary follow-up is discussed with the mentor and mentee.

9. Celebration

Mentors and mentees (and their supervisors) participate in an awards luncheon, to celebrate their participation in the program.

Contact Desdemona Cole, HR, Suite 219, extension 7447, for additional information about the mentor program.

MEMO WRITER TIPS

1. The specifics of a company's mentor program will vary. This memo attempts to outline some steps agencies might consider.
2. In a step-by-step fashion, discuss the specifics of the mentor program.
3. Include information about whom to contact with questions or comments.
4. Define what a mentor is and outline the objectives of the program.

EMPLOYEE MENTOR PROGRAM ASSIGNMENTS

To:
From:
Date:
Subject: Mentor Program Assignments

Welcome to the Mentor Program for new associates at Learning Fundamentals, Inc.! You have been selected to serve as a mentor because of your experience, expertise, and willingness to help others learn and grow.

Your mentee for this year will be _____ in the _____ Department. She has been with the corporation for only six months; her resume is attached. You were selected as her mentor because of similar skills and interests. Please contact _____ at ext. _____ to set up your first meeting and discuss the program with her in more detail.

The enclosed *Mentor Handbook* explains the program thoroughly. Use it as a guide as you undertake this important project. If you have any questions or comments, please contact me at 444-4444 or drop by the human resources office, LL106.

Also enclosed is the evaluation form you will return to HR by the end of the year. Thank you for your input on the evaluation form; your comments on the program will help us improve it in subsequent years.

Again, don't hesitate to contact me regarding the Mentor Program. Best wishes for a successful experience for both you and your mentee.

MEMO WRITER TIPS

1. Name the mentee, the mentee's department, and where/how the mentee can be reached.

2. Provide a little background on why these two individuals were paired.

3. Enclose any handbooks or information which will help the two through the process.

PHRASING ALTERNATIVES

Paragraph 1

Congratulations on your selection as a mentor for new employees. Your experience will enable you to help new employees adjust to our company and manage their careers more successfully.

As an outstanding employee, you are to be commended for volunteering to serve as a company mentor. Your record, skills, and knowledge will doubtless help your mentee succeed in our organization.

Paragraph 2

Because your mentee hopes to someday move into management, you have been matched with _____ in the _____ division. Please give him a call at ext. _____, so the two of you can meet and outline your plans for the next six months.

Your apprentice for the next year will be _____. He works in the _____ department and has been with the company for nine months. He's expecting your call. I suggest that the two of you meet at a mutually convenient time to discuss how you both feel the Mentor Program can be of benefit.

Paragraph 3

The *Mentor Handbook* you both received at the orientation session should answer any questions you have about the process. If you have additional questions, call me at ext. 555 or bring your questions for discussion at our monthly mentor meetings.

Use your pamphlet, *An Effective Mentor,* to guide you through the process. I'll be happy to answer any other questions you may have. Drop by my office, Suite 506, or call me at ext. 312.

Paragraph 4

The mentor evaluation form is included at the back of the handbook. Feel free to make notes throughout the year and return the completed form by December 31. Your comments and suggestions will be used to improve next year's activities.

You'll receive quarterly assessment forms throughout the year. The data from these forms will be used to make the mentor program more effective.

Paragraph 5

Again, thank you for agreeing to participate in this program. Through your own and other mentors' efforts, we hope to build a solid cadre of new associates. Good luck!

Your service as a mentor is greatly appreciated. Our objective is to groom potential management candidates and, as a successful manager, your help will be invaluable. I hope your mentor experience will be rewarding and mutually beneficial.

7

Model Memos about Teams

If one picture is worth a thousand words, then one team is worth a thousand lone employees. The whole is, indeed, greater than the sum of its parts. Its parts—high-functioning teams—can build a "whole" organization much greater, more efficient, and more effective than an organization inhabited by lone employees who have neither common vision nor goals.

Getting things done in the century to come will involve getting things done by teams. High-performance teams: self-regulated, self-directed, specific-issue teams.

Memoranda in Chapter 7 address a wide range of team issues:

- How to establish a team
- How to guide a team
- How to select a team leader
- How to structure teams for optimal effectiveness
- How to reassure traditional managers that teams won't make them obsolete

Use the team memos in this chapter to communicate with members of the teams in your organization. Use them to write to others about the teams in your organization. Use them to clarify your own thinking about the benefits of doing business—team-wise.

Teams, not lone employees, will provide the needed structure for tomorrow's businesses, today. Use the team-wise memos in this chapter to write effectively about the issues that will help teams form, develop, and perform.

BENEFITS OF THE TEAM APPROACH

To:
From:
Date:
Subject: Benefits of Work Teams

For more than four decades, UBS Electronics has manufactured switches, cables, and fibers for telephone systems. Each individual on the production line has done the specific task required of him or her. And each member has done this well. This year, we're going to try something different: the team approach.

What is a team? Lots of groups are called teams, but all groups are not teams. A team is two or more individuals who (1) are given or develop a common mission, goal, or task; (2) can achieve better results interdependently than individually; (3) give and get open feedback from each other; (4) have or have access to the skills and resources needed to accomplish the task at hand; (5) optimally, have the authority to act on their suggestions and plans; and (6) are concerned with both task, goal, or mission accomplishment, as well as the process that leads to task completion.

Here are some of the benefits of teams. High-performing teams

- Have a common purpose and focus
- Can tap into the collective wisdom of team members
- Play off each other's strengths and fill in for each other's weaknesses
- Motivate individual members
- Out-perform even the best individual
- Are focused jointly and also accountable jointly
- Select their own leaders and coaches
- Swim or sink together
- Have more collective power than do individuals

These are just some of the benefits of the team approach. If you've ever been on a team outside of work, you know the feeling of community and accomplishment effective teams can achieve. Let's give the team approach our best efforts.

MEMO WRITER TIPS

1. These are just some of the benefits of teams. Use the useful ones for your organization and add others.

2. If available, include specific examples of things teams have accomplished in your company or organization.

3. Well-structured teams are established generally to handle tasks or projects that require the buy-in of team members, or tasks that will affect and/or change the work environments, operations, or structure of a group of employees greatly.

4. Teams, once formed and trained adequately, should be allowed to learn from both their successes and failures. If a manager plans to override the work of a team, why bother to establish the team in the first place?

5. Teams generally go through conflict as they transform themselves from groups into teams. Constructive resolution of this conflict is an essential part of team-building.

6. Teams require open and honest communication and feedback. Managers should take steps to ensure that teams function in an environment that has these features.

SPELLING OUT A NEW ROLE FOR SUPERVISORS

To:
From:
Date:
Subject: Supervisors and Their Teams

Since we began using a team approach to concrete pouring, supervisors have expressed some concern about their new roles. Supervisors feel that they are no longer needed and that, ultimately, they will be let go. This is not going to happen. Supervisors must adjust their thinking and acting in order to work *with*, not against, the other members of the team.

Since teams began pouring concrete, we've saved many dollars on concrete purchases and have reduced pour time by 15.7 percent. The teams obviously work, not because they aren't "supervised," but because they've assumed responsibility for making the pours in the most efficient way possible.

As a supervisor, you are there as a member of your team. Your job is to contribute to and lead the team, keeping company objectives in mind. You are a very necessary part of the team, and your skills are needed more than ever.

> **MEMO WRITER TIPS**
>
> 1. Supervisors may be very threatened by the introduction of work teams.
> 2. Write your memo using a reassuring tone.
> 3. Tell supervisors what their new role is and what you expect from them.

SPELLING OUT A NEW ROLE FOR MANAGERS

To:
From:
Date:
Subject: The Role of Managers in Team Operations

Several managers have voiced concern about their roles since self-directed work teams will soon be responsible for train dispatching. Let me assure you that these teams in no way detract from the role of effective managers. In fact, the advent of teams requires even keener management skills.

To begin with, your management role will involve much more of the coaching you already do. Instead of managing a group or groups of individuals, you will now be responsible for managing a team or groups of teams. Individuals perform much differently when they are part of a team. In most cases, their performance and productivity improves markedly.

Just remember that your role has simply shifted. You are part of the team; you are its leader. Your role has become even more challenging and critical than it was before. You will rise to the occasion, I'm sure.

As always, I'm here to help if your team needs to brainstorm or bounce ideas off me.

> **MEMO WRITER TIPS**
>
> 1. Supervisors and managers may feel very threatened when teams are implemented. Therefore, it's important to address these fears candidly.
> 2. Your memo should have a reassuring tone and should outline the new role for managers specifically.
> 3. Include your expectations for managerial performance.
> 4. Close on a positive note, offering managers your coaching assistance.

DETERMINING TEAM STRUCTURE

To:
From:
Date:
Subject: Structure for the Registration Process Team

The team structure that makes most sense for the Registration Process Team is as follows:

- One representative from the admissions office
- One advisor
- One financial-aid counselor
- One cashier from the business office
- One representative from student assessment
- The director or assistant director of each area

This structure will provide input by all departments involved in student registration. That's what we need if we're going to develop a student-friendly process and handle student problems more quickly and efficiently.

I'd like departments to select a representative at their next staff meeting. Tracy Wilson is scheduled to begin team-process training on July 21, so I'd like the team to be in place by then. I'll meet with the team before their first training session. Let me know when you get the team formed.

MEMO WRITER TIPS

1. Explain the structure you'd like and explain why you think this structure is most effective.

2. If the team is going to develop its own structure, provide the team with its constraints and any concerns about structure you may have.

3. Add dates or deadlines.

PHRASING ALTERNATIVES

Paragraph 1

I'd like to see the Insurance Claims Task Force develop its own structure. I do have several issues I'd like to share about structure, however. I'd like each member of the team to share equal authority. I think the team would work most effectively without the presence of management, so I'm suggesting that the team be composed of no personnel at the supervisory or managerial level. Other than these things, the team is free to structure itself for maximum interchange and effectiveness.

Here are my thoughts about how the Compensation Survey Committee should be structured. The team should select a team leader, whose role it is to keep the team focused on its goals, stay within the timeline, move the team forward when it gets bogged down, and see to it that all team members contribute fully. I'd also like the team to select someone as a team coach. The coach's job will be to navigate team process and mediate conflict.

Paragraph 2

If you'd like to discuss my ideas, let me know before my November 14 meeting with the team.

Other than these items, I want the team to set up a workable structure. This is a lot of work, and I commend each of you for agreeing to serve on this team.

ESTABLISHING A TEAM

To:
From:
Date:
Subject: Formation of the Recruitment Task Force

Our client base has continued to decline for the past three months. With all the downsizings in the area, I don't think we're getting our market share. To investigate community resources, make contacts with area employers, and uncover sources we may be missing, I'm putting together a group of account executives to serve on a Recruitment Task Force.

This will be an ongoing Task Force that will continue to recruit new clients, at least for the coming year. I've asked Will Jones, Ed Addison, and John Abbott to be on the Task Force. I know they'll do a great job.

They'll have their first meeting on June 14. If you have ideas or suggestions, call one of these members. I'm sure they'll welcome suggestions from us all.

MEMO WRITER TIPS

1. Outline the team's area of responsibility. Name members, if appropriate.

2. If you want other staff members to provide the team with information, tell them when and how to do so.

3. Include information about why the team has been established and what your expectations for team efforts are.

PHRASING ALTERNATIVES

Paragraph 1

A new-employee orientation team is being formed. This team will develop a structured orientation plan and make the necessary contacts to carry it out.

In order to deal with job bids more quickly and efficiently, I'm putting together a team to take a look at our current bid procedures and policies. I think some of our methods are outdated, and they're making us lose work.

Paragraph 2

If you'd like to be a part of this team, let me know by Friday, October 22. I'd like the team to get going as soon as possible. Anyone with good ideas is invited to participate, with their supervisor's endorsement.

Joe Vance has volunteered to put this team together. If you want to be on it, call Joe at ext. 717 by Monday, May 5. This team is going to come up with a streamlined bid procedure that should make more money for us all. Participate if you have the time and interest.

ESTABLISHING SELF-DIRECTED WORK TEAM STANDARDS

To:
From:
Date:
Subject: Self-Directed Work Team Standards

As members of the Vantage production division, you are the company's pilot self-directed work team. This is an exciting new venture. The eyes of the entire plant are on your team.

Because we're all committed to making this venture work, here are some standards I expect from the team. Use them to guide your efforts:

- Production is *your* issue, not someone else's. Since you work on the Vantage team every day, you know best what produces a quality automobile.

- Team members must openly communicate with each other about problems, defects, or flaws *when they arise.* I hope to see a marked improvement in quality control.

- This is a first. Your team is going to make mistakes and have difficulties. You may find that you learn as much from your failures as you do from your successes.

- If your team, after carefully studying a problem, determines that the line needs to be shut down, shut it down! "Ask for forgiveness, not permission!"

- The team will meet at the beginning and end of each work shift to discuss issues and pass on information to the next shift.

- The team will be responsible for its own quality control and continuous service improvement.

- Team members will identify and solve production problems as they arise.

- The production quota will remain as is, but I anticipate there'll be a decrease in rejects.

- The team will order its own parts and negotiate for services with other production lines.

- Be creative about your solutions to problems. Just because it hasn't been thought of or done before doesn't mean your team can't try it. If it seems like the best solution, try it and see what happens.

- Have your team recorder keep a log of problems solved, activities completed, concerns identified, successes, and innovations.

- Ahmad Jones will be the team's point of contact for decisions that need management input.

I hope your team is as enthusiastic about this pilot project as I am. I will meet with the team each month to review its progress and handle any obstacles it needs me to troubleshoot. I'm confident you'll do a superb job that will increase productivity, decrease errors, and solve problems more quickly.

MEMO WRITER TIPS

1. A self-directed or self-managed work team is one that takes responsibility for accomplishing identified tasks. A self-managed team directs itself, rather than being directed by a supervisor or manager. Unlike the typical hierarchy, self-directed teams work from bottom-up rather than from top-down. Team members are equally responsible for the accomplishment of tasks and are generally given responsibility for managing, inventing, or reinventing their own processes, methods, strategies, and innovations.

   Consensus-building, trust, and autonomy are important components of self-directed teams. Self-managed work teams may have a team leader, a team coach, and/or a team reporter. The team itself usually selects people to fill these roles and establishes what the duties of each role are. Team members require a great deal of skills training in communication, consensus-building, team-building, conflict resolution, and self-direction in order to operate effectively.

2. Be as specific about standards—what's expected of the self-directed team—as possible.

3. If this is a new venture, express your enthusiasm and affirm team success.

4. Include information about how, when, and by whom the team's efforts to maintain standards will be evaluated.

5. If this is a first for your organization, applaud team members for being risk-takers.

PHRASING ALTERNATIVES

Paragraph 1

Listed below are the standards I expect your self-directed work team to maintain. I will meet with the team next week to discuss any questions you may have about these standards.

Concrete standards will provide your self-directed work team with tangible methods for evaluating the team's performance. I have listed the standards the team should uphold below.

Paragraph 3

Next month, I look forward to reviewing with the team how well these standards have been maintained. This is an exciting new venture for the company, and I'm confident it will produce creative solutions to problems. Thank you all for your participation.

In a highly competitive market, we need all the leverage we can get. Self-directed work teams will provide us with that leverage. The people directly involved with tasks are the ones most likely to design creative solutions to problems and to forge innovations. I wish the team success.

COMMUNICATING THE TEAM MISSION

To:
From:
Date:
Subject: Computer-Installation Work Team

Many order takers have suggested that desktop computers would speed up order processing. Staff say these computers will (1) decrease wait time for customers, (2) provide employees with faster access to inventory information, (3) and enable order takers to log pertinent details more efficiently.

Since this would be a significant expense, I am establishing a Computer Installation Work Team to study and make recommendations about:

- The best computers to purchase
- How other companies process similar orders
- The impact computer installation will have on operations
- How problems can be resolved proactively
- The training required for both order takers and fillers, should terminals be installed
- The pros and cons of computer installation

Management will use the team's recommendations to decide whether to install the computers, which computers to purchase, what kind of training to conduct, and how to minimize disruptions to order-taking operations (should computer purchase be the work team's recommendation).

Work-team recommendations will be completed by April 5. They will then be distributed to key personnel for review. I look forward to reviewing the team's report.

MEMO WRITER TIPS

1. Briefly describe how and why the team was formed in the first paragraph.

2. List the goals, tasks, decisions, or problems the team is to address. Be as specific as possible.

3. Tell the team how its work will be used.

4. Provide the team members with guidelines about how long their work should take, if this is appropriate.

PHRASING ALTERNATIVES

Paragraph 1

Your work team has been formed, and you've selected a team leader and a team coach. Over the next several months, you'll prepare a plan to address how the new managed-care regulations will affect hospital operations. This is an important study, one I'm sure you'll all give your best efforts.

Before you attend your first team-building session, here are my expectations for the Electronic Data Interchange (EDI) Task Force. EDI installation will greatly affect department operations. Your work on this team will minimize disruptions of day-to-day operations, once EDI is installed.

Paragraph 2

Your team's plan should address the following:

1. How should managed-care regulations be communicated to various hospital constituencies: physicians, nurses, laboratory personnel, support staff, patients, insurance providers, and so on?
2. What impact will these new regulations have on hospital operations in general and departments and employment classes, in particular?
3. What challenges will these regulations produce for patient services?
4. How can the regulations be implemented while preserving excellent patient care?
5. What effect, if any, will managed care have on current staffing patterns and/or on hospital structure as a whole?
6. What is the best way to implement managed-care requirements? Develop a specific narrative plan and/or flowchart.

Here's the team mission:

- Look at how EDI installation will affect current operations.
- Discuss current procedures that will be eliminated.
- Design a chart that outlines how EDI should be implemented.
- Gather information from the affected departments. Discuss the impact EDI conversion will have on each of these departments.
- Develop a pre- and postinstallation training plan.
- Address how EDI conversion will affect customers and how information about the conversion should be communicated to customers.
- Pinpoint areas of major resistance or problems and give recommendations for overcoming them.

Paragraph 3

Hospital management will use your team's plan to implement managed care. While fiscal concerns must be considered if managed care is to be a financial success, your recommendations will be adhered to if at all possible.

Your team will implement the Electronic Data Interchange. Using a training-for-trainers model, each team member will communicate information discussed in team meetings with his/her department staff. Your team will select a member(s) to work with Training and Development to prepare and implement an effective pre- and postinstallation training plan. The team will also evaluate its effectiveness and assess the success of EDI's implementation, once the conversion has occurred.

Paragraph 4

Managed-care regulations take effect January 1. Your team plan should be completed at least nine months before then, so we'll have adequate time to review and implement your recommendations. Thank you for your work on this very important endeavor.

The EDI conversion is slated to occur July 1. Your team should develop a timeline so you have adequate time to inform and train staff and alert customers. I commend each of you for working on this team.

SETTING TEAM SCOPE OF RESPONSIBILITY

To:
From:
Date:
Subject: Team Responsibilities—Accidental Damage Team

The Accidental Damage Team will be responsible for these services:

1. Investigation of accidental damage when it occurs.
2. Interviewing involved employees within 24 hours after the incident.
3. Completing the "Accidental Damage" report form and submitting it to the department manager within 48 hours after the incident.
4. Contacting clean-up services and monitoring damage clean-up.

These guidelines should clarify any questions you may have.

MEMO WRITER TIPS

1. Name the team the responsibilities are for.
2. List or bullet specific responsibilities.
3. Include pertinent deadline information.

PHRASING ALTERNATIVES

Paragraph 1

> The plant inspection team is responsible for the following duties:
>
> I am assigning the following responsibilities to the Inventory Control Team:

CROSS-DEPARTMENTAL WORK TEAMS

To:
From:
Date:
Subject: Cross-Departmental Work Team Guidelines

You have volunteered to serve on the interdepartmental Marketing and Promotions team. Getting the perspectives of manufacturing, distribution, repair and service, and product returns should give us a more systemic view of how to best market our product.

I'm looking forward to seeing the result of your team's efforts.

MEMO WRITER TIPS

1. Cross- or interdepartmental teams are comprised of staff from different departments, usually staff whose work is interdependent. Cross-departmental teams are necessary when correcting problems or creating plans that affect more than one department and/or staff. Some teams are both cross/interdepartmental and cross-functional. These teams can best address problems that overlap functional and departmental lines.

2. Discuss briefly why the cross/interdepartmental team was established, if this is not already known.

3. Discuss the benefits of interdepartmental perspective.

4. Close by thanking members for their participation.

PHRASING ALTERNATIVES

Paragraph 1

The return rate for catalog orders increased 14 percent during the last sale season. That's why I've asked you to put together a cross-departmental team of supervisors and order-takers. If we can get those on the front-line involved, I'm sure we'll be able to decrease our return rate.

There have been major foul-ups in the past month's real-estate closings. Documents have been missing from buyer files, appointments have had to be canceled and rescheduled, and documents have contained typographical errors. Because of these problems, I'm asking you to serve on an interdepartmental team to study how these problems can be corrected. The team will be composed of staff from closings, finance, and document preparation. I'm hoping this team can help correct our problems with closings.

Paragraph 2

Thank the members of the team for me. We've never tried this before, and I'm anxious to pinpoint and correct this problem area. Their work will benefit us all.

I look forward to solving this problem once and for all. I appreciate your willingness to work on this team.

CROSS-FUNCTIONAL WORK TEAMS

To:
From:
Date:
Subject: Guidelines for the Cross-Functional Work Team

Legal briefs are being prepared incorrectly, so I'm forming a team of word processors, secretaries, paralegals, associates, and a partner to determine what we can do to prepare error-free documents. Each time we have to correct faulty briefs, it costs this firm three to five billable hours, often much more. We must get the problem corrected, and I think involving all the players can help save dollars.

I expect to see the team's recommendations no later than September 1. Thanks for helping with this project.

MEMO WRITER TIPS

1. Cross-functional teams involve people in the same department who perform different tasks. Their work is interdependent. Therefore, problems in one area create problems for workers in another. Cross-functional teams are best used in areas where systemic, intra-departmental problems need to be corrected or when an entire department needs to generate ideas. Some teams are both cross/interdepartmental and cross-functional. These teams best address challenges that overlap functional and departmental lines.

2. Describe the job functions of the team members. List names, if appropriate.

3. Discuss why a cross-functional team will solve a problem better than a single-function team would.

4. Thank members for their work on the team and let them know about any deadlines.

PHRASING ALTERNATIVES

Paragraph 1

Client calls are often being misrouted. Therefore, I'm setting up a cross-functional team, with representatives from each of the functions involved. I'd like to see Jan Foster, Valerie Abrams, Sam Watson, and John Hamilton serve on the team.

Account executives, real-estate developers, and contract negotiators seem to be having problems communicating client information. I want you, Susie Black, Bob Throll, Wes Johnson, and Pat Haines to work together on a task force to improve intradepartmental communication.

Paragraph 2

I'd like the team to present its procedure at the February 18 support services staff meeting. Thanks.

Let me know what you come up with by August 6. I appreciate your help on getting this thing fixed.

INTRODUCING/SELECTING A TEAM LEADER

To:
From:
Date:
Subject: Janice Macelroy—Team Leader

Our team has selected Janice Macelroy to be its leader. We're sure she'll provide us with the leadership we need to improve routing procedures.

MEMO WRITER TIPS

1. Name the team leader.
2. Include information about why he/she was selected if you'd like.
3. Give the team leader a vote of confidence.

PHRASING ALTERNATIVES

Paragraph 1

Doug May will be the team leader for the Minigil Telemarketing Team. Doug has been here the longest and has the skills we need to help us perform at higher levels. We think he'll make a great team leader, and we look forward to working with him.

Please join me in congratulating Trudy Espinosa on her selection as leader of the graphics production team. Trudy is an excellent choice, and I'm certain she'll make a fine leader.

TELLING A TEAM TO BEGIN WORK

To:
From:
Date:
Subject: Team—Ready, Set, Go

After months of planning and training, your team is now ready to begin operations. There are good problem-solvers on the team, and I'm confident you will perform well together. You've come a long way, but your efforts will doubtless pay off in the form of better working relationships, increased productivity, and heightened efficiency. Good luck. If you need my help in any way, just ask.

MEMO WRITER TIPS

1. This memo should have a positive, enthusiastic tone.
2. Reemphasize the team's goals, tasks, or challenges, if necessary.

PHRASING ALTERNATIVES

Paragraph 1

I know each of you has been looking forward to this day for some time. On Monday, July 17, the Product Recycling Team will begin operations. I'm proud of the hard work you've already put in on this project and look forward to future benefits of your work.

Let me, first, thank each of you for agreeing to be a member of the Safety and Risk Management Team. I understand your training went smoothly and that the team is beginning to "gel." I'd like you to officially begin functioning Wednesday, October 17. I'm looking forward to solid accomplishments from the team.

GETTING A SELF-DIRECTED WORK TEAM STARTED

To:
From:
Date:
Subject: Self-Directed Work Teams—Let's Get Started

Research and Development has studied the feasibility of using self-directed work teams on the production floor thoroughly. As you know, the implementation of these teams requires a great deal of training if the team is to be effective. Based on R & D's feasibility study, I need you to do the following:

- Interview workers and select members for a pilot implementation team. Get the names of workers who are outspoken, good communicators, risk-takers, and experts at their tasks. Ask supervisors for recommendations, if necessary.
- Work with the Training Department to draft a training schedule and plan for the team.
- Meet with supervisors to discuss what a self-directed team is and assuage any fears they may have about diminished roles for themselves.
- As a part of training, have the pilot team draft an action plan for itself with timelines.
- The team should also develop ways to evaluate its performance.

Once these steps have been completed, we'll be ready to put our first self-directed production team into operation. Thanks for your help on this.

MEMO WRITER TIPS

1. A great deal of study and discussion will precede the actual initiation of self-directed work teams. These teams are not right for every task, nor for every environment. Training will be a major precursor to the actual implementation of such teams.

2. List the steps involved in establishing the self-directed work team.

3. Include any requirements to which your particular organization must adhere.

RECORDING TEAM MEETING MINUTES

To:
From:
Date:
Subject: Team Minutes—January 30 Meeting

Team Members Present: Al Evans, Bobbie Vance, Amy Ortega, Wu Lan, Doug Hammer
Team Members Absent: None
Meeting Chair: Wu Lan

Meeting Recorder: Doug Hammer

Topics Discussed: Hold flags, phone coverage, data mailers

Solutions Developed:

1. Al suggested that hold flags be put on only those accounts that are more than 60 days past due. The team concurred.
2. Bobbie suggested that Sue, Mel, and Marvin rotate coverage during the lunch hour, the most difficult time to provide adequate coverage. Bobbie will help the three operators develop a workable schedule. The team concurred.
3. Amy Ortega noted that we need more information from the mail room and from accounts payable before a decision can be made about data mailers. Amy will get this information and bring it back to the next meeting.

New Problems: Customer wait list, canceled-check processing.

These problems were discussed, but the team decided to table action until the next meeting.

Adjourned 4:00 p.m.

Next Meeting: February 7

MEMO WRITER TIPS

1. Meeting minutes are important for teams, as each member will have a different perception of what occurred during the meeting. Minutes offer the team a way to chart its progress.

2. Keep minutes as brief as possible without sacrificing details. Pages and pages of minutes won't be read, and will likely bog down team functioning.

3. Rotate meeting chair and recorder roles, if the team likes the idea.

4. Another option is to develop and use a standard meeting-minutes format. This format might be structured with "Issue" at the top and each team member's name below, with space to write or word-process comments. Another format might put "Concern" at the top with a list of all the departments represented on the team beneath it. Leave space to summarize each department's input or suggestions. Another format would be a "Problem/Solution" one, where the problem is recorded, and the team's solution is written or word-processed beneath the problem. Have the team develop a format that suits its needs best.

RECOGNIZING TEAM PERFORMANCE

To:
From:
Date:
Subject: Congratulations, Data Processing Team

The Data Processing Team has worked hard to develop new methods for installing, monitoring, and repairing computer networks. The team has developed an ideal solution, which each department will be contacted about soon. Congratulations on some very fine work. I think this creative solution would have been a long time in coming if not for the collaborative efforts of the DP Team.

MEMO WRITER TIPS

1. Congratulate the team and cite what the team is being commended for.
2. Stress team, not individual, effort.

PHRASING ALTERNATIVES

Paragraph 1

The internal auditing team has reduced the amount of outstanding account receivables by 12 percent in just the past six months. This is outstanding progress for such a short period of time. I really appreciate the work the team has done to improve our cash flow. Congratulations!

I want to personally thank the members of the Chemical Control Team for its development of a cost-effective filtering system. The team put in many hours on this project and, as a result, the percentage of hydrogen in the lines has been decreased by 78 percent. You've done an outstanding job and should be very proud of your team and its accomplishments.

Model Memos about Information Technology

Today's manager probably spends considerable time at a personal computer. On the Information Highway, just about everything you ever thought you wanted to know can be accessed with the click of a "mouse."

Mail can be sent electronically—in moments—to just about anywhere in the world. In addition to street addresses and zip codes, managers have e-mail addresses. Memos can be transmitted by fax. Cellular phones make conversations possible in your car, in an elevator, at the health club. Using your personal computer, you can order lunch, pay your bills, make airline reservations. And you've probably traded in your appointment book for a hand-held, electronic wizard that keeps track of your appointments, your "to do" list, and your business associates' phone numbers and addresses.

Today's information technology has everyone plugged in and online. And if you're not, you soon will be. Use the model memoranda in Chapter 8 to help you communicate about information technology:

- Computer security
- Conference calls
- Accessing electronic networks
- Maximizing voicemail
- Announcing teleconferences
- Information overload

Information technology has changed the way we do business forever. As this is being written, new technology is being developed, and more efficient ways to access and transmit data are being planned. As a manager, you probably always said you wanted information at your fingertips. Well, now it's there. And more and more of it is destined to find you on the Information Superhighway in days to come.

DESCRIBING COMPUTER CAPABILITIES

To:
From:
Date:
Subject: Computer Capabilities

You have just been issued a desktop computer. Your computer has a Pentium microprocessor. It has 16 MB (megabytes) RAM (Random Access Memory), and your memory is expandable to 64 MB.

Your desktop computer has a hard drive; 3½-inch and 5¼-inch "floppy" disk drives; and a keyboard with 101 keys.

Your system also has a color, SVGA (Super Video Graphics Array) monitor, which means you can see color in your documents. It also has a CD-ROM (Compact Disc Read-Only Memory), which allows you to retrieve data from compact discs. Your computer also comes equipped with an internal modem. The modem allows you to send and receive information electronically over telephone lines.

Your computer can run many operating systems. This gives you the capability of using thousands of different software packages. WriterWord, Word Touch, DistanceCom, DistanceFax and Blossom software have already been installed on your computer. This provides you with word-processing, graphics, and spreadsheet functions. You can also send and receive electronic messages and faxes.

Additionally, your system has a laser printer.

MEMO WRITER TIPS

1. Write in user-friendly language if your reader is not computer literate.
2. Refer to the *User's Manual* for additional details.

COMPUTER SECURITY ISSUES

To:
From:
Date:
Subject: Computer Security

A user ID and password will be installed and maintained to prevent unauthorized access to your computer. The system requires you to change your password every 90 days. When changing your password, you will be allowed three attempts to enter the correct user ID and password. After the third failed attempt, the system will lock you out. If this happens, you must contact the system administrator to regain access.

If you need assistance with password changes, please call the system administrator at 210-4567. He is available from 8:00 a.m.–12:00 noon and from 1:30–5:00 p.m.

MEMO WRITER TIPS

1. Provide users with information about how to secure their computers.

2. Also provide information about whom to contact for assistance.

USING LICENSED COMPUTER SOFTWARE

To:
From:
Date:
Subject: Use Licensed Software Only

Computer software is protected by copyright laws, as well as laws protecting intellectual property. Software is, therefore, licensed—not sold. This means that you may purchase the rights to use the software only. The software remains the property of the person or company who holds the copyright on it.

These restrictions require that the company purchase licenses for the software it uses. This is the software the system administrator has installed on your computer or provided for your use.

You cannot use other than licensed software on your computer. If you have software other than the software provided by the system administrator on your computer, you are prohibited from using it here at the office. You are also prohibited from copying the software on your computer for home or other uses.

If you currently have unlicensed software on your computer, please delete it now. The company could be held liable if employees are found using unlicensed software on our premises.

Thank you for using only licensed software provided to you by the system administrator.

MEMO WRITER TIPS

1. Write the memo using your organization's policies and procedures on licensed software.
2. Describe the action you want users to take.
3. Close on a positive note.

DETECTING COMPUTER VIRUSES

To:
From:
Date:
Subject: Computer Virus

Another computer virus has hit our section. Be sure to scan your computer for viruses when you start it up. If you have Virus-Clean for MS-DOS on your computer, type **msav** at the command prompt. When the main menu appears, select the drive you want to scan. Press the **Detect and Clean** button. After a virus has been detected and cleaned, a status screen will appear on your monitor. It will tell you whether a virus was found and that it has been cleaned. Press the **OK** button and proceed with your work.

As a precaution, you can set your computer to automatically scan for viruses each time you turn it on. Consult Page 43 of your *User's Manual* for instructions.

If you work on other computers (at home, and so on), scan your disk for viruses before you use it on your desktop. This will help prevent spreading viruses from one computer to another.

If you need further assistance with virus detection and cleaning, contact the system administrator.

MEMO WRITER TIPS

1. Computer viruses are programs designed to replicate and spread. Sometimes, users may not know the virus is present.

2. Outline the procedure used in your office.

3. Let users know where to go for additional assistance.

4. Stress the importance of preserving data by checking for viruses regularly.

CENTRALIZED COMPUTER SERVICES

To:
From:
Date:
Subject: Centralized Computer Services

Effective Monday, October 1, ABC Technology will provide centralized computer services for our branch. You will be able to communicate with ABC from your personal computer once a modem and communications software have been installed on your computer (if you do not already have these) and ABC has supplied you with a user name.

Requests for batch processing will require a three-day (maximum) turnaround. Batches will be picked up each day at 4:00 p.m. and will be delivered no later than 9:00 p.m. Special arrangements for rush jobs can be made by contacting Janice Shoop between the hours of 9:00 a.m.–12:00 noon, Monday through Thursday, at ABC. Her phone number is (246) 333-4444.

ABC will provide assistance through a 24-hour helpline. That number is (246) 333-5555. Please make a note of it.

I think ABC will provide us with better computer service than we have had in the past, once we get used to the new procedures.

MEMO WRITER TIPS

1. Centralized operations provide agreed-upon computer services from a central location. Often this location is off-site. Since centralized operations often process work for multiple entities, your computer services will be provided along with those of many other users.

2. Describe the services provided by the centralized supplier.

3. Give details about how questions can be answered and problems resolved.

4. Be specific about any constraints and/or deadlines.

DECENTRALIZED COMPUTER SERVICES

To:
From:
Date:
Subject: Decentralized Computer Services

Effective January 1, we will change from our previously centralized computer services to a decentralized model. This means computer services will be handled by our in-house Technical Services branch. Technical Services will provide the following:

1. Computer-generated reports (weekly, monthly, and annual)
2. Computer repair
3. Software purchasing and installation
4. Troubleshooting
5. Network maintenance and service

In addition, services handled previously by Central Computing (payroll, accounts receivable and payable, billing) will now be done in-house. A procedure for submitting special requests is attached.

Technical Services will soon provide information about policies and procedures related to computer services. Cyl Butler will head the new operation. While we're making the switch, Cyl asks that users be patient. It will take some time to get the "bugs" worked out of the system and to get everyone on board with the new procedures.

MEMO WRITER TIPS

1. Decentralized services provide local support. Decentralized systems generally focus on services for a specific audience or function, rather than for multiple users at multiple operations.

2. Provide information about which computer services will be offered.

3. Let users know how they can get assistance.

4. Refer users to any applicable policies or procedures.

DESCRIBING MANAGEMENT INFORMATION SYSTEMS

To:
From:
Date:
Subject: Management Information Systems

Pat Thurgood has been hired as our new Director, Management Information Systems (MIS). The MIS Department will provide managers and other staff with a variety of computer support services, including computer-generated reports. You can also work with Pat to design specialized reports you need.

Pat will be scheduling appointments with each of you. I think the new MIS functions will provide us with just the decision-making information we need.

MEMO WRITER TIPS

1. Management Information Systems provides users with a broad spectrum of information processing services.

2. Generally, MIS can design a variety of reports to gather and present data in user-friendly formats.

MANAGEMENT INFORMATION REQUEST

To:
From:
Date:
Subject: Request for Trip-Time Report

In order to develop reasonable delivery standards, I need information about how long it's currently taking our drivers to deliver products. Please provide me with an analysis of the average trip-time per driver. I'll need a breakdown by distance, so I'd like to set up a table: 3–5 miles, 6–10 miles, 11–15 miles, 16–20 miles, 21 miles or more.

I also need this information by day and time of day (so I can see whether some days'/times' trips take longer than others) and by month (for the same reason). I also need to know what the longest trip-time is per week and what the shortest trip-time is per week (on an average), as well as the day of the week and time of day for each (shortest and longest).

I'm trying to put together my recommendations by the end of the month, so I'd like to have your report by August 12. If you have any questions, give me a call at ext. 8888. Thanks for your help.

MEMO WRITER TIPS

1. What managers sometimes want in the way of information may not always provide them with exactly the data they need. Often, it's best to discuss your needs with your computer analyst or MIS person face-to-face. By talking your needs through, you may come up with other information or formats you hadn't considered.

2. Be specific about your needs.

3. Provide applicable deadlines.

4. Tell the person what you need the information for; this often helps the MIS person design more user-friendly reports/data.

GETTING USERS INVOLVED IN COMPUTER SYSTEM DESIGN

To:
From:
Date:
Subject: Computer System Design

Our current computer system no longer meets our needs effectively. Before we purchase a new system, however, I want to make sure a system will meet our current and projected needs.

You may recall that it took considerable time to install our current system; we went over budget and experienced a great deal of frustration. I don't want to see that happen again.

Please provide me with a list of the reports, functions, and software packages (word processing, spreadsheet, graphics, and so on) you currently use, as well as those you need but don't have. I will need your list by Friday, September 3.

I am also putting together a team to study our computer needs and make recommendations for our next purchase. If you would like to be a member of this team, please indicate your interest on the bottom of your computer-needs list.

MEMO WRITER TIPS

1. Getting users involved in decisions about computer systems may save countless hours of wasted time once a system has been purchased. Getting user buy-in accelerates user acceptance and system efficiency.

2. Ask users for information about how they utilize their computers.

3. Explain to them why their participation will benefit everyone in the long run.

PROACTIVELY ADDRESSING CONCERNS ABOUT NEW TECHNOLOGY

To:
From:
Date:
Subject: New Technology

Our new computer system will be operational in a few days. A number of you have expressed concerns about your ability to adapt to the new technology, and a few of you apparently think you're going to be replaced by automation. Let me put your concerns to rest.

This new computer system, one you had input into, has been purchased to speed up operations and eliminate many of the manual functions we presently do. The new system will help you do your jobs faster, more efficiently, and more accurately.

The system cannot take the place of human beings; it must be operated by people. Think of it as a tool you can use to do your work better than you do now. It will take us all a while to become adept at using this new tool. But in a few months, we'll look back and wonder how we ever functioned without it. I'm anxious to see what you will do with this new tool. I hope you are too.

MEMO WRITER TIPS

1. Technology sometimes makes employees fearful. Addressing these fears proactively will diminish the time required to adjust to the new technology.

2. Explain the benefits of the new technology.

3. Reassure workers that they will ultimately come to be as proficient using the new technology as they are now.

ANNOUNCING A COMPUTER NETWORK

To:
From:
Date:
Subject: LAN (Local Area Network) Installation

The new LAN (local area network) for our department will be completed on Wednesday, October 8. It should be ready for use the following Monday. This network will allow all members of our department who have PCs to communicate from their work stations with other members of the department.

Trudi will conduct a hands-on orientation to the LAN in the computer lab on Friday, October 10 from 8:00 a.m.–12:00 noon. She will also be available for individual appointments, beginning Monday, October 13. Call Trudi at ext. 770 to sign up for the orientation and/or to schedule an appointment.

MEMO WRITER TIPS

1. Computer networks allow one computer to communicate with another. Currently, there are LANs (local area networks) and WANs (wide area networks).

2. Mention when the network will be installed and when it will be operational.

3. Provide information about assistance for users.

4. Describe the benefits the network will have for the department.

5. Include any other details peculiar to your network or organization.

ACCESSING ELECTRONIC NETWORKS

To:
From:
Date:
Subject: WIN Dial-In Procedures

To access the WIN (Wordsmith International Network), follow this procedure:

1. Be sure your computer is set up and ready to communicate. Check to be sure your

   - Modem is properly connected to your computer
   - Phone line is connected from the modem to the phone jack

- Computer is on
- Modem is on (if you have an external modem)

The parameters for your communications software are:

- 8 data bits, 1 stop bit
- Odd parity
- "Xon/Xoff"
- Full duplex

2. Dial the TeleNet access number closest to you. For Phoenix, the 9600 baud number is (246) 960-9999; the 2400 baud number is (246) 240-4444; the 300/1200 baud number is (246) 312-3333.
3. Once you are connected (the word **CONNECT** will appear at the top of your screen), hold down the **"shift"** key and tap the **"4"** key; then press <**return**>.
4. At the **USER NAME** prompt, type in your user name. This is the 8-digit name you've been given by Central Computing.
5. At the **PASSWORD** prompt, type in your password. If you are using WIN for the first time, enter a password of your choosing, one you can remember readily. Your password should be between 6 and 8 characters long.

Once you have logged on, you will see a screen that looks something like this:

WELCOME TO WIN!

The Wordsmith International Network

You have six unread messages.

What would you like to do?

   (R) Read your mail

   (S) Send a message

   (C) Check the bulletin boards

   OFF Disconnect from WIN

Please enter your selection:

You are now ready to do business on WIN. Prompts will appear at each selection to guide you through the electronic network. If you run into trouble, consult your WIN *User's Guide* or call the Central Computing HelpDesk, at (246) 426-4264.

When you are ready to sign-off WIN, simply put a comma **(,)** on a line by itself and press **<return>**. On the very next line, type **OFF.** A message announcing that you have been disconnected will appear on your screen.

I hope these guidelines help. If you have any questions, don't hesitate to call me at (246) 321-9933. Have a productive time on-line with WIN.

MEMO WRITER TIPS

1. Of course, procedures for accessing electronic networks will vary.

2. Be explicit, precise, and clear about your instructions.

3. List them in sequential order.

4. If you're writing a memo to employees who are not familiar with computers, write in user-friendly language; avoid technical jargon.

5. Include information about how users can receive assistance.

ELECTRONIC BULLETIN BOARD SYSTEM (BBS) USE

To:

From:

Date:

Subject: Electronic Bulletin Board Use

Our electronic bulletin board system (BBS) plays an integral role in communicating effectively. To familiarize users with the BBS, a workshop titled, "The BBS: A User's Guide," will be held on Thursday, November 15, from 7:30 a.m.–12:30 p.m., in Room 202. Sarah Eckert, Computer Support Specialist, will conduct this hands-on session.

In the workshop, you'll learn how to:

1. Log on and off
2. Change your password
3. Send and receive files
4. Connect with the BBS
5. Use all popular file-transfer protocols and terminal emulations

6. Scan your downloaded files for viruses
7. Manage compressed files

Please plan to attend this informative session. Call ext. 5608 (by Tuesday, November 13) to register.

MEMO WRITER TIPS

1. Electronic bulletin board systems vary. Provide users with your system specifics.
2. List steps in sequential order.
3. Tell users how to get additional help.

INSTRUCTIONS FOR USING ELECTRONIC MAIL (E-MAIL)

To:
From:
Date:
Subject: Using Electronic Mail (E-Mail)

Here are the steps for using e-mail:

1. Log on the main menu.
2. Click on **mail.**
3. At the prompt, type in the user identification code assigned to you by computer support services.
4. At the next prompt, type in your 6–8-character password; this will open your mailbox.
5. Read your electronic mail by clicking on the appropriate entry.
6. Use the icons on your monitor to reply to, save, or discard each message.
7. Click on the **reply** icon to reply to a message. At the prompt, type in a brief message or upload a longer message from another file. (Consult your *User's Manual* for specific instructions on how to send your message out for review [pages 46–47] or to proofread your message [pages 47–48].
8. To save the message, click on the **save** icon.
9. To discard the message, click on the **discard** icon.
10. Click on the **search** icon to find a specific file. As the search screen indicates, you may search for e-mail by date, sender name, subject, or key word. Click on **open** when you have found the file you want; repeat Steps 6, 7, and 8.

11. A log of incoming and outgoing messages is maintained in your e-mail log. Click on **log** to access it. You can change, add, or erase information; send information to others; search through your log, review it, and/or print out your log.

12. Click on **outgoing** to see if mail you've sent to others has arrived.

13. Click on **exit** to terminate your e-mail session.

14. Contact the system administrator if you experience problems with the system.

15. Call the help desk at (206) 333-4444 with specific questions about operating your e-mail system.

MEMO WRITER TIPS

1. List the e-mail steps in sequential order.

2. Be as detailed as possible; write in user-friendly language.

3. Provide help desk, assistance, and/or user-guide information.

EVALUATING ELECTRONIC MAIL (E-MAIL) SYSTEMS

To:

From:

Date:

Subject: Electronic Mail (E-Mail) Systems Evaluation

An electronic mail (e-mail) system would help us communicate with each other much more quickly and efficiently, in light of our rapid expansion. In order to procure the best e-mail system for our office, I've established an E-Mail Evaluation Team. The team will assess two e-mail systems: the systems' receive, create, send, store, and search capabilities.

Team members will ask each of you for input. To assist with this, they'll provide you with a "fast-track" diagram that shows you how each of the systems works. Please provide the team with your candid suggestions, questions, or comments.

Team recommendations will be used to acquire the most efficient system for us. Once an e-mail system has been selected and installed, you will receive hands-on training on how to use the e-mail system.

MEMO WRITER TIPS

1. Assessing user input on electronic mail systems before one is acquired accelerates user acceptance and system use.

2. Outline which aspects of e-mail systems should be assessed.

MANAGING INFORMATION OVERLOAD

To:
From:
Date:
Subject: Suggestions for Managing Information Overload

"Be careful what you ask for, lest you get it!" We all wanted more information, and now we have more than any of us could have imagined. I think this may be causing information overload for some people.

Here are a few suggestions for managing the reams of information that cross your desk and/or your computer monitor each day:

1. Try to touch information only once. Read/scan it, pass it on to a peer or subordinate (put an FYI sticker, name, dept., and so on on it and put it in your "out" box), file it, put it in a box for future use, throw it away, or delete it from your computer the first time you read it. I always go through my mail with a wastebasket nearby.

2. Keep only information you absolutely need. If someone else needs it more than you do, pass it on to them.

3. Plan time each day to just read and think. Use this time to go through your mail; answer/send e-mail messages; scan your reports, information, brochures, and so on; route outgoing info. If you don't put this time in your schedule, you'll find you won't get around to it.

4. Realize no one can retain all this information (unless he/she has a photographic memory). Read and keep what you need; route the rest, toss it away, or delete it from your computer.

5. Keep chronological "to do" stacks on your desk or "to do" files in your computer. As you're going through your mail, put information you need in the appropriate stacks or files.

6. Assign appropriate subordinates to read and report back to you (face-to-face or in a written summary) on essential information contained in

longer documents. They may need the information, too. (Remember, information is power!). Most times, they'll be glad you asked, and you'll get the details you need.

7. Relax. There's so much information and so little time. One thing's for sure. If you don't get to the information on your desk or in your computer, no one else will do it for you. It will be right where you left it when you come back.

MEMO WRITER TIPS

1. All of us probably have more information than we ever needed, so information overload is a very real occupational hazard.

2. The important key is to sort out useful information from information you don't need.

SCHEDULING A TELEPHONE CONFERENCE CALL

To:
From:
Date:
Subject: Conference Call—February 3, 7:30 p.m. (CST)

I have scheduled a conference call for you, Donna Albright, John Stevens, and me, to discuss the budget for the Macambridge Project. The conference call is scheduled for Tuesday, February 3, at 7:30 p.m. (CST). Dial 1-800-999-8888 at 10:30 p.m. and tell the operator you're joining the Rae Bishop conference call. She'll connect you.

I'm glad we'll have this chance to finalize the budget before our presentation. I look forward to talking to you Tuesday.

MEMO WRITER TIPS

1. Tell the reader when (day, date, time, time zone) the conference call will take place.

2. Discuss the purpose of the conference call.

3. Provide the access number and information about the procedure.

ANNOUNCING A TELECONFERENCE

To:
From:
Date:
Subject: Learning Organization Teleconference

Please plan to attend the teleconference titled *Learning Organization* on Thursday, February 14, 8:00 a.m.–5:00 p.m., in the Green Auditorium. The teleconference, hosted by Peter Senge, author of *Fifth Discipline*, will feature executives and managers from major corporations who have applied learning-organization principles in their organizations.

Registration will begin promptly at 7:30 a.m. and will continue until 8:00 a.m. A continental breakfast will be served from 7:30 a.m. until 8:30 a.m., and the teleconference will begin promptly at 8:30 a.m.

All Level-1 and Level-2 managers should plan to attend, if at all possible. The teleconference will cover topics related to our strategic plan and will provide managers with an overview of learning organization principles and practices. Question-and-answer segments will provide participants from all over the United States with an opportunity to call in their questions and have them addressed by the teleconference presenters.

Accompanying workbooks will be distributed at the registration desk. A buffet lunch will be served at 12:00 noon. If you plan to attend, call Jan Singleton at ext. 642 by Monday, February 11. This will be an informative session, one I hope you'll all attend.

MEMO WRITER TIPS

1. Describe the teleconference and provide information about the presenters.
2. Give details about day, date, time, place, contact person, and suggested audience.
3. If the teleconference is interactive, provide this information as well.

SENDING/RECEIVING FAXES
ON YOUR PERSONAL COMPUTER

To:
From:
Date:
Subject: Steps for Sending/Receiving Faxes on Your PC

To send and/or receive faxes on your personal computer, be sure you have DistanceFax or another fax software package installed on your computer properly.

To send a fax from your personal computer, follow these steps:

1. Find the file you want to send in your word-processing program. Set your printer up for **DistanceFax on Com 2.** Click **OK.**
2. Press the **Alt and Tab keys** simultaneously until **DistanceFax** appears in the window. Release the **Alt-Tab** keys.
3. Click on **send fax** on the DistanceFax main menu.
4. Choose the appropriate option on the send screen.
5. On the send screen, type in the name, company, area code, and telephone number of the person you're faxing (if you've never faxed this person before) or click on **telephone** to retrieve a preentered telephone listing.
6. When all information on the send screen is correct, click on **send fax.** A status screen will appear to let you see the progress of your fax transmission.
7. When 100 percent of your fax has been transmitted, you can click on **log** to verify that your fax has been sent.
8. Click on **close** to return to your standard-use menu.

To receive a fax on your PC, follow these steps:

1. Set up your printer for **DistanceFax Com 2.**
2. Click on **DistanceFax.**
3. Click on the **receive** icon on the DistanceFax main menu.
4. Click on **receive fax.**
5. A status screen will now appear. When "ready to receive fax" appears, you are ready to receive your fax.
6. As your personal computer is receiving a fax, a status screen will track its progress.
7. Click on **look** to see the fax.
8. If you want to print the fax, make sure your printer is on and click on **print.**
9. Click on **close** to return to your standard-use menu.

If you need more help, check your *DistanceFax User's Manual* or call computer support services at ext. 3490.

MEMO WRITER TIPS

1. Fax procedures will vary.
2. List the detailed steps in sequential order.
3. Write in user-friendly language.
4. Tell the user where additional assistance can be found.

VOICEMAIL POLICY

To:
From:
Date:
Subject: Voicemail Policy

Please observe the following guidelines when using the voicemail system:

1. Update your message frequently, particularly if you plan to be away from the office for an extended period of time.
2. Restrict your message length to no more than 20 seconds. Listeners "tune out" after a certain period of time and won't hear what your message says anyway.
3. Be sure your messages have a professional tone, free of slang and trite phrases.
4. Respond to messages within 24 hours, if at all possible. If you will not be able to return calls within 24 hours, say when you *will* return calls on your voicemail message.
5. Always provide callers with a way to access a human being. Leave your secretary's, receptionist's, or assistant's name, title, and telephone extension at the end of your voicemail message.
6. Never leave voicemail messages that could create conflict. Handle these conversations face-to-face.
7. Never reprimand subordinates on voicemail. Handle this face-to-face.
8. When leaving voicemail messages for others, provide as much detail as possible. This will prevent unnecessary follow-up calls. For example, if you want the caller to meet with you at 3:00 p.m., say that in your message. If you want them to send you a report, ask for the report in the message.

9. Retrieve your voicemail messages several times a day, whether you are on-site or off-site. Remember, voicemail messages are purged after seven days.

This policy is provided to help us all use voicemail wisely, courteously, and efficiently.

MEMO WRITER TIPS

1. Be as explicit as possible.
2. Provide voicemail users with a list of do's and don'ts.

VOICEMAIL PROCEDURES

To:
From:
Date:
Subject: Procedure for Voicemail Users

To update your voicemail message, follow this procedure:

1. Dial into your voicemail box.
2. Press * 9 and you will hear a menu.
3. Press 1 at this point to update your voicemail message.
4. Press 5 to rerecord your message.
5. Record a new message, informing callers about your current day's schedule, including when you can be reached and/or when you will return their calls.
6. Once you have recorded your new message, press the * key.
7. You will hear a menu; press 1 if your message is acceptable. If you want to record your message again, press 5 and rerecord; repeat steps 6 and 7.

Additional voicemail training sessions have been scheduled for Tuesday, November 19; Thursday, November 21; and Friday, November 22. All sessions are from 10:00 a.m. until 12:00 noon in Suite 407. Plan to attend one of these sessions to familiarize yourself with voicemail operations. If you have specific voicemail problems or questions, call Tina Vincent, ext. 222.

MEMO WRITER TIPS

1. Detail the voicemail process.
2. Provide the reader with information about resources for help.

9

Model Memos about Training

Chapter 9 Model Memoranda target the training functions of your operation:

- Announcing training sessions
- Approving/disapproving conference attendance
- Preparing a schedule for cross-training
- Requesting educational reimbursement
- Making training requests
- Scheduling new-employee orientation
- Summarizing training efforts for your boss

Formats for writing about both voluntary and mandatory training sessions have been provided. Use your model memoranda to help you discuss the results of your organization's training as well: how you/participants liked it, and whether training was effective.

Memos introducing volunteers or interns, asking for input or for feedback about training, determining training needs, and discussing conferences and retreats have also been included.

Employees who've been trained properly produce better results. Use the model memoranda in this chapter to produce the results you want when you write about training needs, sessions, or quality.

ANNOUNCING AN ANNUAL CONFERENCE OR RETREAT*

Date:
To:
From:
Re: Planning Retreat, November 18, 8:00 a.m.–5:00 p.m., Aurora Public
    Library

Be sure you have marked your calendar for the November 18 Academic Services
planning and development meeting.

In preparation for our November retreat, please review the "Staffing Concepts" (below) we developed at last year's session.

Please bring the following to the meeting on the 18th:

1. Any suggested changes or additions to the six concepts listed below
2. Specific staffing needs or recommendations for your area or Academic
   Services in general
3. Any planned new initiatives, programs, facilities, or equipment for your
   area that might require resources (i.e., $$$$$)

Thank you.

MEMO WRITER TIPS

1. As with any meeting, include the day(s) of week, date, time, and place at the very beginning of the memorandum. Include this information in the "subject" line if you wish. If it's there, it won't get lost in the memo, and people are more apt to see it and pay attention to it.

2. Outline what items will be discussed at the retreat and/or attach a retreat schedule of activities.

3. If the retreat is at a hotel or other conference facility, include a brochure about the facility, information about check-in times, how rooms will be assigned, how meals will be handled, and a map to the location.

4. Let participants know what they should bring with them to the retreat. If the retreat is at an off-site location, advise attendees to bring any special clothing or other materials needed for special conditions.

---

*This memorandum was written by a community college Dean of Instruction.

PHRASING ALTERNATIVES

Paragraph 1

In recognition of your commitment to the goals and objectives of Frenetics Enterprises, I am pleased to announce that the next retreat will be held at the Keystone Resort from Sunday evening, June 23 through Tuesday afternoon, June 25.

Our annual retreat has been scheduled for Friday through Monday, January 3–6, 19____ .

I look forward to a productive retreat this year:

WHEN: Monday–Friday, August 5–9, 19____
WHERE: Lamont Lake Resort, Westridge, Minnesota
WHY: To develop next year's operational plan

Paragraph 2

In a later memo, I will provide you with more details about the facility and the agenda.

Further details will follow.

Specific information about the location, activities, etc., is attached.

ANNOUNCING AN AUDIO-VISUAL TRAINING PROGRAM

To:
From:
Date:
Subject: Audio-Visual Training Program

The training department has prepared a 30-minute video on safety procedures for installers. This video will be shown in Training Room 10 on the following dates:

Friday, August 1   8:00–8:30 a.m.
Wednesday, August 6   1:00–1:30 p.m.
Monday, August 11   5:00–5:30 p.m.

All installers should sign up with Betty for one of these dates. This is an important training session that highlights important safety tips and procedures.

MEMO WRITER TIPS

1. Outline what kind of audio-visual training will be offered.

2. Include information about when training sessions have been scheduled: days, dates, times, locations.

3. Include at least one sentence that explains what the audio-visual training session covers.

4. Specify whether this is mandatory or voluntary training.

PHRASING ALTERNATIVES

Paragraph 1

Plan to attend an audio-visual training segment that will give you an overview of our new computer system and how it operates.

All employees hired since January 1 are required to view an orientation videotape.

We are proud to announce we now have a film on training techniques. The film is entitled "Tips for Effective Training."

Paragraph 2

The audio-visual segment can be viewed Monday through Wednesday from 8:00 a.m. until 12:00 noon in Room 406.

Sign up for this exciting program scheduled for Friday, June 10, 4:00 p.m., Small Conference Room.

A schedule of viewing times is attached. Sign up for the date and time of your choice and return the schedule to your supervisor.

Paragraph 3

This entertaining videotape will acquaint you with step-by-step procedures for completing purchasing contracts.

You will learn how to correctly mount film on file cards.

Audio-visual training is an interesting way to learn the latest procedures.

ANNOUNCING COMPUTER TRAINING

To:
From:
Date:
Subject: Computer Training

The next computer training session has been scheduled for Friday, July 14, 19/20 _____, from 9:30 a.m. to 1:30 p.m. Topics covered will include:

- Creating a document
- Editing a document
- Storing a document
- Retrieving a document

This will be a hands-on session facilitated by Millicent Saul, Computer Training Specialist. To register, call the training office, ext. 876, no later than Thursday, July 13. Box lunches will be provided at the end of the training session.

MEMO WRITER TIPS

1. Include the day, date, time, place, and facilitator of the computer training.
2. Describe briefly what topics will be covered.

ANNOUNCING KEYBOARDING SKILLS TRAINING

To:
From:
Date:
Subject: Training Session—Keyboarding Skills

Several keyboarding skills training sessions have been scheduled:

Beginning Keyboarding—If you've rarely touched a computer or typewriter keyboard, this is the session for you. Attend one session or all three. You'll learn keyboard setup and practice typing by touch:

Monday, February 10	8:30 a.m.–12:30 p.m.	Computer Center
Wednesday, February 12	1:00 p.m.–5:00 p.m.	Computer Center
Friday, February 14	10:00 a.m.–2:00 p.m.	Computer Center

Intermediate Keyboarding—If you type between 20 and 40 words per minute, you'll pick up speed and accuracy in this session. Attend one session or all three.

Monday, February 17	8:30 a.m.–12:30 p.m.	Computer Center
Wednesday, February 19	1:00 p.m.–5:00 p.m.	Computer Center
Friday, February 21	10:00 a.m.–2:00 p.m.	Computer Center

Morrissey Handford, an expert in the Keyboarding-for-Keeps Skills Training Program, will be conducting each hands-on session. Keyboarding-for-Keeps guarantees participants at least a 10-word-per-minute increase in typing speed for every four hours of instruction. Sign up for these fast-paced workshops by calling Hugh Wells, ext. 921, at least one day before your desired session.

MEMO WRITER TIPS

1. Include the day, date, time, place, and facilitator of training.
2. Discuss the intended audience.
3. Provide registration information.

ANNOUNCING A TRAINING SESSION, MANDATORY ATTENDANCE*

To:
From:
Date:
Subject: Communication Workshops for Supervisors (Mandatory)

All supervisors in your department should plan to attend one of the communication workshops listed below. Workshops have been scheduled as follows:

---

*This memorandum was written by the Personnel Director for a municipal government agency.

Session I	Friday, May 25, 19____	9:00 a.m.–12:00 noon
Session II	Friday, June 8, 19____	10:00 a.m.–12:00 noon
Session III	Friday, June 22, 19____	10:00 a.m.–12:00 noon

Sessions will be held in council chambers. An outline of topics to be covered is attached.

MEMO WRITER TIPS

1. State that training is mandatory in the "subject" line or in the first paragraph of the memorandum.

2. Provide essential days, dates, times, and locations.

3. Feel free to include information about what the training will involve.

4. If participants are to bring special items with them, let them know this in the closing paragraph.

PHRASING ALTERNATIVES

Paragraph 1

Mandatory training in "Effective Communication Skills" has been scheduled for Monday, March 3, 19____, 9:00 a.m.–12:00 noon. Training will take place in the 1st floor conference room.

Dr. Peg Walford, a renowned economist, has agreed to conduct a mandatory training session for all account reps on Friday, April 4 from 10:00 a.m. until 12:00 noon. We will meet in the dining room. Dr. Walford will discuss economic trends and forecasts.

Mark your calendars for a training session on billing procedures: Wednesday, October 14, 19____, 8:00 a.m. until 5:00 p.m. Your attendance is required.

ANNOUNCING A TRAINING SESSION, VOLUNTARY ATTENDANCE*

To:
From:
Date:
Subject: Saturday Workshop—Continuity: Assessment and Grading

You are invited to attend a workshop on Saturday, October 24, 19____ , in East Park 108. The session will run from 8:30 a.m. until 1:00 p.m.

Assessment of students, placement, and grading will be discussed. Please submit three samples of student writing—samples representative of good, acceptable, and unacceptable writing. The samples need not be graded.

You will, of course, be paid for your participation. However, I hope the benefits you gain from this workshop will exceed the $8.00 per hour rate you will be paid.

MEMO WRITER TIPS

1. Put the day, date, time, and location of the training session in the first paragraph, preferably the first sentence.

2. Discuss the nature of the training session and how it might be of benefit to participants.

3. Tell readers what they should bring, if anything.

PHRASING ALTERNATIVES

Paragraph 1

The Training Department will conduct a session on "Tools for Effective Management": Monday, March 3, 19____ , 9:00 a.m.–12:00 noon. Training will take place in Room 407.

Please plan to join us for a short course in business writing on Friday, April 4 from 8:00 a.m. until 1:00 p.m., Conference Room B.

If you could use a review of tax changes, come to a training session entitled "Tax Laws: What's New for 19____ ." This session will be held from 8:00 a.m. until 5:00 p.m. on Saturday, July 6 in Suite 406.

---

*This memorandum was written by the Division Chair for a college English department.

ANNOUNCING VOICEMAIL TRAINING

To:
From:
Date:
Subject: Voicemail Training

Voicemail training for all personnel has been scheduled as follows. Sign up for only one training session.

Monday, August 4, 19/20_____, 9:00 a.m.–12:00 noon, Room 304.
Tuesday, August 5, 19/20_____, 1:00 p.m.–5:00 p.m., Room 303.
Wednesday, August 6, 19/20_____, 8:30 a.m.–12:30 p.m., Room 304.
Thursday, August 7, 19/20_____, 1:00 p.m.–5:00 p.m., Room 303.

Voicemail system basics, including sending/retrieving voicemail messages; recording/changing voicemail messages; setting up voicemail groups; voicemail etiquette; and some voicemail do's and don'ts will be covered.

Consultants from our voicemail supplier will conduct the training. To register, call Bill Hones, Training Department, 264-9781. Register at least two days before your selected session.

MEMO WRITER TIPS

1. Include the day, date, time, place, and facilitator of training.
2. Discuss the topics to be covered.
3. Provide registration information.

APPROVING CONFERENCE/ SEMINAR ATTENDANCE

To:
From:
Date:
Subject: Conference Attendance Approval

I've approved your request to attend the National Auditors' Convention next month. Jan will make your airline, hotel, and car rental reservations.

I've attended this conference in the past and found it most helpful. Enjoy your trip.

MEMO WRITER TIPS

1. In the first sentence, let the reader know that his/her training request has been approved. Name the conference or seminar your subordinate has asked to attend.
2. Include a "wish you well" sentence if you like.

PHRASING ALTERNATIVES

Paragraph 1

Your request to go to the State Employees Council computer training workshop has been approved.

I hope you'll learn a great deal at the upcoming management seminar.

I'm pleased to approve your request for training at the Cumberland Training Network.

Paragraph 2

I hope you'll pass on whatever you learn to the rest of us when you return.

Be prepared to conduct a similar training session for your department when you get back.

The knowledge you gain at this conference will benefit your entire section.

DISAPPROVING CONFERENCE/ SEMINAR ATTENDANCE*

To:
From:
Date:
Subject: Conference Attendance Disapproval

I am currently unable to approve your request to attend this year's Police Records and Communications Conference. Limited travel funds as we approach the end of the fiscal year make a trip of this nature unfundable right now.

---

*This memorandum was written by the Acting Chief of Police of a police department.

When you find out the particulars about next year's conference, resubmit your request. Funds may be available then.

MEMO WRITER TIPS

1. Let the reader know which request is being denied and why.
2. Close by telling the reader when such attendance might be permitted.

PHRASING ALTERNATIVES

Paragraph 1

Unfortunately, you will not be able to attend the November 22 workshop sponsored by the American Management Association.

I'm sure you'd benefit from attending the annual realtors conference in Dallas this year, but adequate funds simply aren't available at this time.

Your request to attend the Production Managers' Seminar in Oakland cannot be approved.

Paragraph 2

All travel requests submitted after August 15 cannot be approved this fiscal year.

Your department has exceeded its conference/travel budget for this year.

The funds required for a trip of this kind are not available.

You have already attended two conferences this year, and I'd like to make funds available for others in the department to travel.

Paragraph 3

Please submit your request again when funds are available.

Perhaps this conference will be offered again and funds will be available for you to attend.

Let me know if there are other seminars you'd like to attend later in the year. We will have the new travel allowance by then, and you may be able to go.

DISTRIBUTING AN INFORMATIONAL BROCHURE

To:
From:
Date:
Subject: Informational Brochure

Copies of the brochure about our Employee Assistance Program are attached. Please see that everyone in your department receives one. Thanks.

MEMO WRITER TIPS

1. Include the name and/or nature of the brochure in the first sentence.
2. Tell how distribution is to be handled and who should receive a copy.

PHRASING ALTERNATIVES

Paragraph 1

"On the Firing Line" is an informational brochure for first-line supervisors. I think you'll find some helpful information in it and hope you'll enjoy reading it.

Please distribute a copy of the enclosed brochure, "Tips for Effective Word-processing," to the secretaries and clerks in your section.

All the auditors in your unit will want to read "Auditing: The Bottom Line" (copies attached); make sure each auditor gets one.

FAILING A TRAINING SESSION

To:
From:
Date:
Subject: Unsatisfactory Performance, Supervisory Training

Satisfactory completion of Supervisory Training requires a 70 percent overall average. Your average was 65 percent.

This training will be offered again, beginning January 15. Plan to attend the next session if you want to receive credit.

If you have any questions, call me at ext. 650.

MEMO WRITER TIPS

1. To soften the blow, say what satisfactory completion standards are. Then let the employee know what his/her score was.

2. Include details about how/when the course can be retaken and what steps the employee may take to rectify the situation.

PHRASING ALTERNATIVES

Paragraph 1

An 80 percent grade on the final performance test was required in order to receive credit for "Workplace Etiquette" training; you scored 65 percent on the final examination.

In the typing course, you achieved an average speed of 55 words per minute. In order to pass the course, a speed of 65 words per minute is required.

Your performance in the "New Managers" course did not meet requirements for satisfactory completion.

Paragraph 2

A passing grade in this course is required for promotion to Data Entry Operator II. Brush up on your skills and enroll in the next session.

You cannot be given credit for having taken the course until you achieve a passing grade. Contact this office to find out when the course will be offered again.

Failure to pass this course may delay your promotion to the next grade. Since the course will not be offered again until next year, I suggest you contact the local community college and, perhaps, enroll in a similar course there.

INTRODUCING AN INTERN OR VOLUNTEER

To:
From:
Date:
Subject: Summer Intern

Ms. Agnes Cochrane will work as a summer intern in the Marketing Department from June 1, 19____, until August 18, 19____. Agnes is a third-year journalism major at Cayahoga State University.

She will be working primarily with Jack Copperfield, to develop the new promotional brochure. Jack will coordinate any other assignments you might want Agnes to tackle.

Let's make good use of her talents.

MEMO WRITER TIPS

1. Name the volunteer or intern in the first sentence, and provide the reader with information about how long this person will be working.

2. Briefly describe what kind of work the intern or volunteer should be doing and include who the intern will be reporting to in the memo.

PHRASING ALTERNATIVES

Paragraph 1

Kris Thompson has volunteered for duty in the Pediatrics Department. She can volunteer 10 hours per week, beginning Monday, January 4, 19____ .

Please make the summer intern, Mr. Jonathan Peale, feel welcome in your department. He will begin work on Monday, May 14 and continue working through Friday, August 18.

Your intern will begin work on June 1 and work through August 14. Her name is Janet Crenshaw.

Paragraph 2

You will have primary responsibility for coordinating her work assignments. Ms. Jones, a finance major, is a junior at Welsh College.

Brad Dillon in Volunteer Services supervises all volunteers. Meet with Brad and work out duties and assignments for Ms. Gleason.

Your intern has a fairly good background in copy writing, so I hope you'll use him in this area as much as possible.

PREPARING A CROSS-TRAINING SCHEDULE

To:
From:
Date:
Subject: Cross-Training Schedule

As you know, cross-training will begin in our department on Monday, April 1. The following schedule outlines cross-training assignments:

Employee	Training Assignment	Trainer
Meryl Johnson	Data Entry Operator II	M. Martin
John LaPointe	Wordprocessor III	A. Avery
Dorine Camp	Data Analyst	J. Foster
Mark Stamper	Data Analyst	J. Foster
Peggy Jones	Data Supervisor	M. Martin

Please report to the trainer with whom you'll be working at 8:30 a.m. Monday morning. Cross-training will last for two weeks. I hope you all will take advantage of this valuable opportunity to learn about other positions within the department.

If you have any questions, see me by 5:00 p.m. Friday.

MEMO WRITER TIPS

1. Let workers know when cross-training will begin. Then list the schedule, outlining which employees will be learning which jobs and with whom they will be working.

2. Tell workers whom they should report to when cross-training begins, and close with a positive note about how valuable this experience will be.

PHRASING ALTERNATIVES

Paragraph 1

The following schedule details the cross-training program that begins next week.

You are scheduled for cross-training, according to the schedule below. Training will begin Monday, January 4, 19_____ .

Your cross-training will begin on Wednesday, November 11, 19_____ , as outlined in the schedule below.

Paragraph 2

Come to Conference Room 1 on Monday, February 11 at 10:00 a.m. for a brief orientation. Cross-training will begin immediately following this meeting.

See your trainer on Monday, March 3 at 8:00 a.m. Together, you will work out details.

You will have a chance to meet your trainer at 8:00 a.m., Monday, August 1 in Room 311.

Paragraph 3

Many of you have requested cross-training, and I'm certain the entire department will benefit from this undertaking.

What each of you learns can only serve to enhance overall operations in our unit.

This unique training opportunity will go a long way toward familiarizing each of you with the work done by your team members.

PRESENTING A TRAINING SCHEDULE*

To:
From:
Date:
Subject:

Ladies:

Here is the training schedule for Friday. We will still meet at City Hall at 7:15 a.m. and try to arrange rides.

TIME/TOPIC	FACILITATOR
8:00 a.m.–9:15 a.m. Panel Discussion	S. Canter J. Smith
9:30 a.m.–10:45 a.m. Upward Mobility Continuing Education Stress Management	E. Grenata J. Greenspan B. Martin

---

*This memorandum was written by an Assistant to a City Manager.

TIME/TOPIC	FACILITATOR
Communication	C. Barnes
Marketing an Image	C. Planet
Retirement	E. Sherman
11:00 a.m.–12:15 p.m.	
Irate Public	A. Jamison
Stress Management	B. Morschum
Upward Mobility	E. Green
Family and Career	N. Havel
12:15 a.m.–1:30 p.m.	
Lunch/Discussion (Lunch will be provided.)	
1:30 p.m.–2:45 p.m.	
Upward Mobility	E. Green
Stress Management	B. Martin
Communication	C. Barnes
Marketing an Image	C. Planet
3:00 p.m.–4:15 p.m.	
Communication	C. Barnes
Conflict Resolution	A. Sanchez

On the slip below, write in the name of the session you would like to take next to the time indicated. Fill this form out and return it to Cindy Thatcher by 5:00 p.m., Thursday, March 15, so we'll have an exact count of how many people will be attending each session.

We will be back at City Hall by 5:00 p.m. on Friday or shortly thereafter. I'm looking forward to seeing you on Friday for a productive, stimulating day.

Return to Cindy Thatcher by 5:00 p.m., Thursday, March 15.

I plan to attend the following sessions:

9:30 a.m. _____   11:00 a.m. _____

1:30 p.m. _____   3:00 p.m. _____

My name: _____   Dept. _____

MEMO WRITER TIPS

1. Outlines and lists work best for schedules of this kind. Include the time, session title, presenter's name, and any other pertinent information.

2. If attendees need to indicate their preferences for sessions, provide a tear-off form for this purpose.

3. Include a location for sessions, as well, if attendees have not already been informed where training will take place.

PHRASING ALTERNATIVES

Paragraph 1

The schedule for next Monday's training sessions is listed below:

Here's the training schedule for Friday, January 18, 19_____ . Attached is an outline of the times, topics, and facilitators for next week's training course.

Paragraph 2

Call Bev in Training, Extension 2042, and let her know which sessions you plan to attend. Do this by 5:00 p.m. Friday, August 5.

Indicate the session(s) you plan to attend on the tear-off sheet below and return this sheet to John Himson in Training by 5:00 p.m. Friday.

REPRIMAND: FAILURE TO ATTEND TRAINING

To:
From:
Date:
Subject: Failure to Attend Training

Why weren't you at the 8:00 a.m. training session on safety practices yesterday? All lathe operators are required to complete this training, so you are hereby directed to contact the Training Department and register for the next available course.

Training helps all of us perform our jobs more efficiently. Take it seriously and don't let an absence like this one occur again.

MEMO WRITER TIPS

1. Tell the employee which training session was missed and briefly describe why this session was important.

2. Use strong language that conveys your displeasure, as well as your expectation that the employee will not miss future training.

3. If company policy has specific disciplinary action for such infractions, include what this policy is and what action will be taken.

4. Tell the reader what the next step will be.

PHRASING ALTERNATIVES

Paragraph 1

Your absence from the 9:00 a.m. training course on bookkeeping procedures disturbs me a great deal. I'd like to know why you could not or did not attend.

Training is an important part of all our jobs; therefore, your unexcused absence from the mandatory training session held yesterday afternoon is very disturbing.

I would like to believe you have a good reason for missing Tuesday's training on equipment handling, but whatever your reasons, don't be absent again.

Paragraph 2

Contact the training office to find out when you can make up what you missed, and don't let this happen again.

Come to my office today so we can discuss why you were absent and what you plan to do about it.

Call Mitch Haverd in the Training Office for a schedule of future sessions. When the next training session is offered, be there!

REQUESTING EDUCATIONAL REIMBURSEMENT

To:
From:
Date:
Subject: Request for Educational Reimbursement

I am requesting educational reimbursement in the amount of $82.41 for the Principles of Supervision course I recently completed at Langston Community College. I received a grade of "A" in the course, and a copy of my transcript is attached.

MEMO WRITER TIPS

1. Say that you are asking for educational reimbursement and name the dollar amount requested.

2. Your memo should also include the name of the course you took, and what grade you received.

3. Since most companies need proof of satisfactory completion, make reference in your memo to whether such substantiation is attached or will be forwarded, etc.

PHRASING ALTERNATIVES

Paragraph 1

Reimbursement for educational expenses in the amount of $312.00 is requested. I satisfactorily completed the following courses at Wayne University last fall:

Principles of Management	B
Sales and Marketing	A

Please prepare an educational reimbursement check for $256.00 for coursework I completed at Harbor Community College last semester. The two courses I took were Business Communication and Technical Writing. The college is sending an official transcript, and it should arrive within two weeks.

I request educational reimbursement for $75.00, the amount it cost me to take a course titled Women in Management. A letter from my instructor at Hammond College is attached. Thank you.

REQUESTING TRAINING

To:
From:
Date:
Subject: Request for Supervisory Training

Since I have recently been promoted to a supervisory position, I would like to enhance my formal training in management. Grosspointe College offers a 15-week course in Management and Supervision, and I would like to take this course Fall Semester, 19_____ .

The course costs $125, which would be reimbursed by the company educational benefits plan. The class meets Monday through Thursday, from 11:45 a.m. until 1:00 p.m. Classes begin August 28 and end December 14.

I feel this course would equip me with the skills needed to be a more effective supervisor. Do I have your approval to take it?

MEMO WRITER TIPS

1. A brief explanation of why you think the course would enhance your job skills should be included.

2. Include the title of the course you'd like to take and who offers it, as well as how long the course will run, when and where it meets, and how much it will cost.

PHRASING ALTERNATIVES

Paragraph 1

I request you approve the following training:

Effective Communication Skills
March 3–4, 19_____ , 8:00 a.m.–5:00 p.m.
Better Training Institute
Grand Palace Hotel
Cost: $295.00

Better Training has a reputation for providing outstanding business training, and I think this course would do a lot to help me enhance my communication skills.

Hubbard Management Consultants is conducting a one-day seminar in Auditing Practices, and I'd like to attend. The seminar will be held on Friday, January 17, 19____ , from 8:00 a.m. until 5:00 p.m. at the Westoffer Inn.

May I have your approval to attend an in-house training session on the new billing procedure? The session is scheduled for Friday, August 4, 19____ , from 10:00 a.m. until noon in Suite 406.

Paragraph 2

I use my computer quite a bit and believe this session will give me more information about computer applications.

This course will provide me with an overview of techniques useful in my present position.

Frankly, I could use a good review of business writing and oral communication.

REQUIRING TRAINING

To:
From:
Date:
Subject: Training Session

Plan to attend the upcoming training session on Account Executive responsibilities. The session will be held on Monday, October 1 from 1:00 p.m. until 5:00 p.m. in Conference Room C. The Training Department can give you additional details.

I think this class will give you a solid understanding of what an Account Executive does and what tools you can use to make your job more functional.

Call me if you have questions.

MEMO WRITER TIPS

1. Tell the employee the specific kind or title of the training you'd like him/her to take. Include details about the day, date, time, and place.

2. Include at least a one-sentence explanation of why you think this training will be beneficial for the employee.

PHRASING ALTERNATIVES

Paragraph 1

I'd like you to go to an Effective Communication course sponsored by Communication Consultants: Wednesday, November 1, 19_____ , 8:00 a.m. until 5:00 p.m., Jarvis Street Hotel, Banquet Hall A.

Our Training Office has scheduled a series of classes on Management Excellence, and I want you to attend. Contact Sue Nivens in the Training Department for further details.

You have had two accidents in the past month, so please plan to attend a Defensive Driving course offered by the Training Department. The next class will meet on Monday, October 18 from 8:00 a.m. until 12:00 noon, Bus Terminal 11. Be there.

Paragraph 2

I think this class will provide you with some motivational techniques you'll find useful in dealing with your subordinates.

Communication skills can always be improved, and this training may acquaint you with some methods you hadn't considered.

This very important new procedure will be discussed in detail, and since you'll have to train other employees in its use, this training should prove very helpful.

RESPONDING TO A REQUEST FOR TRAINING

To:
From:
Date:
Subject: Training Request

I received your request for training and will let you know whether you can attend after I've had a chance to review the training budget.

I'm glad you're interested in upgrading your skills and will do all I can to help you in this regard. Expect to hear from me by next week.

MEMO WRITER TIPS

1. Acknowledge that you have received the request for training and explain what action you plan to take.

2. Encourage the employee's initiative by affirming the positive aspects of training and reassuring the employee that you respect his/her efforts in this regard.

PHRASING ALTERNATIVES

Paragraph 1

Your training request has been received. Ms. Johnson has final approval for all training requests, and as soon as I talk to her, I'll get back to you to let you know what her decision is.

Your recent request for training should be approved, if funds are available. I'll be able to let you know whether they are or not by close of business on Friday.

I'm happy to see you're interested in additional training. As soon as I can arrange adequate coverage for your absence, I'll let you know.

Paragraph 2

In such a rapidly changing field, each of us can use all the training we can get. Your efforts to seek such training are commendable.

I'm pleased you're interested in seeking training that will enhance your job performance.

Thanks for wanting to do a better job and using training to help you do that.

RESPONDING TO FAVORABLE COMMENTS ABOUT TRAINING

To:
From:
Date:
Subject: Training Comments

Thanks for letting me know you found the Office Practices course helpful. We do our best to offer training that employees will find useful, and it's always gratifying to hear we've succeeded.

I hope you'll take other training and that it will be equally beneficial.

> **MEMO WRITER TIPS**
> 1. Acknowledge the favorable comments and let the reader know they are appreciated.
> 2. Invite the employee to take other training that she/he feels will be beneficial.

PHRASING ALTERNATIVES

Paragraph 1

I'm glad you learned a great deal in the installation course you took last month.

It's so nice to hear you found the training you recently took helpful to you.

I'm pleased to learn the course you took last semester proved beneficial to you.

Positive feedback about training is always nice to hear.

Paragraph 2

Since you found this course so useful, I'm confident you'll sign up for other training you'll find helpful, as well.

Feel free to request similar training when it is offered again.

I hope this will be the first in a series of successful training undertakings for you.

RESPONDING TO UNFAVORABLE COMMENTS ABOUT TRAINING

To:
From:
Date:
Subject: Training Comments

Thanks for sharing your comments about the training, even though you seem to have found it not as helpful as you had hoped. Feedback about training sessions, both positive and negative, is necessary, if courses that meet employee needs are to be developed.

Your suggestions for improvement have been forwarded to the Training Section, and I'm sure they'll take these into consideration when they offer this course again.

MEMO WRITER TIPS

1. Keep the tone positive, as a way of encouraging employees to offer honest input about training sessions.

2. Assure the employee that his/her negative comments will be used in a constructive way.

PHRASING ALTERNATIVES

Paragraph 1

I'm sorry you found the recent training session primarily a review of things you already know.

Even though you weren't pleased with the training you recently received, your comments are helpful.

Although the training you took wasn't as useful as you had hoped, your comments are appreciated.

Paragraph 2

I'll be sure to use your suggestions as I revamp the course for future attendees.

Your suggestions will help make this a better course.

I'd like to discuss the strengths and weaknesses of the training with you in more detail before this course is offered again.

SCHEDULING NEW-EMPLOYEE ORIENTATION

To:
From:
Date:
Subject: New-Employee Orientation

Orientation for employees hired since December 15, 19_____, will be held on Monday, January 4, 19_____, from 9:00 a.m. until 11:00 a.m., Training Room 14. Please plan to attend.

This session will acquaint you with company policies and procedures, give you a chance to meet other new employees, and answer any questions you may have regarding benefits, salary, etc.

MEMO WRITER TIPS

1. Put the day, date, time, and place for new orientation in the first sentence. Be sure you include a description of what constitutes "new employee."
2. Include a brief explanation of what topics will be covered during orientation.

\PHRASING ALTERNATIVES

Paragraph 1

All new employees who have not attended an orientation session are required to do so: Wednesday, October 5, 19_____, 1:00 p.m.–3:00 p.m., Room 304.

As a new employee, mark your calendar for a mandatory orientation session scheduled for Friday, September 5, 8:00 a.m., Personnel Office.

Employee orientation is an integral part of getting off to the right start. Plan to attend the next orientation session, Tuesday, December 1, 19_____, 4:00 p.m. Orientation will be held in the small conference room, 2nd floor; light refreshments will be served.

Paragraph 2

Basic policies and procedures, as well as other information helpful for new employees, will be discussed.

All you ever wanted to know about being an employee for Compton Associates will be discussed.

Come find out information about benefits, company practices, and other data necessary for successful employment at XYZ Corporation.

SOLICITING COMMENTS ABOUT TRAINING

To:
From:
Date:
Subject: Needed: Comments About Training

I am interested in getting feedback from you about the "Sales Pro" training you took recently. Specifically, I'd like to know (1) what the strengths of the training were, (2) what weaknesses you found, (3) whether the course held your interest, (4) what suggestions you have for improvement, (5) and whether you would take a similar course in the future.

Write me a brief memo addressing these points, adding any other comments you would like. Your input can help improve future training.

Thank you.

MEMO WRITER TIPS

1. Ask for feedback and name the specific course you're interested in.

2. If at all possible, list specific questions you have or comments you would like employees to give about the training.

3. Describe whether you want comments to be given to you in oral, memo, report, and other fashions.

4. Be sure to thank the employee for providing you with this information.

PHRASING ALTERNATIVES

Paragraph 1

Please let me know how useful you found the training session on "Marketing Tools."

I'd like your reactions to the teller training program.

Your assessment of the Strategic Planning course you recently took would be appreciated.

Paragraph 2

I'm primarily interested in knowing whether

1. the training will help you perform your job better.
2. the instructor was well prepared and organized.
3. the course met your expectations (why or why not).
4. you'd structure the course differently next time.

Tell me what was most useful and least helpful about the class. Include any recommendations you have for improving the class next time.

In your response, include (1) what you had hoped to learn, (2) what you actually learned, and (3) what you'd like to see future sessions include.

Paragraph 3

Let's sit down and discuss your reactions to the training some time this week.

Call me and share your comments with me.

Prepare an informal report that addresses the questions I've outlined.

SUMMARIZING TRAINING EFFORTS FOR A SUPERIOR

To:
From:
Date:
Subject: Training Summary

Training efforts during the past year have offered the employees in my department a wide range of training, tailored to the information we received in our needs assessment.

The following courses were offered during Fiscal Year 19_____:

1. Amplifying Your Job Aptitude
2. Stress Management
3. Planning for Effective Operations
4. Telephone Techniques
5. Writing Business Letters and Memoranda
6. A User-Friendly Approach to Mini-Computers
7. Communicating with Impossible People
8. Time Management
9. Problem Solving and Decision Making
10. Becoming a Team Player

Of the 58 people in my department, 94 percent participated in at least one training class. Sixty-four percent took five or more classes, and 12 percent took them all.

Participants were asked to evaluate the training sessions. These results were averaged, with the following results:

Excellent— 50 percent
Good   — 36 percent
Fair   — 9 percent
Poor   — 5 percent

These results indicate employees' highly favorable response to training, and we hope to duplicate or exceed these results next year.

If you'd like additional information, just let me know.

MEMO WRITER TIPS

1. In preparing this memorandum for your boss, specify what period of time or what specific training program you are summarizing.

2. Include information about the kind of training that was offered, how many employees participated in this training, and what their responses to the training were.

PHRASING ALTERNATIVES

Paragraph 1

As you requested, I have summarized our training efforts for 19_____ .

Here is a brief summary of (1) training programs offered, (2) level of employee participation, and (3) evaluations of training courses for the past quarter.

I am pleased to provide you with the following summary of training activities in my section, January 3–June 30, 19_____ .

10

Model Memos about Diversity Efforts

By the year 2000, most of the people who supply and buy your goods and/or services will be people who don't necessarily look just like you. Progressive leaders and managers will strategize now proactively, in order to plan effectively for the changing needs of these diverse stakeholders.

While Corporate America will still be controlled largely by people who look like its present owners, only 15 percent of the individuals entering the workforce will be white males. Females, who currently comprise more than half the workforce, Hispanics, African-Americans, Asians, and others will comprise the remaining 85 percent. By the year 2010, one-third of the American population and the workforce will be comprised of people of color: African-Americans will make up 14 percent, Hispanics nearly 15 percent, and Asians about 5 percent. By the year 2025, people of color are expected to make up nearly 40 percent of all 18–24-year-olds. This, admidst the retirement of aging "Baby Boomers" and the takeover of, some "me, my and mine" Generation X-ers.

Diversity—the predispositions, values, and behaviors internalized by members of any group that has a common set of experiences, can mean an ongoing, counterproductive battle between opposing forces. Or it can mean the preservation of tactics that work, the elimination of old-guard strategies that impede, and a celebration of organizational coming-of-age in a climate of diversity. Instead of fearing and rejecting what appear to be differences, the players in a diverse workforce must uncover and capitalize on commonalities. Then, and only then, will agencies thrive.

The model memos in Chapter 10 recognize the nature of this changing workforce. They can help you write about:

- A definition of diversity
- Diversity-related issues

- The needs of disabled workers
- The mandates of the Americans with Disabilities Act.

Use these memos to communicate effectively about a host of issues that will arise in the diverse workforce—and changing buying public—that will lead your organization into the next century.

DEFINING DIVERSITY

To:
From:
Date:
Subject: A Definition of Diversity

Over the past year, we've talked a great deal about "diversity." Each of you probably has your own definition of what diversity means. Here is mine.

Diversity means difference; differences in experiences and beliefs, values and behaviors, attitudes and interests. Differences in age, color, sex, religion, national origin, ability or disability. Differences in thinking, or in viewing the world and the work we need to do in it.

In a group of people who look alike, there is diversity. Each of us is unique. No other person who has ever lived has our same genetic coding, background, experiences, or talents. Each of us has special gifts to give, and it is through tapping those special gifts that our organization can become stronger and better than it has ever been.

Though each of us is an individual, we grow up and live in groups. These groups share common heritages, experiences, values, and beliefs. It is from these groups that we develop our attitudes and skills. It stands to reason that individuals who have had similar experiences may also have similar values and attitudes. These values and attitudes may differ markedly from those of individuals who have grown up in different groups.

The values, attitudes, beliefs, and experiences we learned from the group we grew up in are not worse nor better than those of someone who grew up in a different group. People are simply different, not more than or less than.

Diversity doesn't necessarily mean color differences or sex differences or age differences, though it can mean all these things. Diversity, in my view, simply means difference. And difference, in my mind, has far greater potential than sameness. Think how boring it would be to live in a world where all flowers were yellow, where all animals were beige, where all cars were green.

It is our individual and collective differences that make this company what it is—a viable, successful force in our field. Our strength comes from our diversity.

MEMO WRITER TIPS

1. Develop a common definition to begin or continue your diversity efforts.
2. Include information from your organization's policies in your definition memo.
3. Discuss your definition with others in your workplace.

DIVERSITY: CELEBRATION OF VERSUS TOLERANCE FOR

To:
From:
Date:
Subject: My View of Celebrating, Not Tolerating, Diversity

Thanks for your support, as we continue to cultivate our diverse workforce. As we move closer to our goal, I'd like to tell you what I mean by valuing/celebrating diversity, rather than simply tolerating it.

We *tolerate* interruptions when we're in our closed-door offices, trying to think and get our work done. We also tolerate bosses we don't like, weak coffee from the vending machines, and (infrequent) irate calls from disgruntled customers.

We *celebrate* promotions, associate achievements, company holidays, performance bonuses, and year-end profits.

Our goal is to value and embrace the differences that make our company productive. Personally, I can't stand weak coffee.

MEMO WRITER TIPS

1. There is a major difference between valuing and tolerating diversity. If these issues have come up in your company, use this memo or one like it to help you clarify the difference. Talk to employees face-to-face, if possible.

2. To celebrate diversity effectively, members of your organization will need to pay close attention to their language: phrases like "tolerance for diversity," "managing diversity" (how does one "manage" the attributes of another that are not subject to change?), "affirmative action," "token," and talking about diversity only in terms of people of color may have potentially negative connotations to some and may, unintentionally, thwart your diversity efforts.

OUTLINING DIVERSITY GOALS AND RATIONALE

To:
From:
Date:
Subject: Diversity—Goals and Rationale

Rationale

By the end of this decade, more than 40 percent of our current staff members will have retired. Since we work in a cutting-edge industry, we will not survive unless we can find qualified replacements. If we are to ensure a smooth transition that preserves our market niche and solid financial base, we must now begin to find, train, retain, and promote the members of tomorrow's workforce. In order to do this successfully, we will need to hire and retain the most qualified candidates in the field.

Goals and Objectives

Specific goals and objectives will help us find these qualified candidates:

1. Publicize position vacancies in newspapers and magazines with diverse readerships.
2. Recruit potential candidates at college fairs at historically black, Native American, Latino/Latina, female, and other schools.
3. Make every effort to fill vacant positions with a qualified candidate—female; white; Latino/Latina; disabled (man or woman of any ethnicity, and

so on); Asian; African-American; or young. Personnel statistics at the end of the year should reflect at least a 10 percent increase in the number of diverse staff in the company overall and at least a 10 percent increase in diverse management hires and/or promotions, as well as the retention and promotion of 10 percent of all white, male new hires.

4. More than 75 percent of all staff should participate in diversity training and on-the-job implementation.

5. Performance appraisals will include a review of diversity efforts. Next year, managers and supervisors will codevelop (with their managers) specific diversity objectives for their sections. Subsequently, promotions, bonuses, and pay increases will be linked to their achievement of diversity objectives.

6. Fully 70 percent of our new hires should be retained the next and succeeding years.

7. Employee satisfaction surveys should indicate at least a 5 percent improvement in responses to questions related to an organizational climate supportive of diverse persons.

8. The number of discrimination complaints will be reduced by at least 10 percent.

We have our work cut out for us, but I'm confident, if we all work together, we can achieve these goals.

MEMO WRITER TIPS

1. Write goals and objectives in specific, measurable terms.
2. Encourage workers to support diversity efforts.
3. Write about the rationale for diversity efforts as sound fiscally, as well as correct morally or politically.

INITIATING DIVERSITY EFFORTS

To:
From:
Date:
Subject: Diversity Goals

Creating a more diverse workplace is a major goal of this year's annual plan. As we've discussed, diversity means hiring, retaining, and promoting people from different backgrounds. Diversity also means fair hiring and treatment practices with respect to male and female employees, as well as to associates of varying ages, religions, disabilities, sexual orientations, and beliefs.

Our major objective is to hire the most qualified and talented people in the cable industry. If we do not, we will not be able to keep pace with technological and other changes in this ever-changing environment.

To find and keep the most talented people, we will need to make our company more welcoming and inclusive. In order to accomplish this, I am announcing the initiation of a major diversity effort. This effort will include the following:

- The formulation of a comprehensive diversity plan. A cross-functional/departmental work team will be formed to develop this plan and obtain input on it from all staff.
- Organization development work to assess our current climate and design interventions to improve its potential for inclusivity.
- The integration of diversity objectives into our performance appraisal system.
- Diversity hiring goals and objectives.
- A mentoring program to help new workers acclimate to our environment.
- Comprehensive diversity training, including projects designed to apply the skills learned.
- Pilot projects designed to help us achieve our diversity goals.
- Ongoing monitoring and evaluation of diversity efforts.
- Expansion of our current selection sites and methods.
- Regular forums to discuss diversity issues.

I know each of us is committed to enhancing our current practices in this way. I look forward to working with you to achieve our diversity goals.

MEMO WRITER TIPS

1. Serious diversity undertakings will require careful, long-term planning, implementation, and evaluation; employee buy-in; specific incentives; and in-depth training, if it is to be successful.

2. Initiate diversity efforts by soliciting participation from current staff and involving them in the design and implementation of diversity programs.

3. Use a positive, supportive tone in your memo and either precede the memo or follow it up with face-to-face communication.

MOTIVATING EMPLOYEES TO SUPPORT DIVERSITY INITIATIVES

To:

From:

Date:

Subject: Your Support for Diversity Efforts Is Needed

Our diversity initiative is well underway. I appreciate the exemplary work of the Diversity Task Force and the support of staff who have helped to make our efforts successful thus far.

This will not be an easy undertaking, nor will it happen overnight. It will take consistent attention, and we will need to allow sufficient time for our work to pay off. Our efforts will enable us to remain fiscally sound and prepared to meet the challenges ahead.

I encourage each of you to give this your best. If we do, we will uncover previously untapped potential.

MEMO WRITER TIPS

1. Use an upbeat tone in your memo.

2. Lay out your expectations for staff members and enlist their support.

3. Remember, however, that a memo, while it can put your commitment to the effort on record, can only go so far in motivating others.

PHRASING ALTERNATIVES

Paragraph 1

I am writing this memorandum to enlist the support of all staff for our ongoing commitment to diversity. Only by making the best use of the great talent in our organization and actively seeking to find more of that talent can we hope to remain competitive.

While we have taken the first steps to operationalize our diversity plan, its success will depend on consistent effort on each of our parts. Therefore, I want each of us to give the project the time and attention it will certainly require and to put forth maximum effort to make it a success.

Paragraph 2

Show your support for this initiative by participating in training sessions, coaching colleagues, and discussing these issues openly and honestly.

If we fail, it is only we and our organization that will suffer. If we succeed, we will doubtless reap untold benefits. The ultimate outcome depends on the commitment of each one of us.

Paragraph 3

I am counting on each one of us to make this work. I know you won't let me down.

I will show my commitment in ways that count. I hope you will, too.

ANNOUNCING DIVERSITY TRAINING

To:
From:
Date:
Subject: Prejudice Awareness Training—February 4

The upcoming prejudice awareness training has been scheduled for Monday, February 4, 9:00 a.m. to 5:00 p.m. in Conference Room A.

We are pleased to have Dr. Jacob Firestone, noted prejudice-reduction expert, as our facilitator. Dr. Firestone has planned engaging activities, as well as "homework" that will help us apply what we learn back on the job.

I hope to see you there. Please call Mel Larkin, ext. 403, to register. The registration deadline is Wednesday, February 27.

MEMO WRITER TIPS

1. Describe the diversity training and introduce the facilitator.
2. Include details about day, date, time, and place.
3. Encourage attendance.
4. Give a point of contact.

PHRASING ALTERNATIVES

Paragraph 1

Noted human rights advocate, Dr. Lois Bateman, will be on campus Thursday, April 20, 19/20____ , 12:00 noon–1:30 p.m., in Lecture Hall C. Dr. Bateman will be giving a lecture titled "Diversity: Rhetoric or Reality."

A Diversity Workshop has been scheduled for all department managers. If we are to remain competitive in our industry, we must learn to find, hire, and retain the top talent in our field.

Paragraph 2

Department chairs, division directors, deans, and vice-presidents: please plan to join me for what appears to be an excellent opportunity to examine issues critical to our continued success. Call Pat, ext. 404, for registration details.

Contact Jan or Steve in Training and Development for additional details and to register for the session. I look forward to seeing you there.

DIVERSE CELEBRATIONS

To:
From:
Date:
Subject: Diversity Celebrations

This year, your Diversity Promotion Team is considering a number of exciting activities:

- Martin-Luther-King, Jr. Reflection March
- African-American-History-Month Readathon (parents and their children)
- Presidents' Day Lecture
- Trip to the Chinese New Year Parade
- Women's-History-Month Fair
- Holocaust-Awareness-Month panel discussion
- Cinco-de-Mayo Bazaar
- Fourth-of-July Fireworks and Picnic
- Labor-Day Telecommute
- Veterans'-Day Recognition Ceremony
- Presentation by co-workers who belong to Parents of Gays and Lesbians
- "Who Discovered America?" Forum
- Indian Perspective on Thanksgiving Forum
- Pilgrim's Progress Update
- Religions-Around-the-World Quilt (to be sewn together by employees)
- Company Celebration Benefit (to raise scholarship money for associates' children)
- "Politically Incorrect" Dress-Down Day

Please let us know which of these activities you would be interested in attending. If you or your team would like to sponsor an activity, call Ito Nakimura, Diversity Promotion Team Leader, at ext. 999.

GENDER DIVERSITY ISSUES

To:
From:
Date:
Subject: Gender Discrimination

Our agency promotes respect for all its associates, regardless of gender or sexual orientation. This means that every person will be valued and respected for his or her contributions to our organization.

Thanks for your continuing support of this and other gender-related issues.

MEMO WRITER TIPS

1. As more and more women move into management ranks, you will need to continue to resolve gender-related conflicts. Handle these face-to-face, when possible.

2. Point out what the issue is and how you'd like to see it resolved. Maintain a positive tone.

DETAILS ABOUT THE AMERICANS WITH DISABILITIES ACT

To:
From:
Date:
Subject: The Americans with Disabilities Act: Some Details

ADA Titles

The Americans with Disabilities Act (ADA) has four Titles:

1. *Title I* prohibits *employment discrimination* against individuals with disabilities. *Private employers with 15 or more employees must comply.*

2. *Title II* prohibits any *state or local government or their agencies* (police and fire departments and government agencies) from discriminating on the basis of disability.
3. *Title III* guarantees persons with disabilities *access* to private entities that make goods and services available to the public (restaurants, theaters, amusement parks, and health clubs).
4. *Title IV* mandates that *telecommunications relay services* must be provided for individuals who have hearing or speech impairments.

ADA Requirements for Employers

With respect to employment, the ADA requires the following:

- Questions such as health history or direct questions about a disability cannot be asked on the employment application.
- Questions related to workers' compensation history or questions related to how the person's condition would affect job functioning are tantamount to asking for disclosure of a disability.
- An employer may ask if a person has a need for an accommodation.
- During the interview process, interviewers are prohibited from asking questions about a disability.
- Questions about how an individual would perform job-related functions can be asked.
- A person with a disability can also be asked questions about how he or she would perform essential and nonessential job functions.
- If an applicant chooses to disclose that he or she has a disability, the interviewer can ask only questions related to how the individual became disabled or about the prognosis for the disability.
- Questions about needing time off or the need for treatment or other disability-related matters are prohibited.
- Medical examinations can be required only if a conditional offer of employment has been made and only if all employees in the same work categories are required to have the same medical examination.
- All information obtained from preemployment testing is confidential and can be disclosed only to staff who need this information to provide accommodations directly related to job functions or employment testing.
- Drug testing is not considered medical testing or examination under the provisions of ADA.
- Employers cannot release information that reveals a medical condition or disability as the result of drug testing.

- A positive drug test should always be confirmed by a second, independent test to verify illegal drugs, since many prescription drugs can cause false-positive results.

- An individual may wish to disclose prescription drugs to avoid a false-positive result.

- Employers may not refuse to hire applicants because of projected or actual increases in insurance costs.

- An employer does not have to provide insurance, but if the employer provides insurance for all other employees, a person with a disability is entitled to the same amount of coverage provided to all other employees.

- The ADA does not eliminate preexisting condition clauses included in insurance policies, but the existence of preexisting conditions cannot be used to evade the purposes of the Act.

ADA Discrimination Charges

To bring discrimination charges under the ADA, an individual must prove (1) that he or she has a disability covered by the Act; (2) that the employer in question is an entity required to comply with the ADA; (3) that the employee is qualified to do the essential functions of the job; (4) that the employer violated one or more prohibitions of ADA. In cases where discrimination is charged, the employer has the burden of proof.

Prospective/Employer Defenses Against ADA Claims

Generally, employers have three defenses to an ADA claim:

1. **Direct Threat Provision**
   This defense requires that the employer prove that employment of a disabled individual poses a direct threat to his or her safety or to the safety of others; a threat that cannot be eliminated by reasonable accommodation.

2. **Undue Hardship**
   This defense limits an employer's obligation to provide a reasonable accommodation to an applicant or employee with a disability, and stipulates that such employment would impose an undue hardship on the business, company, or organization.

3. **Disparate Impact Defense**
   This defense stipulates that an employer's uniformly applied criteria have an adverse effect on an individual with a disability or a disproportionately negative impact on a class of individuals with a disability.

> **MEMO WRITER TIPS**
>
> 1. For specific information about ADA, refer to The Americans with Disabilities Act (Public Law 101-336) or consult an attorney.
>
> 2. These are intended as general guidelines and should not be used as the basis for making decisions regarding prospective or other employees who have disabilities.

REQUESTING ADAPTATIONS FOR DISABLED EMPLOYEES

To:
From:
Date:
Subject: Request for Screen Magnifier

One of the applicants for the Administrative Data Entry Clerk III position has disclosed he has a vision problem. In order for him to take the examination, I will need a screen magnifier for the computer he will be using. The exam will be administered on August 14.

If you cannot locate one in time through normal purchasing channels, let me know at ext. 707. Thanks for your help.

> **MEMO WRITER TIPS**
>
> 1. Be specific about the accommodation you need.
>
> 2. Write your memo in enough time to make sure the accommodation will arrive by the desired date.
>
> 3. If you have any questions about ADA or the law regarding reasonable accommodation, contact your attorney or legal department.

PHRASING ALTERNATIVES

Paragraph 1

One of your employees is a self-disclosed epileptic. This employee's medication makes her tire easily. Please see that she is allowed to take more frequent breaks during the day. This will help prevent seizures and ensure continued productivity.

Since several of our associates are deaf, please hire a certified interpreter for next month's general meeting. The meeting is scheduled for Monday, June 20, 9:00 p.m., in Room C203. The meeting will last approximately two hours. Please pay for the interpreter services out of the 113-0446 cost center.

Paragraph 2

This is a reasonable accommodation, as outlined by the Americans with Disabilities Act. Let me know whether more frequent breaks help.

We provide reasonable accommodations, as necessary. Owen in Personnel has a list of certified interpreters. Thanks for your help on this.

ADDRESSING DIVERSITY-RELATED CONFLICT

To:

From:

Date:

Subject: Managerial Responsibility for Promoting Teamwork and Respect for the Individual

Some of the new hires in your section have apparently had difficulty getting along with our more experienced technicians.

As you know, our corporation values teamwork and respect for all individuals. Your section is comprised of qualified technicians, some of whom have been here for many years and others who have just started with us. As their manager, I encourage you to model and foster corporate commitment to respect individual expertise and experience.

I know I can count on you.

MEMO WRITER TIPS

1. Conflict resulting from diversity-related issues should usually be discussed face-to-face, rather than addressed in a memo.

2. If you write a memo to managers and/or supervisors about diversity-related conflict, coach them on how to diffuse it and handle it positively.

3. Maintain a positive tone, keeping in mind that conflict around diversity issues, while similar to other workplace conflicts, is often charged with additional issues (of which managers are sometimes unaware themselves). For this reason, diversity conflict may be potentially more volatile and more difficult to identify and correct.

4. Affirm your commitment to the resolution of the conflict and to the reinforcement of corporate values and policies.

PHRASING ALTERNATIVES

Paragraph 1

Since Ms. Cho started work as our new operations manager, she has done an exceptional job. Please pass along my praise to Ms. Cho, and tell her how happy I am to have her on our team.

Once again, I must reiterate our company's commitment to diversity and respect for the individual, regardless of creed, national origin, race, sex, religion, or sexual orientation.

Paragraph 2

As you know, our company has a strong commitment to hiring the most qualified managers we can find.

Our new facilities manager has done an exemplary job in his tenure with us. He was hired to do a job, and he is performing well above my expectations.

Paragraph 3

I know you will continue to give Ms. Cho your full support.

I know I can count on you to model and promote your team's commitment to team success and respect for all individuals on that team. Thanks.

REPORTING ON PROGRESS TOWARD DIVERSITY GOALS

To:
From:
Date:
Subject: Diversity Progress

I am pleased to announce that this year's diversity efforts have been successful. We have been able to increase managerial hirings by 12 percent, technical hirings by 15 percent, and support-staff hirings by 8 percent. Of the employees hired last year, 89 percent continue to work with us.

These results reflect your continuing support of the project. Thanks for a job well done. We expect even greater results in the coming year.

MEMO WRITER TIPS

1. Report progress in measurable terms, if possible.
2. Congratulate workers on their efforts.
3. Enlist their continued support.

PHRASING ALTERNATIVES

Paragraph 1

Our efforts to create a diverse workforce are beginning to show results. Of the 14 employees hired last year, two are women, six are people of color, one has a disability, and two are white males. This group of new hires helped us achieve a 34 percent increase in sales last year. Several of them personally generated more than $500,000 in sales and have been inducted into the Half-Century Club.

I am sorry to report that we fell short of our diversity-related objectives for the year. We were not able to attract qualified applicants at the planned rate and, sadly, 60 percent of the people we did hire are no longer with us. Discrimination complaints increased by 25 percent, and we spent considerable sums to settle several substantiated claims.

Paragraph 2

I told you our efforts would pay off, and they have—in a big way. This could not have happened, however, without your ongoing support and participation. I congratulate you on such fine work. Let's keep it up.

I am not pleased with our results thus far. We will continue to work on these issues, as they are, obviously, ones we need to address. I am asking once again for your support of our diversity initiative. I will be meeting with department heads and senior management staff to discuss ways we can improve.

11

Model Memos for Policies and Procedures

Policies and procedures standardize operations in your company. If you compare what happens in your organization on a daily basis to a game, policies and procedures provide the rules and guidelines needed to play the "game" successfully. Even skilled players need information about how a "game" gets played.

Policies and procedures spell out work processes, outline communication channels, establish organizational structure, and present lines of authority.

Having too many policies and procedures can constrict workers and stifle creativity. But in any organization, certain boundaries must be set, and these boundaries must be communicated effectively throughout the organization.

The model memoranda in Chapter 11 deal with a host of policies and procedures, ranging from price increases to signature authority, from changes in work hours, to what happens when the rules of the "game" are violated.

Of course, rules of the game change as the organization changes. So a number of the models in this chapter deal with the issue of change: how to communicate changes in policy, how to help employees deal with frequent changes, how to elicit employee buy-in before changes are made.

Models for writing a policy and procedure have been included, as have memos about routine procedural matters like coffee breaks, lunch hours, and smoking areas. Memos about appeal and grievance procedures have also been provided.

Add specific details about your company's policies and procedures to the model memo of your choice. The rules for writing policy and procedure memos outlined in this chapter may help you play the game more effectively.

ANNOUNCING A PRICE INCREASE

To:
From:
Date:
Subject: Price Increase

Effective Monday, July 3, 19____, prices on the following items will be increased:

STOCK #	DESCRIPTION	NEW PRICE	CURRENT PRICE
D-18945	Athletic Shoe, Men's	$65.98	$54.29
D-38426	Sweatshirt, Men's	$21.95	$18.99
D-48361	Sweatshirt, Ladies'	$20.99	$17.95
D-38122	Jogging Suit, Men's	$48.99	$44.95

See to it that all price tags are changed accordingly. Familiarize yourselves with these new prices.

MEMO WRITER TIPS

1. Put the effective date of change at the beginning of the memo.

2. Include a brief description of the item, the new price, and the current price.

3. If the prices for several items are being changed, listing them will make the changes easier to read.

4. Be sure to tell employees what action, if any, they must take to initiate this change.

PHRASING ALTERNATIVES

Paragraph 1

The price of our Deluxe Stranborg 2 Mini-Computer will be raised from $2895.00 to $3199.00, beginning Monday, August 4.

Note the following price increases, which will take effect January 2, 19____.

Beginning Monday, June 1, 19____, clients will be billed $125.00 per hour for Associate Partners' legal services. This represents a $25.00 per hour increase over our present rates.

Paragraph 2

Be sure you quote these new prices to customers when they call, beginning January 2.

Modify the computer program to reflect these price increases.

Add this list of price changes to your price list.

DEALING WITH FREQUENT CHANGES IN POLICY

To:
From:
Date:
Subject: Policy Changes

Changes, changes, and more changes! The cash receipt policy has once again been changed. The latest—and, hopefully, final—change in policy directs the following:

1. Count all cash.
2. Put the counted cash in a receipt envelope and seal the envelope.
3. Write the total amount enclosed on both the back and front of the envelope.
4. Date-stamp the envelope.
5. Rubber band cash-receipt envelopes into groups of 10.
6. Deposit each group of 10 in the accounting vault.

I appreciate your patience through this series of changes. Eventually, I'm sure we'll get a procedure that works. Thanks for your cooperation.

MEMO WRITER TIPS

1. Giving this memorandum a humorous tone may take some of the edge off, since people are apt to be disgruntled about frequent changes.

2. Spell out—step by step—what the new procedure calls for.

3. Acknowledge the fact that patience is required in implementing these changes, and thank workers for their compliance with the new policy or procedure.

PHRASING ALTERNATIVES

Paragraph 1

Your cooperation is required if we are to implement the latest change to Policy #741.

Guess what? The procedure for billing clients has been changed—again.

The microfiche processing procedure has been changed as follows:

Paragraph 2

Thank you for your cooperation in this matter.

I realize a number of you are becoming frustrated with the frequency of changes to this procedure, but be assured we will have a procedure in place soon.

Thanks for working efficiently while we iron out the bugs in this latest policy change.

DISCUSSING PROPER OFFICE ATTIRE

To:
From:
Date:
Subject: Office Dress Code

Several employees have adopted a dress style more casual than is appropriate for our office environment. Proper office attire includes the following:

WOMEN

1. Dresses, suits, skirts/blouses, preferably in solid colors or stripes, but no bold designs.
2. Hosiery is to be worn even in warm weather.
3. Heels, pumps, or flat shoes—no sandals.
4. No flashy or gaudy jewelry—hoops, dangling bracelets, large earrings, etc.

MEN

1. Suit, sportcoat and shirt. Ties are to be worn at all times.
2. White shirts or solid pastels.
3. Dark shoes.
4. Haircuts no longer than the tip of the ear lobe.

Adhering to this dress code ensures that our company will project the professional image we want to convey to our clients.

If you have questions about the dress code, refer to Page 25 in your Employee Handbook.

Thank you for helping us "dress for success."

MEMO WRITER TIPS

1. State that inappropriate dress has been noticed but avoid phrases like, "It has come to my attention . . ."

2. Focus more on what proper attire is, rather than on what the dress code violations have been. If necessary, list in the memo what constitutes proper office attire, in as much detail as is practicable.

3. Close by assuring employees that you recognize they will adhere to these dress standards.

PHRASING ALTERNATIVES

Paragraph 1

The onset of warm weather causes me to once again stress how important it is for you to dress appropriately.

Proper office attire is a necessary cost of doing business, so I must reiterate our dress code.

A few problems with office dress have prompted me to spell out what proper office attire is.

Paragraph 2

I'm certain each of you wants to project a professional image, and adhering to these policies will ensure that this happens.

If violations persist, individuals will be asked to go home and change clothes. Annual leave time will be deducted accordingly.

Your assistance in creating a professional-looking work environment is greatly appreciated.

DRAFTING A POLICY

To:
From:
Date:
Subject: Gasoline Purchase Policy

Some employees have been buying gasoline at full-service pumps, rather than purchasing gasoline at self-service pumps, which offer lower prices. This practice is contrary to a basic directive of this administration. We should deliver high quality, responsive service at the lowest possible cost. Therefore, cost savings should be achieved whenever possible.

Therefore, I am directing each of you to take immediate steps and require the following of all employees who use vehicles to conduct official business:

1. Purchase gasoline at the lowest possible price, and always use the lower-priced, self-service pumps.
2. Gasoline purchases made at full-service pumps are prohibited unless self-service pumps are not available.

Please bring this memorandum and its directive to the attention of all personnel in your departments who use vehicles (either company-owned or employee-owned) for official business.

MEMO WRITER TIPS

1. Explain what practices have motivated the development of the policy. This will give employees a better understanding of why the policy is needed.

2. List, if possible, the major points of the policy.

3. Cite any applicable rules or regulations in manuals, handbooks, etc.

4. Close by specifying which employees should see this policy and what action they should take.

PHRASING ALTERNATIVES

Paragraph 1

The following policy/procedure is to be implemented immediately.

Please make all employees aware of the following procedure and see that it is implemented on Monday, July 5, 19_____ .

Problems with purchase orders have yielded the following procedure, which is to be implemented on Friday, October 10, 19_____ .

Paragraph 2

Make sure that all employees affected by this procedure follow its guidelines.

Inform your subordinates of this policy directive and follow up to ensure its successful implementation.

Distribute a copy of this policy to all the employees in your section and stress the importance of complying with it.

DRAFTING A PROCEDURE*

To:
From:
Date:
Subject: New Warrant Procedure

Jennifer Slaughter has developed a new warrant procedure, which should save you time and work. Effective today, warrants will be processed according to the following procedure:

1. Entries in the Warrant Ledger will include:
    a. Warrant Control Number
    b. Suspect Name
    c. Date of Birth
    d. Charge
    e. Bond
    f. Crime Report Number (entered at time of arrest)
    g. Disposition (entered at time of arrest)
2. You will not fill out a Warrant Information/Check-Out Form for each warrant.
3. The Warrant Control Number will be written in the upper right hand corner of the warrant after it has been logged.
4. The Felony/Misdemeanor Warrant Card will be filled out as before and entered on the computer.
5. The warrant, with summons copy attached, will be filed (without cover sheet).

---

*A court clerk wrote this procedure.

6. The new Warrant Information Sheet (SEE SAMPLE) will be filled out only when it is to be used as an offense report in the file (when party bonds at another agency).
7. Summons copy will be filed with Custody Report or Warrant Information Sheet when used as an offense report.

If you have any questions about this new procedure, call me at ext. 104.

MEMO WRITER TIPS

1. Give a brief rationale for the new procedure.

2. List the steps involved in the procedure, in the same order in which they are to be performed; i.e., the first step should be first on the list, etc.

3. Any new procedure, unless it is fairly simple, should be discussed orally with those who are to implement it.

4. If the new procedure involves filling out forms or other paperwork, attach a sample of how the completed form should look.

5. Make sure all employees have received a copy of the procedure and understand how it is to operate.

PHRASING ALTERNATIVES

Paragraph 1

Because of the large volume of decals we now have to process, the following procedure should save time in processing these decals:

The number of clients checking into the hospital in recent months has increased dramatically; therefore, the following procedure is to be implemented immediately. This will save time in processing new clients.

As a cost-saving measure, the following procedure is to be adopted on Monday, August 5, 19____ :

Paragraph 2

We will meet on Wednesday, March 3 to discuss this new procedure.

Direct any questions you have about this procedure to Mary Morgan in the Billing Department.

John Avery will be happy to answer any questions you may have about this new procedure.

ENFORCING SIGNATURE AUTHORITY

To:
From:
Date:
Subject: Signature Authority

The Vice President of Operations is the only individual authorized to sign travel vouchers. In her absence, her assistant has signature authority. No travel vouchers will be processed without one of these signatures.

MEMO WRITER TIPS

1. Name the individual(s) who has signature authority and name the document or forms over which this person has signature authority.

2. Include information about who can sign in this person's absence.

3. Explain that paperwork cannot be processed without this signature.

PHRASING ALTERNATIVES

Paragraph 1

Don Abbot, Department Manager, has signature authority for petty cash reimbursement checks.

Purchase orders can be approved only if they are signed by Bill Whitaker, Purchasing Manager, or Jane Akron, Assistant Purchasing Manager.

Checks in amounts over $10,000 must have two (2) signatures: the director of field services and the financial vice-president.

Paragraph 2

Purchase requisitions that lack this signature will be returned to the requester, unprocessed.

Obtaining the approved signatures will avoid delays in processing payroll checks.

If you want petty cash vouchers to be processed promptly, make sure they have the proper signature on them.

GIVING SUBORDINATES GUIDELINES FOR WORKING AT HOME

To:
From:
Date:
Subject: Work-at-Home Guidelines

Since you will be completing most of your work at home for the next two months, follow these guidelines:

1. Check your message board daily and respond promptly to those who are trying to contact you.
2. Call the office at least twice per week to pick up any telephone messages, and return these calls promptly.
3. Transmit any work you do on the computer to Terry Trump in Computer Services. She will disseminate the work you produce.
4. Provide me with monthly reports on your progress.

I know this will be a satisfactory working assignment. Following these basic guidelines should help you accomplish your work and provide the office adequate contact with you.

MEMO WRITER TIPS

1. More and more employees will begin doing work at home, as new technology makes this more feasible.

2. Specific guidelines should be given to these employees, including any special requirements you have about contacting the office, picking up messages, or transmitting information via computer.

PHRASING ALTERNATIVES

Paragraph 1

I've listed a few guidelines I'd like you to follow as you complete this project at home.

Though you'll be doing much of your work at home, following these guidelines will make that a more profitable experience for us both.

Adhering to these instructions will ensure that you accomplish the work you're doing at home while allowing us contact with you.

HANDLING CONFIDENTIAL CORRESPONDENCE*

To:
From:
Date:
Subject: Confidentiality of Employee Information

I have been contacted recently by two employees who expressed concerns that their supervisors had shown a lack of discretion in sharing confidential information. In both cases, the employees shared information of a very personal nature with their supervisors. The employees did this because they felt personal problems were having an impact on their job performance. In each case, the employee found out later that this information had been shared with others, persons who had no need to know.

I request that you emphasize to your staff that divulging such confidential information can have a negative impact on the supervisor-employee relationship, as well as on peer relationships within the work group. While there may be a temptation to share personal concerns of others, this is rarely necessary or appropriate.

Thank you for your assistance in emphasizing the importance of preserving confidentiality.

MEMO WRITER TIPS

1. Describe briefly the breach in confidentiality and how it has occurred.

2. Let employees know that this is not appropriate and tell them what action you expect them to take.

PHRASING ALTERNATIVES

Paragraph 1

Several breaches in confidentiality have occurred in recent months.

Confidentiality of information is an important part of doing business successfully with clients and co-workers.

A trust once violated is difficult, if not impossible, to repair. Consider this when you next think about violating someone's confidence.

---

*This memorandum was written by the Director of Administration of a metropolitan transit district.

Paragraph 2

I expect no further breaches of this kind to occur.

Let's offer subordinates the same respect we demand for ourselves. Keep confidential information private.

I direct you to see that such infractions do not occur again.

HANDLING RUSH ORDERS*

To:
From:
Date:
Subject: Rush Supply Orders

WE CAN NO LONGER PROCESS RUSH SUPPLY ORDERS! Beginning today, we can only order supplies from state-approved vendors. These vendors generally deliver merchandise to our office in one to three weeks.

If you have special orders, please notify us at least two weeks in advance. With proper lead time, we can continue to fill your supply needs.

Thank you.

MEMO WRITER TIPS

1. Explain what the policy is regarding rush orders, and whether these can or cannot be processed.

2. Let readers know what action they need to take in order to get the items they need as expeditiously as possible.

PHRASING ALTERNATIVES

Paragraph 1

All rush orders must be processed according to the following guidelines.

If rush orders are not stamped "RUSH," they are likely to be overlooked.

We'd like to process rush orders as quickly as possible, but cannot guarantee speedy delivery on these items unless they are ordered at least seven working days prior to the time you need them.

---

*This memorandum was written by a supply clerk for a governmental agency.

Paragraph 2

Please make sure all rush orders are hand-carried to this office at least 48 hours before you need rush items.

Be sure to stamp all special orders with the "RUSH" stamp. Our office will need three working days to process special orders.

As long as we receive rush orders five working days in advance, we will be able to process these orders and deliver your items promptly.

HELPING SUBORDINATES FOLLOW AN UNPOPULAR POLICY

To:
From:
Date:
Subject: Hiring Freeze

I realize the new policy on hiring freezes is not likely to win great support. However, I'd like to explain that this policy is absolutely necessary if we are to remain fiscally sound this year and fill the positions we desperately need for next year.

Your cooperation in implementing this unpopular policy will make long-term goals possible, even though things may be slightly more difficult right now. Thanks for your cooperation.

MEMO WRITER TIPS

1. Acknowledge that the policy is unpopular, but explain why it must be done anyway.

2. Enlist your subordinates' support in carrying it out, explaining to them what the benefits of doing so will be.

PHRASING ALTERNATIVES

Paragraph 1

The new smoking policy has doubtless ruffled a few feathers.

This may not be the most popular policy in the world, but it is a necessary one.

Your failure to follow this policy, no matter how unpopular it may be, will only delay our getting past this issue.

Paragraph 2

Though this policy may cause short-term difficulty, long-term benefits will be derived from enacting it right now.

Adhering to this policy will allow us to save considerable money now, money we can use to make capital expenditures next fiscal year.

These temporary belt-tightening measures will allow us to continue to operate, saving both jobs and money.

INFORMING SUBORDINATES ABOUT A POLICY CHANGE

To:
From:
Date:
Subject: Purchasing Policy Change

In the past, individual account reps could purchase supplies from whatever vendor they deemed most appropriate. However, in order to receive the lowest prices and highest quality for goods, this policy will be changed, effective Monday, February 5, 19____ .

The new policy directs that all purchases be made by the Purchasing Department. Employees in this department are tasked with finding the most competitive vendor and ensuring the fastest delivery time.

Beginning February 5, send all purchase requisitions to the Purchasing Department. They will order your supplies and make sure they are delivered to your office.

Thank you for complying with this cost-saving measure.

MEMO WRITER TIPS

1. State what the current policy is.

2. Explain why the policy has been changed and what benefits the change is likely to produce.

3. Spell out the new policy, including the effective date for implementation.

4. Clarify what action readers must take in order to comply with the new policy.

PHRASING ALTERNATIVES

Paragraph 1

Policy #245-B in your procedural manual has been changed as follows:

This change is effective today.

Please note the following change in policy:

Your cooperation as we implement the following policy change is greatly appreciated.

Paragraph 2

I'm certain you will make every effort to implement this policy as soon as possible.

Thanks for your cooperation in making this new policy work.

I really appreciate your efforts to make this new policy save us both money and time.

HANDLING A POLICY VIOLATION

To:
From:
Date:
Subject: Policy Violation—Gasoline Purchases

The use of full-service gasoline pumps and related costs represents an inefficient expenditure of state resources and will be stopped immediately. We are managing state government in a time of scarce resources, restricted reserves, and uncertain revenues. Every dollar available to us must be used in the most cost-effective manner possible.

With the level of gasoline services available in today's market, there is no reason for using full-service pumps and paying the premium price related to that service. I am directing all managers and boards to instruct their employees to CEASE ALL USE OF FULL-SERVICE GASOLINE STATIONS IMMEDIATELY. We must curtail this financial abuse. Further, use of state-operated fueling pumps whenever possible should be encouraged for additional savings.

Our efforts to provide prudent, cost-effective management of state government have been and will continue to be successful. The Motor Vehicle Advisory Council will be responsible for following up on this directive and other cost-saving measures.

MEMO WRITER TIPS

1. Explain which policy has been violated and state clearly that such violations will not be tolerated.

2. Explain why it is so important to follow the established procedure.

3. Give the reader information about how you expect to follow up to ensure the policy has been followed.

4. Give the consequences for any further violations, if applicable.

PHRASING ALTERNATIVES

Paragraph 1

In direct violation of policy, some field representatives have been using their company credit card for personal expenses. This practice cannot be tolerated.

Certain expendable supplies have been ordered from other than approved vendors, a violation of company policy. Such violations of policy must be discontinued immediately.

Exempt employees have been asked to work mandatory overtime; this violates personnel regulations. This infraction must be brought in line with existing policy right away.

Paragraph 2

These measures were taken to ensure efficient operation.

Significant time and money savings are realized through following existing policy.

Continuing this practice may result in increased grievances and problems within your work area.

Paragraph 3

I will monitor this situation for the next 30 days, to ensure that no further infractions occur.

A task force has been formed to study this matter, and they will report to me on their findings.

Each department manager is directed to follow up on this matter and make sure no additional violations of policy occur.

Paragraph 4

If this practice continues, section chiefs will be held accountable.

Continued violations may result in adverse publicity for the company, a problem we all want to avoid.

We can all live without the additional grievances sure to be filed if these practices continue.

MAKING AN EXCEPTION TO POLICY

To:
From:
Date:
Subject: Exception to Policy

An exception to policy is being made to allow shop employees to drive their company-owned vehicles from their last appointments to their places of residence. This measure should reduce fuel costs, as well as the amount of mileage currently being used to drive vehicles back to the company after the last appointment.

This practice will begin on Monday, August 8, 19____, and continue until further notice. I will review how this procedure is working after 30 days and reevaluate its effectiveness at that time.

MEMO WRITER TIPS

1. Say what kind of exception to policy is being made, and briefly explain why the exception is being granted.
2. Explain the new procedure or practice, and tell how long the practice should be followed.
3. Include information about how/when the exception will be checked and followed up on.

PHRASING ALTERNATIVES

Paragraph 1

Your request for an exception to policy in the matter of hiring an employee not on the hiring list has been granted.

I am granting your request for an exception to policy.

A one-time exception to policy will be made concerning the purchase of legal services from a sole-source provider.

Paragraph 2

For the next 60 days, you may advertise the position in local newspapers, interview qualified applicants, and select the new-hire from these candidates.

You may choose a sole-source consultant to provide services on the negotiation of the upcoming labor contract. These services may be contracted for no more than 90 days.

Exempt employees may be granted compensatory overtime—1½ hours compensatory time per one hour worked—until the end of this fiscal year.

Paragraph 3

Review the hiring process carefully and let me know how things go.

I anticipate no further exceptions in this regard, but I will monitor the practice on a case-by-case basis.

Give me a written report on the impact of this exception.

INFORMING SUBORDINATES ABOUT A PROCEDURAL CHANGE*

To:

From:

Date:

Subject: New Format—Arrest Ledgers

Janet Havers has developed a new format for the arrest ledger. Effective January 1, 19____ , entries should be made as follows (see attachment):

Column 1—Date of Arrest

Column 2—Date of Birth

Column 3—Charge

Column 4—Disposition

Column 5—Crime Report Number

Column 6—Arresting Officer's Name

Column 7—Dispatcher's Initials

This new procedure will save time and provide the court clerk with only that information necessary to execute bonds and track court disposition. New, smaller ledgers have been formatted in this new way. If you have questions, let me know.

---

*This memorandum was written by a Communications Supervisor of a police department.

MEMO WRITER TIPS

1. In the first sentence, describe what procedure is being changed. If the change was initiated by someone other than you, give credit to the developer/initiator of the change.

2. Include the date on which the change is to become effective.

3. List the steps involved in the new procedure. If the change involves a form, attach a sample copy of how the form should be filled out, consistent with the new procedure. Flowcharts may also be helpful in diagramming new procedures, particularly if procedures are fairly complex.

4. Give a brief explanation of why this change is being made and how it will help those tasked with implementing it.

5. Follow up to make sure the change is being implemented properly.

PHRASING ALTERNATIVES

Paragraph 1

A new billing procedure will be implemented effective Monday, August 1, 19____ .

The process for securing bids will be changed in three weeks, Monday, January 14, 19____ .

Dan Avalon in the Accounting Department has devised a more efficient way to order supplies from vendors. He will discuss this new procedure with all Supply Clerks in a meeting scheduled for Friday, March 14, 2:00 p.m., Room 704. I anticipate using the new procedure beginning with our new purchasing cycle, July 1, 19____ .

Paragraph 2

Follow these steps to implement this procedure successfully:

The new process is detailed as follows:

All forms will be filled out according to the steps listed below (see attached sample):

Paragraph 3

This change will eliminate the duplication of effort currently taking place.

The new procedure should save you at least five (5) work hours per week.

A smoother paperwork flow will be one result of this new process.

CORRECTING ERRORS RESULTING FROM A PROCEDURAL CHANGE

To:
From:
Date:
Subject: Errors—Change in Hiring Procedure

One major problem has resulted from the change in hiring procedure implemented last month. Each department is placing newspaper advertisements for new-hires when all such requests should be routed through the Personnel Office. ONLY THE PERSONNEL OFFICE IS TO ADVERTISE FOR JOB VACANCIES.

Effective today, (1) write an ad for the position, (2) take the ad to the Personnel office and discuss it with one of the counselors, (3) let personnel place the ad in the newspaper, (4) get applicant folders from the Personnel Office the day following the closing date provided in the ad.

Following these guidelines will save you work and will also allow personnel to process applications more quickly. Thank you for your compliance with this procedure.

MEMO WRITER TIPS

1. In order to refresh readers' memories, mention the change in procedure that has caused the error.

2. Explain what the error is and how it should be corrected.

3. Include the date when this practice is to begin and, if necessary, reiterate how the process works.

4. Include a brief explanation of why the change must be implemented in this way.

PHRASING ALTERNATIVES

Paragraph 1

Instead of delivering hospital equipment to the nurses' stations on each floor, some supply clerks are delivering equipment to patients' rooms. This is not the procedure spelled out in last week's memo.

Tellers should tally each day's receipts before closing out their cash drawers, as outlined in the procedural change given to you several weeks ago.

A minor "glitch" has occurred as a result of the change in procedure made this month. From now on, teachers should give copies of their weekly lesson plans to the Assistant Principal, rather than to their Department Chairperson.

Paragraph 2

Please see to it that this new practice is followed, beginning today.

Follow the steps listed below, effective immediately:

All is working well except for this one error, which should be corrected immediately.

Paragraph 3

Correcting this error will help the system work smoothly.

When this flaw is corrected, the new procedure will allow all requests to be processed within 10 days.

Thanks for your help in managing this change.

INFORMING EMPLOYEES ABOUT A CHANGE IN WORK HOURS*

To:
From:
Date:
Subject: Change in Work Hours

Effective Monday, February 19, 19____ , full-time sales associates will work from 9:00 a.m. until 6:00 p.m. Lunch hours may be taken at 12:30 p.m. or 1:30 p.m.; coordinate this with me.

This change in work hours will allow us to provide better service for our customers.

MEMO WRITER TIPS

1. Tell which employees are being affected by the change, when the change is to begin, and what the new work hours will be.
2. Give a brief explanation of why the work hours are being changed.

PHRASING ALTERNATIVES

Paragraph 1

Beginning Monday, June 1, 19____ , shop employees' work hours will be 7:30 a.m. to 3:30 p.m.

---

*This memorandum was written by the manager of a clothing store.

On Saturday, October 9, 19____, new work hours will be established for stock clerks: 5:00 a.m. to 2:00 p.m.

Work hours for part-time data entry operators will be changed on Monday, March 3. The new hours will be 5:30 to 9:30 p.m.

Paragraph 2

These new hours will provide better office coverage during peak hours.

The results of our customer survey show that these hours are the most convenient for them.

This change in work hours will enable us to have vehicles ready for service when drivers report for duty.

INFORMING SUBORDINATES ABOUT A COMPANY BUY-OUT

To:
From:
Date:
Subject: Company Buy-Out

Negotiations to sell XYZ Enterprises have been going on for the past two months, as most of you know. Well, it's official. Dostrum Industries has purchased our company, and the sale should be finalized within the next 30 days.

Panic is not necessary, as Dostrum has agreed to retain as many of our current employees as possible. A meeting to discuss the buy-out has been scheduled for this Friday, 8:00 a.m., Employee Cafeteria. All employees should plan to attend.

MEMO WRITER TIPS

1. A buy-out makes people nervous at best, so keep this memo short and to the point, but write it in such a way as to allay people's fears.

2. Tell who the company has been purchased by and give an approximate date of final sale.

3. A brief explanation of why the sale is taking place should be included.

4. Include in the memo how employees will get more specific information about how the buy-out will affect them.

PHRASING ALTERNATIVES

Paragraph 1

Acme Enterprises has purchased our company. The anticipated date of sale is August 1.

Our company is being purchased by Randle Foods, effective May 8, 19____ .

Operations in your department are being sold to a sub-contractor, Mercury Management Corporation. Mercury will assume rights on or about July 1, 19____ .

Paragraph 2

As you know, we have been in financial difficulty for the past two years, and this buy-out will once again make us solvent.

The sale of this portion of the company was necessary to save money and as many jobs as possible.

Our operation has grown too large for our current status. This buy-out will allow us to expand into new markets.

Paragraph 3

Details about how this buy-out will affect you will follow shortly. In the interim, know that we are doing everything possible to preserve as many jobs as we can.

You will be given the option of going to work for the new company or remaining with the parent company. ABC Corporation will conduct informational sessions on site next Tuesday, 1:00 p.m.–3:00 p.m., to better help you make your decision.

Each department head will be meeting with his/her employees to discuss the buy-out and how it is likely to affect you.

INFORMING SUBORDINATES ABOUT COMPANY REORGANIZATION

To:
From:
Date:
Subject: Company Reorganization

Effective Monday, January 3, 19____ , the company will be reorganized as outlined on the attached chart. This means you will report to Dot Hanrey in the Technical Services Division. Both Data Entry and Data Verification will be merged into one unit, headed by Bill Donald.

If you have questions about the reorganization, let me know.

MEMO WRITER TIPS

1. Give the effective date of the reorganization and explain how it will affect the reader. Keep in mind that matters of this importance should be discussed face-to-face, so the memorandum should only be used as a follow-up or forerunner to this discussion.

2. In most cases, a chart of the reorganization should be prepared and attached to the memorandum.

PHRASING ALTERNATIVES

Paragraph 1

As we've discussed previously, the reorganization will take place on Monday, August 8. Your department will be relatively unaffected by this change, except that your manager will now report to the Superintendent of Business Services.

The attached chart outlines the proposed reorganization of several units, one of them yours. As you can see, you will now be supervising ten (10), rather than eight (8) employees. Let's sit down and discuss the change next Tuesday at 8:00 a.m., my office.

Since the maintenance and services operations of the company are being sold off to expand production, the new structure will be the one described on the attached chart, beginning Monday, June 1, 19____ . Please contact me if you have questions regarding this plan.

INFORMING SUBORDINATES ABOUT INCLEMENT WEATHER PROCEDURES*

To:
From:
Date:
Subject: Inclement Weather Procedure

In the event of inclement weather serious enough to pose a safety hazard to base personnel, the Base Commander will close the base and notify local radio and television stations to announce the closing.

---

*This memorandum was written by a Public Affairs Officer at a military installation.

On bad weather days, the following radio and television stations will carry the cancellation announcement:

KJOW	KHJR	KOB-TV
KLOB	KWRE	KJR-TV
KMON	KBUI	KLX-TV (Close-captioned)

In the event of base closure, only essential personnel will report for work. All other personnel will report the following day, if weather conditions permit.

Only those closures officially announced will be considered official closings. Employees who do not report for work on other days will be charged eight (8) hours of annual leave.

MEMO WRITER TIPS

1. Spell out briefly what constitutes inclement weather.

2. Explain how employees can find out whether the company or operation has been officially closed: radio/television announcements, calling a recorded or special number, etc.

3. Outline what employees are to do.

PHRASING ALTERNATIVES

Paragraph 1

Winter is approaching, so the following procedures should be followed on days when weather conditions make it hazardous for employees to report for work.

This memorandum outlines the procedure to be followed on hazardous weather days.

When inclement weather occurs, follow these steps:

Paragraph 2

Call the contact person listed on your Emergency Conditions list.

Call the company's recorded message line, 333-9999, for instructions.

Listen to local radio and television stations for closure announcements. Essential personnel will be contacted and arrangements made for getting these employees to work safely.

Paragraph 3

You may be called to report for work later in the day, if weather conditions improve.

Missed work days because of inclement weather will be made up at a later time.

Full-time employees will be granted emergency leave for bad-weather days.

INITIATING SUBORDINATE "BUY-IN" OF A PROPOSED CHANGE

To:

From:

Date:

Subject: Proposed Change in Claims Processing

As you know, there is a plan on the table to change the way claims are processed in your office. If this change occurs, the best way to ensure its successful implementation is to solicit input from those responsible for making it happen.

To that end, I have scheduled a meeting for Monday, October 2, 19____, 10:00 a.m. to 12:00 noon in the conference room. Review the attached proposal and come to the meeting prepared to go over it carefully. Also, discuss the plan with the other members of your department and get their feedback, as well. See you on Monday.

MEMO WRITER TIPS

1. The easiest way to initiate "buy-in" from subordinates about a proposed change is to get information from them before the change occurs. This memorandum then should ask for that input.

2. This memorandum may be a cover letter for a questionnaire or the proposal itself.

3. Tell employees what you want them to do relative to the proposal and let them know when their feedback is needed.

PHRASING ALTERNATIVES

Paragraph 1

A change in work hours is scheduled to occur in two weeks, and I'd like to go over with you any possible problems you think may result from this change. This way, we'll have a chance to avoid problems before they occur.

Your input on the proposed change of the quality control process is needed.

I need some information from you about the upcoming change in the customer complaint procedure, before we put the procedure into operation.

Paragraph 2

Since you handle these activities on a day-to-day basis, who would know better how or even if the process should be revamped.

This change will go much more smoothly if each of you has the opportunity to give it a fair trial.

Any change, no matter how minor, is difficult to make. You can help me a great deal by giving this proposal your support and letting me know what problems, if any, you find with it BEFORE we go any further.

Paragraph 3

Look over the attached flowchart and contact me this week to let me know if you see any problems in it.

Please go over the attached proposal with a fine-tooth comb and tell me what you think.

Complete the survey as honestly as you possible can. Your input will determine whether this proposed change is successful or not.

OUTLINING THE PROCESS FOR RECEIVING SHIPMENTS

To:
From:
Date:
Subject: Receiving Shipments

Follow these steps when receiving incoming shipments:

1. Open the package and match the delivery ticket with the copy of the purchase order.
2. Make sure all items listed on the purchase order are contained in the package.
3. Check each item for damage.
4. Route the items to the appropriate department.
5. Date-stamp the delivery ticket and forward it to the Accounts Payable Department.

By following this process, you can make sure that items received are correct, free of damage, and that they reach their correct destination.

MEMO WRITER TIPS

1. Outline whatever your organization's receivable process is, and list this process step by step.

2. Explain briefly the purpose of following the procedure.

3. Follow up to make sure instructions are being carried out properly.

PHRASING ALTERNATIVES

Paragraph 1

The receipt and distribution of products should be handled according to the procedure listed below:

When you receive shipments, process them as follows:

The steps listed below will explain to you how shipments should be processed when you receive them:

Paragraph 2

Following these steps will cut down on the number of lost or damaged shipments.

You must make sure goods received are what we ordered, and this method will help you do just that.

This receiving process will help you process goods more quickly and get them to the office where they belong.

REFERRING A SUBORDINATE TO THE PROCEDURE MANUAL

To:
From:
Date:
Subject: Procedure—News Releases

The Procedure Manual, Volume 4, outlines the process for writing and distributing news releases. If you still have questions after reading this, let me know.

MEMO WRITER TIPS

1. Describe what procedure or process the employee should find.

2. If the information is found in a specific volume or section of the manual, include this information.

PHRASING ALTERNATIVES

Paragraph 1

Check the Operations Manual for an updated version of purchasing procedures.

You'll find the information you need in the Procedures Manual, Section 8.

Regulation 21-C, Paragraph 4, outlines the procedure you need to follow when documenting substandard work performance.

REMINDING SUBORDINATES ABOUT THE SMOKING POLICY

To:
From:
Date:
Subject: Smoking Policy

Smoking is permitted only in designated smoking areas. These are found on the 1st, 3rd, and 5th floors of the building, as well as in a section of the employee lounge. Smokers, confine your smoking to these areas.

Adhering to this regulation will help make this a healthier work environment for us all.

MEMO WRITER TIPS

1. Outline where smoking is permitted.
2. Make it clear that smoking is prohibited, except in these areas.

PHRASING ALTERNATIVES

Paragraph 1

Some violations in our new smoking policy have occurred, so here it is again: Smoking is permitted only in the smoking lounge on the 1st floor or outside the building in areas where ash cans have been provided.

Smoking is prohibited except in offices designated as smoking areas.

No smoking is permitted inside the building—period!!!!

Paragraph 2

Please adhere to this policy.

Following these guidelines will preserve the rights of smokers and non-smokers alike.

Thank you for smoking only in approved smoking areas.

REPORTING THE RESULTS OF APPEAL/GRIEVANCE PROCEEDINGS*

To:
From:
Date:
Subject: Grievance #89-6246

Herbert Greeley, Mechanic III, filed this grievance, claiming pay for two hours of unauthorized overtime. At the first-step hearing, Horace Manley and Susan Griffin agreed that the immediate supervisor (Paul Jones) and the Union representative (Harvey Demaio) should resolve the issue. This was done and Mr. Jones requested that Mr. Greeley's pay be adjusted by two hours of overtime.

This grievance settlement has been made in accordance with the Collective Bargaining Agreement. Please make the recommended pay adjustment.

MEMO WRITER TIPS

1. Name the employee who has filed the grievance in the first sentence and summarize the gist of the grievance or appeal.

2. In one or two sentences, recap what action has been taken at each step of the grievance process used by your organization.

3. Summarize the results of the proceedings and then ask for the recommended action or follow-up.

---

*This memorandum was written by an Operations Superintendent of a public-sector entity.

PHRASING ALTERNATIVES

Paragraph 1

Grievance #1024, filed by Marilyn Jenkins, Psychiatric Social Worker, alleges that the immediate supervisor used abusive and threatening language during a counseling session held January 1, 19_____.

Morris Calvin, appeal #90-495, requests back pay in the amount of $1780.83.

Ms. Anna Kasteel (Grievance #4789) reports she was ordered to work mandatory overtime, in violation of Section 4, Paragraph 32, of the union agreement.

Paragraph 2

To date, the following actions have taken place, in accordance with grievance procedures:

The matter was heard by the appeal board, with these results:

The mediator found the grievance to be unfounded, and Ms. Jones has been informed of this ruling.

Paragraph 3

Please authorize payment of $2,894.00.

Consider this issue closed.

Mr. Smith is to be reinstated, effective immediately, and back pay in the amount of $246.00 should be paid on his 7/15 check.

SHARING COMPUTER TIME

To:
From:
Date:
Subject: Shared Computer Time

Your department will be sharing the new VAX System 3045 computer. Based upon the projections you sent me, four (4) hours of computer time will be needed by your department, three (3) times per week. Since the nature of your work requires that it be done early in the day, you will have access to the computer from 8:00 a.m. to 12:00 noon each day.

This arrangement should provide you with adequate computer time. If it does not, let me know.

MEMO WRITER TIPS

1. Let the reader know with whom the computer time will be shared. This way, if problems arise, the departments can coordinate their needs more efficiently.

2. Inform the reader how many hours of computer time have been authorized and when and how this time should be scheduled.

3. Close by commenting on the productive nature of this arrangement.

PHRASING ALTERNATIVES

Paragraph 1

Two hours of computer time have been authorized for your department. You'll be sharing the computer with the legal and customer relations departments.

I have worked out the following schedule for computer usage:

Billing Department	2:00 p.m.–4:00 p.m., Mon., Weds., Fri.
Claims	1:00 p.m.–5:00 p.m., Tues., Thurs.
Adjustments	5:00 p.m.–6:00 p.m., Mon., Weds.

Computer time will be split between your department and Engineering. You will have access Mondays and Wednesdays from 9:00 a.m. to 3:00 p.m.; they will use it on Tuesdays and Thursdays from 9:00 a.m. to 3:00 p.m.

Paragraph 2

If problems with this arrangement should arise, contact my office.

This schedule should allow all departments to enter and retrieve the information they need each day.

This shared arrangement will allow us to provide computer access while defraying costs for additional equipment.

SHORTENING EXTENDED BREAKS

To:
From:
Date:
Subject: Breaks

Two (2), 20-minute breaks are authorized, one in the morning and the other in the afternoon. Confine your work breaks to 20 minutes, no more, no less.

MEMO WRITER TIPS

1. Reiterate what the coffee break policy is.

2. State clearly that the subordinate should limit his/her breaks to this approved time period.

3. If this has been a persistent problem, include in this memo what disciplinary action will be taken if the problem persists.

PHRASING ALTERNATIVES

Paragraph 1

Coffee breaks have been getting too long, too often: ONLY 15 MINUTES is allowed. So enjoy your break, but confine it to 15 MINUTES.

You may take one 20-minute break in the morning and another in the afternoon, the latter only 15 minutes. Your compliance with this policy is appreciated.

Please limit your break time to the 20 minutes twice a day that has been authorized. Taking longer breaks puts an added, unfair burden on the other members of your department.

SHORTENING EXTENDED LUNCH HOURS

To:
From:
Date:
Subject: Lunch Hours

Lunch hours are 30 minutes long. If you need more time, arrange to take annual or personal leave, but keep your lunch hour to the 30 minutes approved for this purpose. Thank you.

MEMO WRITER TIPS

1. Point out how long lunch hours are to be.

2. Make it clear that you expect the employee to confine his/her lunch period to this time frame.

3. If this has been a persistent problem, spell out what disciplinary action may follow if the problem goes uncorrected.

PHRASING ALTERNATIVES

Paragraph 1

Please confine your lunch hours to the 60 minutes approved for this purpose. If you continue to take extended lunch breaks, your paycheck will be docked accordingly.

Each employee is authorized 45 minutes for lunch. In the future, please limit your lunch break to this 45 minutes.

Recently, your lunch hours have become longer and longer, far in excess of one hour. Correct the problem now. If you are having special difficulties that I need to be aware of, please see me.

TELLING EMPLOYEES HOW LEGISLATION WILL AFFECT THEIR JOBS

To:
From:
Date:
Subject: Legislative Ruling

Last week, the State legislature (HB89-102) cut all funding to outreach social services agencies. The long-range impact of this funding cut will be elimination of our program. We currently have funds to operate through the end of the fiscal year. A bare-bones crew of two to three people will work for 90 days past the end of the fiscal year, and that, as they say, will be that.

We will make every effort to help you find new places of employment and trust that you will continue to provide the excellent service you have rendered over the past three years.

I have scheduled a meeting for this Friday at 9:00 a.m. in the conference room to discuss this matter in greater detail. Please plan to attend.

MEMO WRITER TIPS

1. Cite the legislation and explain what its impact will be right away.
2. Outline both the long-range and short-term results of the legislation.
3. Schedule a meeting or conference to discuss this matter with employees face-to-face.

PHRASING ALTERNATIVES

Paragraph 1

As most of you know, the Buttman-Turner Act passed by the U.S. Congress last week has direct impact on the services we offer.

Just yesterday, Congress voted to renew our funding for another three years (SB89-303-856).

The recent Supreme Court ruling on set-asides for minority contractors will greatly influence our current operations.

Paragraph 2

Each of you will have to sign the attached "Drug-Free Workplace" agreement, as a result of this ruling.

Twenty-five positions will have to be eliminated immediately, based on seniority rights and other applicable lay-off policies.

This bill means we'll have to revamp our procedure for securing bids from female/minority-owned businesses.

Paragraph 3

This means we can continue to offer the exemplary program we've developed. Congratulations on a job well done.

The full impact of this legislation is currently being studied, and you will receive additional information as it becomes available.

If you have questions about how this will affect you directly, please see me.

TELLING SUBORDINATES ABOUT THEIR APPEAL/GRIEVANCE RIGHTS

To:
From:
Date:
Subject: Appeal Process

Labor Contract (Section 64, Article 4) entitles you to appeal rights if you disagree with the ruling made by your immediate supervisor. The process works as follows:

1. Complete your appeal package (see attached guidelines) and submit this within 30 days to your unit manager.
2. The unit manager then has 10 working days to respond to your appeal, in writing.

3. If you are not satisfied with his/her ruling, you may then petition for a hearing before the Appeal Board. You have 14 days after notification by your unit manager to initiate this action.

4. The Appeal Board then has 20 days to act on your appeal. The decision of the Appeal Board is final and binding.

If you have questions about this process, consult the Labor Contract for additional clarification.

MEMO WRITER TIPS

1. Usually, the appeal process will be outlined in one of your organization's publications. You may either refer the employee to this publication or spell out the procedure in a memorandum.

2. List the steps involved in the appeal process.

3. Let the employee know where he/she can find additional assistance if that becomes necessary.

PHRASING ALTERNATIVES

Paragraph 1

In accordance with company policy, your appeal rights are as follows:

The appeal process is outlined in the Employee Handbook. Please read this information carefully and prepare your appeal according to its guidelines.

The ruling of the Appeal Board is final; therefore, you have no further recourse in this matter.

Paragraph 2

The legal department can provide you with assistance should you desire it.

If you have additional questions, contact the personnel office.

This process has been designed to resolve complaints and problems as quickly and effectively as possible. Following the appeal process carefully will ensure your access to these rights.

WARNING AN EMPLOYEE ABOUT EXCESSIVE PERSONAL TELEPHONE CALLS

To:
From:
Date:
Subject: Personal Telephone Calls

You may make personal telephone calls on your break or lunch periods, not during regular business hours. Making excessive personal telephone calls distracts you from your real business of performing work for this company. Please limit your personal phone calls to YOUR time, not ours.

MEMO WRITER TIPS

1. Let the employee know when/where personal telephone calls may be made.

2. Include a one-sentence explanation of why this policy is important.

3. Make it clear that you expect the employee to adhere to these guidelines.

4. If this has been a persistent problem, tell the employee what disciplinary action may result if the problem is not corrected.

PHRASING ALTERNATIVES

Paragraph 1

Please confine your personal telephone calls to your personal time; that is, make them while you are on break or lunch at the public telephone located in the lobby.

Your constant use of the telephone for personal business has become a real nuisance. I have spoken to you about this before, but let me make it clear that NO PERSONAL TELEPHONE CALLS are to be made from your desk during business hours.

You may make personal phone calls only during times when such calls will not interfere with your regular work duties. Please do not make excessive personal telephone calls.

Paragraph 2

Obviously, we can't pay you for conducting your personal business on the job. You are therefore directed to stop making excessive use of the telephone for personal business—NOW!

If everyone in the office made as many personal phone calls as you do each day, we'd rarely get any work done. Please comply with this policy today.

I trust you'll find it possible to limit your phone calls to these approved times.

12

Model Memos for Money Matters

Money always matters in business. Budgets must be prepared and sometimes revised. Cutbacks must be made when funds contract. Purchases can be made when funds expand.

And tracking money must be done on a continuous basis. Supplies are ordered on the correct purchase order or requisition form. Materials get lost, damaged, or stolen, and this must be reported. Production and sales figures must be compiled and presented. Purchases must be justified.

The model memoranda in Chapter 12 will help you write memos about a variety of money matters:

- Travel expenses
- Cost centers
- Expense accounts
- Purchase requests
- Contract payments
- Damage and theft losses

Whatever your money matters, you will find memoranda in this chapter that you can use as they are, or adapt them to suit your needs.

ANNOUNCING BELT-TIGHTENING MEMOS MEASURES

To:
From:
Date:
Subject: Spending Cutbacks

As we approach the end of the fiscal year, money is in short supply. Until next fiscal year, therefore, closely monitor any expenditures, and delay the ordering of expendable supplies until more money is available.

Any action you can take to save dollars over the next 30 days will help us make it to the end of the fiscal year intact.

Thanks.

MEMO WRITER TIPS

1. Explain why you are requesting belt-tightening measures.
2. Outline, specifically, what the reader can do to save money.
3. Let the reader know how long this period of low dollars will last.

PHRASING ALTERNATIVES

Paragraph 1

Until we can land some new accounts, each of us will need to do what we can to save funds. Reduce travel and entertainment expenses. Delay the start of any new projects. Within the next three months, cash flow should improve, and we should be able to resume normal operations.

Expenditures will be reduced for the next 60 days because we have simply not had the cash receipts we anticipated. Until further notice, a hiring freeze becomes effective, and no additional part-time employees are to be given full-time positions.

The following cost-saving measures are being taken in order to make sure we have ample funds to complete the Kirkwood Project:

Paragraph 2

Your cooperation during this period of tight funds is greatly appreciated.

If significant reductions in expenditures are made now, we can avoid a money crunch later.

Thanks for doing all you can to get us through this temporary shortage of funds.

ANNOUNCING A BUDGET EXCESS

To:
From:
Date:
Subject: Budget Excess

Excess budget funds are currently available from now through June 30, 19_____. These may be used for Priority 4 and 5 items you have not purchased.

Any equipment you purchase must be received by June 30; otherwise the equipment will encumber 19_____ funds.

Let's use this extra money wisely and purchase some items to get us off to a great start next fiscal year.

MEMO WRITER TIPS

1. Announce the budget excess and explain what can and cannot be done with the funds.

2. If funds must be used within a certain time period, let the reader know what this period is.

3. Advise the reader how funds should be used.

4. Caution the reader to use the funds appropriately.

PHRASING ALTERNATIVES

Paragraph 1

Additional dollars in the amount of $41,546.78 are now available, if you have capital needs not yet taken care of. These funds must be spent, however, before December 31, 19_____.

This must be your lucky day. A budget excess has resulted in the authorization of additional spending for your section. Perhaps you can use these dollars to fill the two technician vacancies you have in your department.

A budget excess this year makes it possible for you to purchase goods and/or services in the amount of $3,890.72 before next budget cycle begins.

Paragraph 2

I'm happy to report this sudden windfall and trust you will use the funds to bring your staff up to full strength.

Your diligent efforts have helped make this excess possible. Thanks for a job well done.

Who knows when another overage will occur, so use these monies to upgrade equipment in your section.

ANNOUNCING A BUDGET SHORTFALL

To:
From:
Date:
Subject: Budget Deficit

Expenditures for this year exceeded allocations by $57,800. In order to maintain operations until next funding cycle, the following cost-saving measures are being taken immediately:

1. No expendable supplies will be ordered from now until next fiscal year. Contact other departments if you need supplies not in stock.
2. No new personnel will be hired until after July 1, 19____ .
3. No new travel requests will be authorized.

Thank you for your cooperation in handling these cost-saving measures. Your efforts will help us continue to function.

MEMO WRITER TIPS

1. Explain that money is not available, and include the amount if that is appropriate.
2. Outline, specifically, what measures are being taken to conserve funds and for how long these measures will be in effect.
3. Thank workers for their compliance.

PHRASING ALTERNATIVES

Paragraph 1

Because of a budget shortfall in excess of $200,000, no new capital projects can be started for the next 60 days.

Cost overruns in the amount of $97,000 have seriously jeopardized our ability to complete the Taft Construction project on schedule. Until further notice, no new expenditures in the following areas will be authorized:

Sadly, I must announce a budget shortfall again this year. For this reason, only those purchase requisitions dated before June 1, 19____, will be processed.

Paragraph 2

Our financial situation should improve within the next 90 days. Your cooperation until then is appreciated.

Thanks for doing everything you can to get us through this difficult period.

Next year's funds should arrive soon. Until then, do what you can to make ends meet.

APPROVING A REQUEST FOR FUNDS

To:
From:
Date:
Subject: Approval—Request for Funds

Your request for an additional $6,854.00 has been approved. This money should provide you with the additional software you need.

MEMO WRITER TIPS

1. Tell the reader the funds have been approved.
2. Be sure to include the amount.
3. If applicable, make some statement about how the funds are to be used.

PHRASING ALTERNATIVES

Paragraph 1

I have approved your request for $439.32. This additional money should fund travel for at least one conference attendee.

The $18,624.00 you requested has been approved. Accounting will prepare the necessary budget transfer.

You'll get the $9,246.00 you asked for just as soon as this month's books are closed out.

APPROVING TRAVEL EXPENSES

To:
From:
Date:
Subject: Authorization for Travel Expenses

I have authorized travel funding in the amount of $7,843.00 for your department. Several employees who need additional training should be able to attend training sessions and conferences this year.

MEMO WRITER TIPS

1. Say how much you have authorized and for what purpose.

PHRASING ALTERNATIVES

Paragraph 1

Your travel expenses for $212.00 will be reimbursed. Accounting should have the check prepared by next Tuesday.

Your request for travel expenses in the amount of $578.00 has been approved.

I am happy to approve your request for travel expenses: $142.00.

ASKING SUBORDINATES FOR BUDGET INPUT

To:
From:
Date:
Subject: Budget Preparation

Please prepare budget projections for your department for Fiscal Year 19_____.
Forward these to my office by Friday, March 3.

The final budget must be submitted for initial review by April 15.

> **MEMO WRITER TIPS**
>
> 1. Ask for budget calculations and give a specific due date.
> 2. Let the reader know when the final budget must be submitted.

PHRASING ALTERNATIVES

Paragraph 1

Your input for the preparation of next year's budget is needed by February 28. The entire budget must be submitted to City Council no later than April 1.

Calculate your budget needs for next year and submit these to me on the attached forms by Monday, April 1. This will help me complete the budget, which must be ready by May 15. Thank you.

Review the attached budget proposal and add any items you think your department will need next year. Return the amended budget proposal to my office by Friday, March 4. Getting these in promptly will help me prepare the final budget, due in the president's office by April 1.

CHANGING A SECTION'S COST CENTER

To:
From:
Date:
Subject: Change in Cost Center Number

The cost-center number for your project is being changed from 91-014550 to 91-015335, effective Monday, July 1, 19_____. All cost center numbers had to be changed because of the new organizational structure.

Please make a note of this change.

> **MEMO WRITER TIPS**
>
> 1. Tell the reader what the cost-center number is being changed to.
> 2. Give a brief explanation of why this change is being made.

PHRASING ALTERNATIVES

Paragraph 1

Effective Monday, June 1, 19____, your cost-center number will be changed to 10856. The entire numbering system has been changed to speed up data entry operations.

Your section will begin using #31-645 for purchases, beginning Monday, July 1. Since you are now a part of the engineering branch, you need to use their costing code.

Notify the employees in your section that they should begin using Cost Code #48-45613 on Monday, October 1, 19____. This change has been made to help accounts receivable automate their procedures.

DEALING WITH EXPENSE ACCOUNT ABUSE

To:
From:
Date:
Subject: Questionable Expense Account Purchases

An audit of your expense account receipts for the past month indicates your company credit card was used to purchase personal items, in clear violation of company policy.

If you have an explanation for these unauthorized expenses, I'd certainly like to hear it. Remember, your credit card is a privilege extended to you as long as it is used properly and for legitimate business expenses.

You are directed to reimburse the company $128.90. Deliver the check to the accounting office, and make sure this doesn't happen again.

MEMO WRITER TIPS

1. Stick to the facts when reporting the expense account abuse. Say how much money was used improperly and why these expenses are not allowable.

2. Tell the employee what action should be taken now and remind him/her what action may result if further abuse occurs.

PHRASING ALTERNATIVES

Paragraph 1

Accounting has checked your expense receipts for July and found several irregularities. Purchases totalling $478.00 cannot be directly tied to business purchases or travel.

Are all of the expenses you reported on your May travel voucher legitimate business expenses?

Some of the travel expenses you claimed in March—$84.79, to be exact—appear to be disallowable under applicable company policy.

Paragraph 2

See me today to discuss these charges so that you can reimburse the company for any unauthorized purchases.

Your consistent abuse of expense account privileges has resulted in the immediate cancellation of your credit card and the forfeiture of this card for a period of 90 days.

See Karen in the accounting office and make any necessary reimbursements at that time.

Paragraph 3

I trust we will have no further repeats of these unauthorized purchases.

If you value your expense account, confine your purchases to those authorized.

An expense account is a highly valued benefit of your position, one I'm sure you'd like to keep. Purchasing legitimate items on this expense account will preserve this benefit.

DEALING WITH SPENDING OVERAGES

To:
From:
Date:
Subject: Cost Overruns

Spending in your section exceeded the allocation for last quarter by $6,196.48. You will need to adjust this quarter's spending in order to maintain budget reserves to last you through the fiscal year.

I'd be happy to discuss with you what measures you can take to bring spending into line with cost projections. Make an appointment this week to discuss this with me.

MEMO WRITER TIPS

1. Alert the reader that spending has gone over budget and include the amount of the spending overage.

2. Suggest what might be done to bring spending down and set up a meeting to establish specific strategies for doing so.

PHRASING ALTERNATIVES

Paragraph 1

Your department has registered a cost overrun of $12,082.00 for accounting period 9. What can you do to bring these costs under control?

An overage of $845.00 in last month's spending has been noted.

If spending in your unit continues to outstrip budget allocations, you will be in serious financial difficulty as the end of the fiscal year approaches.

Paragraph 2

I noticed that travel authorizations have been extremely high. You might cut costs in this area.

You have used consultative services quite a bit during this period. In-house expertise might be used instead.

The number of raises and promotions granted to workers in your section seriously increased your total outlay. You may want to freeze such practices until your budget balances.

Paragraph 3

Come to the budget meeting scheduled for Friday prepared to discuss ways to cut costs.

Prepare a report for me, outlining how you intend to balance your budget and control expenditures over the next quarter.

Get your spending back on track.

DENYING A REQUEST FOR FUNDS

To:
From:
Date:
Subject: Disapproval—Request for Funds

Although the upgraded steel parts would yield a stronger product, I am unable to approve your request for $28,900 to purchase them at this time.

When you prepare your budget projects for next year, include these in the projections. For now, we will have to use the parts we currently have in stock.

MEMO WRITER TIPS

1. If possible, begin the memo by mentioning the merit of the request.
2. Say that the funds have not been approved, and explain why.
3. Tell the reader if and why such a request might be approved.

PHRASING ALTERNATIVES

Paragraph 1

Unfortunately, I cannot approve your request for $4,500.00. We simply do not have the money to contract outside printing services, even though a contractor could give you a faster turn-around time.

Your request for $1,012 has been denied, pending further study of whether or not your old computer needs a hard-disk upgrade. New computers are due in shortly, and it seems unnecessary to upgrade old computers until the new ones arrive.

Your request for $5,090 will have to be deferred until the beginning of next fiscal year.

Paragraph 2

When added monies become available, I'll let you know. You may want to resubmit your request then.

Perhaps you could have the person attending the conference provide training for the rest of the department, instead of sending two additional people to the conference itself.

Funding for such projects will not be available until our cash flow improves.

DISAPPROVING A TRAVEL VOUCHER

To:
From:
Date:
Subject: Travel Voucher Correction

Your travel voucher will be processed as soon as all expenses are itemized on Form #203 (copy attached). Please complete this form and submit the entire package to the business office.

MEMO WRITER TIPS

1. Take a positive tone by saying what must be done to approve the travel voucher, instead of focusing on what is wrong with it.

2. In one sentence, outline what steps the reader should take now.

PHRASING ALTERNATIVES

Paragraph 1

Your travel voucher cannot be approved for the following reasons:

When your travel voucher package contains all receipts for purchases, you can be reimbursed.

I am unable to approve for payment several items listed on your travel voucher dated June 30, 19_____ . I have circled the items in question and will hold your voucher for two (2) days. If I have not heard from you by then, I will authorize payment for the other items.

ELIMINATING EXCESSIVE PHOTOCOPYING

To:
From:
Date:
Subject: Excessive Photocopying

Photocopying charges for the period ending June 30 ran $5,450.00 over expected costs. Whenever possible, refrain from photocopying large jobs (50 pages or more) unless they are absolutely necessary.

If these expenses go unchecked, we will have to revisit the issue of hiring someone to make copies and to monitor copier use.

MEMO WRITER TIPS

1. Present a convincing argument by telling how much photocopier use exceeded expectations.
2. Set forth guidelines for use of the photocopier.
3. Indicate what might happen if excessive use continues.

PHRASING ALTERNATIVES

Paragraph 1

The photocopier is being used to excess. Last month, we paid $3200.00 for repairs and exceeded paper costs by a significant margin.

In order to better monitor the use of the photocopy machine, an electronic counter is being issued to each department. When you have copies to make, get the counter from your department secretary. This way, we can monitor photocopier use and charge departments accordingly.

Photocopying costs have gone right through the roof, and drastic measures must be taken to bring these costs down.

Paragraph 2

Photocopy only those documents intended for general distribution.

Use the photocopier for official business only. No use for copying personal documents has been authorized.

Let's discuss this problem at next week's staff meeting. Come with suggestions for how we might eliminate excessive photocopier use.

Paragraph 3

If copying volume continues at these high costs, we may have to look into installing coin-operated photocopiers.

These costs must be brought down if we are to have adequate funds for the rest of the year.

Your efforts to limit photocopying to the bare necessities is greatly appreciated.

EXPEDITING A PURCHASE REQUEST

To:
From:
Date:
Subject: Purchase Request—Rush

Please rush the processing of Purchase Request #80944. The items listed on this purchase request must arrive before the July 8 conference I have scheduled.
    Thanks.

MEMO WRITER TIPS

1. Encourage the quick processing of the request by explaining why it needs to be done more quickly.
2. Tell when you need the supplies or equipment.

PHRASING ALTERNATIVES

Paragraph 1

    I need the supplies ordered on June 30 no later than July 24. Could you please put a "rush" on PR #90-20455? Thanks for your help.

    I know most rush orders require 10 days lead time, but I must have the items on Purchase Requisition #908 by the end of next week. These parts will provide the interface for the new computer system, and if I don't get them, computer training will have to be rescheduled. I'd appreciate anything you can do.

    What can you do to speed up the delivery of the equipment ordered on PR #9056? Our current machine is in the repair shop, and if we want to catch up on back-orders, we must have this new equipment. Help me out, will you?

EXPLAINING A THEFT TO A SUPERIOR

To:
From:
Date:
Subject: Theft of Word Processor

On Friday afternoon, July 2, a Lambert Wordprocessor was stolen from the controller's office. The police were called, and they made a police report (copy attached).

As best as can be determined, someone walked into the office while the secretary was out of the room and simply walked out of the building with the word processor. I have instructed all personnel to lock their offices if they are leaving and no one will be present to watch the equipment.

I have initiated an insurance claim and ordered a new word processor. Tighter security measures are being put in place to make sure such a theft does not recur.

MEMO WRITER TIPS

1. Say what was stolen, when, and what action was taken after the theft was discovered.
2. Outline what steps have been taken to reduce the chances of a recurrence.
3. Assure your boss that security measures are being taken.

PHRASING ALTERNATIVES

Paragraph 1

Nan Fabrush's purse was stolen from her desk drawer on November 15. A police report was made, and other workers in the department were questioned by both the police and me.

Two boxes of slides and beakers were stolen from the loading dock on Friday, January 20, 19____, at approximately 7:40 a.m.

Five boxes of typing paper are missing from the supply room. This shortage was discovered on April 19.

Paragraph 2

Nan was away from her desk at the time, and everyone else was out of the office, either on appointments or at meetings.

The police detectives are satisfied that outsiders stole the boxes from the loading dock. Several other thefts of this kind have occurred in the past two months.

Another employee, Bruce Tanner, is a suspect and has been questioned three times by police. Until this investigation has been completed, Bruce has been suspended with pay.

Paragraph 3

I have directed security personnel to make more frequent rounds during late-night hours, in order to make sure this doesn't happen again.

All employees have been directed to keep their valuables in locked desk or cabinet drawers and to lock offices when empty.

Because our building has public access, thefts like this will occur. We have been lucky in the past, but I have had security officers review with my subordinates what precautions they can take to prevent theft.

EXPLAINING A DAMAGE LOSS TO A SUPERIOR

To:
From:
Date:
Subject: Damage Loss

In the process of disassembling the production line for cleaning, an extension was dropped and broken. Cost of repair is $3,500.00. Replacement cost is $2,800.00. Since it would cost more to replace the unit than to repair it, I have ordered a new extension, which should be delivered in approximately 10 days. Until then, I have increased production on the other three lines.

The safety captain has conducted classes on the correct way to disassemble the line so that this doesn't happen again. No negligence can be found. This looks like an accident, pure and simple.

MEMO WRITER TIPS

1. Explain what item or equipment has been damaged and how it was damaged.

2. Include information about repair and/or replacement costs, and outline what steps are being taken to get the damaged item either repaired or replaced.

3. Discuss what is being done to avoid a recurrence.

PHRASING ALTERNATIVES

Paragraph 1

During the relocation of the information processing section, two computers were damaged. It will cost $1,068.00 to have them repaired.

As you asked, here is an explanation of the damage done to the #1 backhoe. Repair costs amounted to $746.00. The backhoe has been repaired and is back in operation.

When the videotape equipment was used at last month's retreat, the video camera lens was damaged. A new lens will cost $208.00. I have ordered one, and it should arrive within the next 10 days.

Paragraph 2

I have talked with the employee responsible for damaging the equipment, provided him with instructions about proper handling, and do not expect that this damage will occur again.

While this damage was unfortunate, it was not due to employee negligence or mishandling.

The amount of the damage is being deducted in increments from the employee's paychecks. The full amount should be reimbursed to the company by December 1.

EXPLAINING PURCHASING PROCEDURES TO SUBORDINATES

To:
From:
Date:
Subject: Purchasing Procedures

Attached is a copy of a sample purchase requisition we will be using to order necessary items for you. You must type in the information in Sections I, II, III, and IV.

All asterisked items must be completed, and the form must be signed by the appropriate cost-center administrator before we can process your orders. Completed forms should be returned to Wanda Copley, Room 207.

Blank forms are enclosed in this package, and additional forms are available in the purchasing office.

If you need information, please contact Wanda at Ext. 741.

MEMO WRITER TIPS

1. Attach a copy of a purchasing procedure form that has been filled out correctly.

2. Include information in your memorandum about what sections must be filled out and what signatures are required.

3. Be sure to provide a phone number if additional questions need to be answered.

PHRASING ALTERNATIVES

Paragraph 1

Here is a sample of how purchase requisitions must be completed before they can be processed.

The purchasing procedure is as follows:

These steps are involved in purchasing goods and/or services:

Paragraph 2

Only Site Managers are authorized to sign purchase requisitions. These signatures must be on the form if it is to be processed.

Be sure you get the proper signatures before forwarding your completed purchase requisition to the accounting office.

Your supervisor must sign the purchase requisition. Then you should send it to David Winslow in purchasing.

Paragraph 3

Dave, Ext. 1102, will be happy to answer any additional questions you may have.

Call me if you have any questions.

Wanda Copley will provide you with additional assistance in filling out the forms, should you need it.

JUSTIFYING AN EXPENDITURE*

To:
From:
Date:
Subject: Justification for Travel Request

I am reducing the 19_____ Administration travel budget request by $5,900; the initial request was for $27,400, the new request is for $21,500.

The remaining trips and conferences in the request are important to the development of staff in areas I consider critical for the accomplishment of department goals.

---

*This memorandum was written by the Director of Administration for a metropolitan transportation district.

> **MEMO WRITER TIPS**
>
> 1. Begin by reiterating what action has been taken to date.
>
> 2. Say what action you would like to take and explain your reasons for wanting to do so. Use specific facts and figures whenever possible, as these will allow you to present a more convincing argument.

PHRASING ALTERNATIVES

Paragraph 1

My request for funds in the amount of $12,500 has been disapproved. I understand that other items have priority right now, but I'd like to explain my reasons for wanting to make this purchase.

In our discussion last week, you indicated you would not approve the purchase of a new forklift for warehousing.

My purchase requisition for an additional printing of the brochure entitled "Teller Training" has been returned unapproved.

Paragraph 2

I have several legitimate reasons for wanting to make this purchase, including . . .

This expenditure is absolutely necessary, considering the age and efficiency of our current machine. We are currently spending as much for repairs ($8,298.00 last year) as it would cost to purchase a new machine outright ($12,476.99).

If we do not hire an additional order clerk this fiscal year, we will be unable to process the $28,540 dollars in back orders we are currently trying to fill. Filling these back orders will generate significant revenue for the company; therefore, the new position is absolutely essential.

JUSTIFYING A SOLE-SOURCE PURCHASE

To:
From:
Date:
Subject: Justification for Sole-Source Purchase

I am recommending the sole-source purchase of services from Hancock, Wry, and Farlow, Attorneys at Law. Their legal services are required to review the new employee handbook scheduled for release July 1.

Hancock has assured me that the services required to review the handbook will be less than $2,000. Since bids are let only for purchases of $2,500 or more, a sole-source acquisition is appropriate in this instance.

We have retained this firm for other legal consultation and have been pleased with their former performance. Your approval of this sole-source purchase is requested.

MEMO WRITER TIPS

1. Say who/what the sole-source purchase will be and what benefit these goods or services will provide to the company.

2. Explain why the sole-source purchase is justified, being as specific about your rationale as possible.

3. If you have used the sole-source firm before, refer to their previous record as part of your justification.

4. Ask for approval of the purchase.

PHRASING ALTERNATIVES

Paragraph 1

A sole-source purchase of janitorial supplies totalling $1,595.00 is required. These supplies are needed immediately, and Acme Janitorial Supplies has promised next-day delivery.

Request you approve sole-source acquisition of consultative services from Lee and Associates, an outplacement firm. Lee and Associates would conduct two outplacement seminars for those employees affected by the recent reduction in force.

I recommend the sole-source use of Todd Developers to revise the blueprints needed for our meeting with Winthrop Construction next week.

Paragraph 2

We are in the process of renegotiating our janitorial supply contract, and until this has been done, we do not have a firm supplier. Of the services contacted, Acme offered a price 20 percent lower than its competitors and a faster delivery time.

Lee and Associates was praised in a recent edition of *Business Times* magazine for the outstanding delivery of outplacement services. Since this is a one-time request, the expenditures required to release requests for proposals and the entire bid process would be almost triple the cost of using this firm.

Our own design department is already overtaxed, completing other priority projects. We need these blueprints revised as quickly as possible and, in fact, the service of Todd Developers will be significantly less expensive than the cost of in-house printing.

Paragraph 3

Please approve this sole-source purchase.

Thank you for considering this sole-source acquisition.

In this instance, this purchase would be the most cost-effective for the company. Do I have your approval to contract for these services?

OKAYING THE PAYMENT OF A CONTRACTOR OR VENDOR

To:
From:
Date:
Subject: Approval to Pay Vendor

Pay Hirschbush Suppliers the $2,806.40 due them for the file cabinets they delivered (PO #90-14877). The file cabinets are free of damage and will meet our needs.

MEMO WRITER TIPS

1. Include the name, amount, and purchase order number (if known) of the request.
2. Keep the memo short and be direct about its purpose.

PHRASING ALTERNATIVES

Paragraph 1

I have approved for payment the $14,809.54 invoice submitted for Overstreet Industries. All work has met specifications.

It's okay to pay ABC and Associates its $150.00 per hour consulting fee for financial analysis services. The contract was executed and completed on January 7.

Process payment for a check in the amount of $546.80 for Newton Printing. The pamphlets were delivered on April 14; they have been proofread and are error-free.

RECOMMENDING THE CANCELLATION OF A CONTRACT

To:
From:
Date:
Subject: Recommendation for Contract Cancellation

I recommend cancellation of the maintenance contract we now have with Lamont Repair. Their performance record has been substandard, to say the least, and on several occasions, I feel they have overcharged us for services.

Below is a list of problems we have had over the past year:

1/7   Service technician responded two days after initial call for service.

1/9   Same problem supposedly repaired on 1/7 recurred. Service rep was called, but did not report until 1/11. We were again charged for repairs.

1/16   When I called to complain about the rebilling for services, I was treated rudely and told, "Well, you all must have broken it again."

1/31   Another call for service.

2/14   Copier was out of service for three days awaiting the arrival of a service technician. When he finally arrived, he had to order a part, which did not arrive for two weeks. The copier was again out of service for two weeks.

3/1   Another call for service.

3/15   Another call for service.

In all, the photocopier was out of service a total of 246 hours, the equivalent of more than six weeks. During these down times, we had to contract with a local printer for copier service. We have been billed $9,840.00 for service calls this year, not to mention the cost of supplies to keep the photocopier operational.

I have surveyed three other repair firms, and the highest quotation I got was half the amount we paid to Lamont this year. Such poor service justifies our cancelling this contract when it expires, June 30. We should then let bids for a new contractor.

MEMO WRITER TIPS

1. Spell out the name of the contractor or vendor and what kinds of goods or services are provided by this company.

2. List specific reasons, based on documentation, for cancelling the contract.

3. Use specific dates and amounts whenever possible and construct a convincing argument by showing the cost:benefit ratio.

PHRASING ALTERNATIVES

Paragraph 1

We should not renew our contract with Logan Enterprises when it expires July 1 of this year. Their products are a full 20 percent higher than goods we could order from local vendors.

The contract we have with Larchton Corporation for concrete deliveries should be terminated immediately. Their chronically late deliveries have caused us delays in pouring at least four concrete slabs.

None of the candidates referred to us by Norton Employment Services has met even minimal qualifications. Therefore, I recommend we cancel our contract with them and secure referral services from another recruitment firm.

Paragraph 2

Some of the problems we have experienced this year include:

During the past six months, the following incidents have occurred:

Their substandard practices are documented below.

Paragraph 3

Securing a new vendor will save us at least $41,000 next year. Let's act to terminate this contract now.

Their contract comes up for renewal in 30 days. Since they obviously cannot deliver the kind of service we require, I suggest we notify them now that their contract will not be renewed.

These incidents highlight a pattern of late and incorrect delivery. Why should we retain the services of a vendor who so obviously cannot meet our needs?

REFUSING TO PAY A CONTRACTOR OR VENDOR

To:

From:

Date:

Subject: Denial of Payment for Window-Fresh Industries

I cannot approve the payment of $3,587.52 to Window-Fresh Industries until they have cleaned windows on floors 15-25. They have billed us the total amount contracted for cleaning windows on all floors, but after seven (7) calls to their office, they have yet to complete the work.

When they have completed the work, I can authorize payment. Notify them of my decision and hold their invoice until further notice.

MEMO WRITER TIPS

1. You will need to include the name of the vendor and the amount of money the company is requesting.

2. Explain why they have not complied with the original contract agreement and spell out when/if payment can be made.

PHRASING ALTERNATIVES

Paragraph 1

Hodgkiss Manufacturing can be paid the $2,080.00 they billed us when they have delivered the 12 doors now on back order (PO # 8053).

I am recommending we not pay Norbert Company their $568.00 fee until the final revisions of the manual they are writing have been approved by our staff.

Do not pay The Atlantis Corporation the amount of their invoice dated 1/9/_____ . Their $43,000.00 contract called for inspection of all equipment once it was put in place, and they have yet to conduct such an inspection.

Paragraph 2

As soon as they comply fully with our initial agreement, I will authorize payment.

If they fail to carry out the full extent of our agreement, they will not receive payment. I have called them and told them this, and they have assured me they will have completed all phases of installation no later than August 1.

Payment will be made when we have approved the final version of their classification study. This should be completed around May 15.

REMINDING SUBORDINATES ABOUT PETTY CASH EXPENDITURES

To:
From:
Date:
Subject: Petty Cash Expenditures

Only pre-approved purchases of $25.00 or less can be reimbursed from petty cash funds. Purchases of more than this amount must be paid by expense voucher and processed through the accounting office. Items that employees purchase without the prior approval of their immediate supervisor cannot be reimbursed.

Thanks for your help in making petty cash an efficient way to pay for authorized small purchases.

MEMO WRITER TIPS

1. Outline the requirements for petty cash use. Keep a positive tone by saying when petty cash expenses will be paid, rather than focusing on what will not be paid.

2. Close by indicating you expect people to comply with these requirements.

PHRASING ALTERNATIVES

Paragraph 1

The petty cash fund is intended for the reimbursement of small purchases ($15.00 and less).

You can be reimbursed for minor purchases of $25.00 and less through the petty cash fund.

This is a reminder that petty cash can only be used for expenses of $30.00 or less that are not expense-account items.

Paragraph 2

Using petty cash for its intended purpose will ensure funds are available quickly.

Following these guidelines enables me to process your petty cash reimbursements promptly.

Thanks for adhering to these guidelines for petty cash purchases.

REMINDING SUBORDINATES ABOUT END-OF-FISCAL-YEAR PURCHASES*

To:
From:
Date:
Subject: End-of-Fiscal-Year Purchases

The end of the fiscal year is rapidly approaching. All purchases ordered this fiscal year must be processed prior to June 15 and must be delivered before June 30, 19_____ . Any goods or services purchased after this date will encumber 19_____ funds.

Purchase anything you may need without delay.

MEMO WRITER TIPS

1. Outline the deadlines required for purchases.
2. Include any specific guidelines that must be followed.

PHRASING ALTERNATIVES

Paragraph 1

As the end of this fiscal year approaches, please make sure you have completed all purchases prior to September 15. No purchase requisitions will be processed between September 15 and September 30.

Purchase the goods and services you need by June 18 if you plan to use funds from this fiscal year. Any purchase requisitions received after this date will be held until next fiscal year and funded with those appropriations.

Thank you for completing all 19_____ purchases by December 15. Any items requisitioned after December 15 cannot be paid for with this year's funds and will encumber 19_____ monies.

---

*This memorandum was written by a purchasing agent for a state government agency.

REPORTING QUARTERLY/ANNUAL PRODUCTION FIGURES

To:
From:
Date:
Subject: Quarterly Production Figures

Production figures for the quarter ending March 31, 19____ , are as follows:

Automobile Make/Model	# Manufactured	# Rejected	Total
1. Quimsby Sedan	3560	37	3523
2. Quimsby Convertible	573	4	569
3. Quimsby Jeep	1493	49	1444
Grand Total	5626	90	5536

These figures reflect a 14 percent increase in production over last quarter's figures and a 3 percent reduction in the reject rate.

If you need additional information, please let me know.

MEMO WRITER TIPS

1. Begin by saying what time period you are reporting figures for.
2. Listing the figures in table form will make them easier to read.
3. Make any necessary comparisons with similar figures from the preceding quarter or year.

PHRASING ALTERNATIVES

Paragraph 1

Here are the production figures for 19____ .

The production figures for the 4th quarter are detailed below:

Here is the report of first-quarter production you requested.

Paragraph 2

Production fell off slightly, 2.3 percent, during this period.

Please note the 14 percent increase in production.

As you can see, production efforts increased output by 8 percent while the number of parts returned by quality control remained fairly constant.

REPORTING QUARTERLY/ANNUAL SALES FIGURES

To:
From:
Date:
Subject: Quarterly Sales

Quarterly sales figures for the period ending June 30, 19_____ , reflect we sold a total of $8,942.31 worth of merchandise. Sales figures for individual products are itemized on the attached computer printout.

    If you need additional information, please let me know.

MEMO WRITER TIPS

1. Report sales figures for a specific period.

2. This may include both an itemized list of specific goods and/or services, in addition to a total figure of items sold.

3. Depending upon your operations, you may also have to report items returned, defective items, or other categories. In this instance, a table of such categories will more clearly convey sales information to the reader.

PHRASING ALTERNATIVES

Paragraph 1

    The following list itemizes sales for 19_____ , by stock number:

    Here are the sales totals for last quarter:

    Sales for the 2nd quarter totaled $11,082.81, distributed as follows:

REQUIRING A SUBORDINATE TO JUSTIFY AN EXPENDITURE

To:
From:
Date:
Subject: Justification for Purchase

The budget printout of last month's purchases for your unit contains costs totaling $3,564.00 for conferences and seminars. I am aware that two members of your department planned to attend the National Telecommunications Conference, but this charge seems larger than the one I'd expected to see.

Could you provide me with details about this expense? I'd like this information no later than this Thursday.

MEMO WRITER TIPS

1. Include the amount and type of expenditure and let the reader know why you have concerns about it.

2. Ask for the justification in a non-threatening way. Often, asking a question will allow you to accomplish this.

PHRASING ALTERNATIVES

Paragraph 1

Please provide me with an explanation of why the lens shipment we anticipated would cost $6,931.00 actually cost $8,473.12. Since we had limited funds available for this purchase, every dollar must be accounted for.

You recently purchased $1,378.00 worth of books for the resource library. This seems a rather high purchase for a single accounting period. Prepare a brief report explaining the nature of this cost.

I have questions about the equipment purchased recently for the medical laboratory. I thought we had agreed Fulhaven Industries would provide us with the lowest prices; however, these items were purchased from another supplier, at what would seem to be a higher price. Fill me in on this.

UNAUTHORIZED FUEL PURCHASES*

To:
From:
Date:
Subject: Unauthorized Fuel Purchases

Only the purchase of gasoline from self-service pumps is authorized for agency vehicles. Purchases of gasoline from full-service pumps is strictly prohibited.

---

*This memorandum was written by the department manager of a state government agency.

In order to spend dollars wisely, gasoline purchases must be made at the lowest possible price. Your cooperation in this matter is needed now. Thank you for your compliance with this policy.

MEMO WRITER TIPS

1. State what the policy is for authorized fuel purchases, rather than beginning with the negative approach of what is not authorized.

2. Explain why the policy is important and affirm your expectation that the policy will be followed.

PHRASING ALTERNATIVES

Paragraph 1

Fuel purchases need to be made at company-operated pumps whenever possible. Purchases made at area service stations cannot exceed the $25.00 limit for such purchases.

Your purchase of gasoline from a vendor not on the approved list of suppliers cannot be reimbursed. Please use only those gasoline stations on your list.

Paragraph 2

Making authorized fuel purchases will help conserve money budgeted for vehicle maintenance.

Thank you for adhering to these guidelines by making only authorized fuel purchases.

13

Model Memos about Sensitive Issues

Writing about sensitive issues challenges even the best business writer. This challenge involves choosing the best words, phrasing them in the most appropriate tone, and conveying what may often be disturbing messages without disrupting operations or placing yourself in legal jeopardy.

The model memoranda in Chapter 13 target a variety of sensitive topics. Whether you're writing a memorandum to announce a strike action, informing employees about drug testing, discussing incidents of racial discrimination, dealing with charges of sexual harassment, or reprimanding an employee for alcohol abuse on the job, the memoranda in this chapter provide you with a framework for communicating your ideas and decisions.

Of course, legal counsel will provide you with definitive guidance about how to handle some of these situations. It's likely your organization also has policies to guide you in your decision making when sensitive topics are concerned. Add information about your firm's policies to the model memos in this chapter, but realize these models do not take the place of adequate legal advice. They can, however, offer you the words, phrases, and structure you need to write memoranda about sensitive issues.

ANNOUNCING A STRIKE ACTION

To:
From:
Date:
Subject: Strike Action

Since agreement cannot be reached with management regarding the renewal of our Contract Agreement, a strike action has been authorized, beginning at midnight, January 15, 19____ .

Arbitration will continue in an effort to resolve our major demands:

1. A pay increase of 7.8 percent.
2. The option of childcare or childcare-referral benefits.
3. Employer-paid medical insurance.

When we have resolved these issues, the membership of Local 271 will once again provide the excellent level of service previously furnished to the company.

MEMO WRITER TIPS

1. Address when the strike is to begin and reiterate the demands of the striking employees.

2. Say under what conditions you will return to work.

3. Make it clear that the strike is the last resort, that you would prefer to return to work as soon as the issues at hand have been settled.

PHRASING ALTERNATIVES

Paragraph 1

A strike vote has been taken of the members of Local 261, the Electrical Workers of America. Since management is not willing to compromise and at least consider the demands we have put forth, we have no alternative but to strike, effective midnight Friday, March 14, 19____ .

Until the issues before management can be satisfactorily resolved, the membership of Local #242, the United Plant Workers of America, will be on strike.

Members of Local 1456, Construction Workers of America, are on strike, pending negotiations on our work contract.

Paragraph 2

The existing demands on the table include (1) safe work conditions, and (2) a pay increase of $.56 per hour.

Binding arbitration should be able to resolve the issues of work hours, pay benefits, and promotional opportunities for employees.

We are ready to return to work as soon as we come to agreement on the $2,400.00-per-year salary increase we are seeking for our members.

ANNOUNCING MANDATORY DRUG TESTING

To:
From:
Date:
Subject: Drug Testing

In our efforts to maintain a safe work environment, we must ensure that all employees are drug-free. To this end, we are announcing a mandatory drug testing program, to become effective on Monday, July 1, 19____ .

Under this policy, employees will be randomly asked to provide urine samples on the premises, which will then be analyzed by Colton Laboratories. Reports of such tests will be held in the strictest confidence, and employees will be notified when a positive drug test occurs.

Such tests are authorized by the agreement you signed when you were hired by the company. If you have any questions about this policy, contact the personnel office at ext. 809.

Thank you for your cooperation.

MEMO WRITER TIPS

1. Let employees know when drug testing will begin and why this policy has been implemented.

2. Tell them what process will be followed during drug testing, and assure them that results will be confidential.

PHRASING ALTERNATIVES

Paragraph 1

Our mandatory drug testing program will begin on Monday, March 15. Since employees handle potentially hazardous materials, the company has the responsibility of protecting all its employees by maintaining a drug-free workplace.

The lives of passengers are in your hands. Only through peak performance and mental and physical health can their safety be assured. For this reason, no employee can be allowed to operate a vehicle while impaired by drugs. Mandatory drug testing will be implemented, effective Monday, January 14, 19_____ .

Paragraph 2

Details of the testing program will be outlined at an upcoming meeting. Test results will be strictly confidential and will be used only to refer employees to appropriate drug rehabilitation programs, when necessary.

The attached pamphlet explains the drug testing program in detail and provides you with specific information about how and when testing will be carried out. Test results will be returned to me, and I will distribute these results to employees. Strict confidentiality will be maintained at all times.

Drug testing will involve the following steps: . . . I can assure you that your drug test results will be made known only to me and to you.

Paragraph 3

Contact the Human Resources Division should you have questions about how this policy will affect you.

Jan Hopper in personnel (ext. 102) will be happy to answer any questions you might have about the drug testing program.

Refer any questions about this testing program to your immediate supervisor.

COMMUNICATING ABOUT HIV AND AIDS

To:
From:
Date:
Subject: HIV and AIDS

HIV and AIDS are life-threatening infections. Those infected may exhibit no symptoms for many years after contracting the virus. There are many myths about HIV and AIDS, but there are also some facts:

HIV and AIDS are transmitted from one person to another through body fluids: blood, semen, vaginal secretions, urine. Neither of these infections is transmitted by casual contact: casual touch, toilet seats, drinking fountains, cups or drinking glasses, and so on. The most common modes of transmission are sexual intercourse/activity, blood transfusions, or tainted hypodermic needles.

Since infected people come in all ages, shapes, sizes, and backgrounds, there is no way to tell whether someone has HIV or AIDS. Medical testing is the only reliable way to diagnose HIV or AIDS infection. Anyone who has had sex, uses or has used a hypodermic needle, has had a blood transfusion, or has exchanged body fluids with an infected person is at risk for getting HIV or AIDS. These infections may incubate for years without any visible symptoms.

We should all do what we can to learn the facts about this serious illness. There are several brochures in the Personnel Office that can provide you with more information.

Let's find out. Let's be safe.

MEMO WRITER TIPS

1. Provide employees with the facts about HIV and AIDS.

2. Take added precautions in occupations that serve HIV and AIDS survivors.

3. Communicate openly and honestly.

4. Obtain legal advice when dealing with employees who are infected. The rights of survivors and others must be protected.

DISCIPLINING AN EMPLOYEE FOR SUBSTANCE ABUSE

To:
From:
Date:
Subject: Substance Abuse

On Saturday, February 15, 19_____, you reported for work while under the influence of drugs, a clear violation of company policy. Effective immediately, you are suspended from duty without pay for the next 14 days. Contact the personnel office before you leave work today, so that they may refer you to drug counseling and rehabilitation services.

You are a valued member of our operation. However, any further incidents of this nature will lead to immediate dismissal (Section 1, Paragraph 14, of the Employee Handbook). I hope you will seek the treatment necessary to overcome this problem.

MEMO WRITER TIPS

1. Provide the employee with specific information about when the infraction occurred. You must be sure of your facts before you can even begin to address this problem. Cite what day the employee reported for work under the influence.

2. Spell out what disciplinary action is being taken.

3. If your company has services designed to treat alcohol and drug abuse problems, refer the employee to these services.

PHRASING ALTERNATIVES

Paragraph 1

When you came to work on Friday, August 8, you were obviously under the influence of some kind of substance. When I confronted you, you admitted that you had used drugs prior to coming to work. The nature of your work requires you to function at peak mental capacity, and substance abuse on the job is cause for immediate termination.

Your work performance has been seriously hampered by your continuous incidents of reporting for duty under the influence of illegal drugs.

Substance abuse cannot be tolerated. Since you were under the influence of drugs last Wednesday evening when you came to work, disciplinary action will be taken.

Paragraph 2

You are terminated from employment with Avery Enterprises, effective today. Under company policy, reporting for work under the influence of drugs leaves you no grievance rights or other avenues for continuing employment with us.

You are, therefore, suspended for 10 days without pay. You will immediately enroll yourself in a drug rehabilitation program, and any further occurrences of this kind will result in immediate dismissal.

A counselor from our Employee Assistance Program will contact you to arrange drug counseling services. If you refuse such counseling, you can no longer remain in our employ.

Paragraph 3

I regret that this action must be taken, but the safety and welfare of your co-workers demands that every employee work drug-free.

You are directed to make use of all services available to you, in order to rectify this problem. Should you refuse, you leave me no alternative but to fire you immediately.

I hope you can resolve this problem and return to work drug-free. You have been a valuable employee, and I hope you want to continue working here.

DOCUMENTING INSTANCES OF SEXUAL HARASSMENT

To: File
From:
Date:
Subject: Sexual Harassment Incident

On Monday, February 22, 19/20____, at approximately, 10:12 a.m., Mr. Hammond called me into his office. He complimented me on my outfit and said he had several "things we need to discuss."

He kept surveying me from head to toe as I walked to his conference table. He sat at the head of the table. He asked me to sit in the chair to his right. I sat down and pulled my dress down over my knees.

He began the conversation.

Hammond: "You know, Honey, I always knew you had a lot of potential."
Wright: "Mr. Carter, my name is Violet, not Honey."
Hammond: "Yeah, you're pretty as a violet. I keep forgetting about all this women's lib junk."
Wright: "Mr. Carter, please call me Violet."
Hammond: "Okay. Okay. Don't make a big deal out of it."
Wright: "What was it you wanted to talk to me about?"
Hammond: "I want to tell you how to get ahead in my department."
Wright: "I'd appreciate any suggestions you could give me."
Hammond: "Well, you know, I have lots of suggestions. I could really help you. I could be your mentor. Maybe you'd like to discuss it further after work, over a few drinks. What do you say?"
Wright: "I don't drink."
Hammond: "Then I guess you don't want to get ahead?"

Wright: "Mr. Hammond, we can discuss my performance right here."
Hammond: "I just thought it would be more comfortable if we were in more informal surroundings. I didn't mean anything by it."
Wright: "Well, perhaps, I misunderstood."

At this point, Mr. Hammond put his right hand on my knee.

I jumped up out of the chair and said, "I think this conversation is over. I feel very uncomfortable. Please don't ever touch me like that again."

Mr. Hammond then said, "Well, your future's in your hands, Honey."

I left his office and went back to my own. I closed the door and cried. This is the third time he's put me in an uncomfortable situation.

MEMO WRITER TIPS

1. Document all incidents of sexual harassment.

2. Be as specific as possible. Include information about days, dates, times, places, circumstances.

3. Quote the harasser whenever possible.

4. Document incidents as soon after they occur as possible.

5. Write thorough, factual information.

6. If the incidents persist, refer to your organization's sexual harassment policy.

DRUG-FREE WORKPLACE GUIDELINES

To:
From:
Date:
Subject: Drug-Free Workplace

As a condition of employment, drug screenings are administered to all new hires. This affirms our commitment to providing a drug-free workplace for all staff.

All employees are expected to be drug-free, except for those drugs prescribed and monitored by an attending physician. Alcohol is also considered a drug. Therefore, alcoholic beverages are prohibited at all company functions and on company premises, including the company parking lot.

Employees suspected of being under the influence of alcohol or drugs while at work will be asked to take a drug screening. Employees who refuse to take the drug screening when asked will be sent home; they will not be paid for that day's work.

Staff who have a positive drug test result will be suspended for three days without pay the first time and referred to the company Employee Assistance Program. Employees who have a second positive test will be suspended for one week without pay and be required to participate in drug and alcohol counseling. Employees who have a third positive test will be terminated on the spot.

Our environment requires that staff perform optimally and safely at all times. To do this, we must be drug- and alcohol-free. We are proud to work for an organization that does its best to preserve a positive, safe working environment for all, and I appreciate your support of these efforts.

MEMO WRITER TIPS

1. Spell out your company's policy in clear, precise terms.
2. Discuss the benefits of a drug-free workplace.
3. Enlist the support of staff.

ENDING A MEMO WAR

To:
From:
Date:
Subject: Stop the Memo War Now!

Fourteen memos are currently sitting on my desk. You and Stan are obviously engaged in a prolonged memo war. This means the issue you need to resolve must be handled face-to-face. If it is not, the memos will continue.

I recall that the original issue involved Stan's reprimanding one of the associates in your section. The war could have ended then, had you simply met with Stan and told him something like, "Stan, I appreciate your interest in my section, but I'd feel much more comfortable discussing problems with staff members myself. In the future, if you'll let me know when a problem arises, I'll be happy to address the issue with my staff, if it is warranted."

Instead, a one-on-one meeting never occurred, and the issue has now gotten out of hand. When an episode escalates to this point, it ceases to be about a tangible incident and degenerates into a personal attack.

I don't care who started the war. I just care that it ends now. Call Stan and arrange a meeting. When you and he have resolved this matter, schedule an appointment with me to let me know how it was resolved.

MEMO WRITER TIPS

1. Call for an end to the memo war and explain why.
2. Specify the actions you'd like the "warriors" to take.
3. Suggest conflict-resolution strategies.

EXPLAINING A DEPARTMENTAL ERROR TO A SUPERIOR

To:

From:

Date:

Subject: Departmental Error

Last month, the central accounting office changed its computer program for payroll processing. When this change was made, some of the stored information was not transferred to the new data base. Consequently, several errors occurred in employee paychecks: (1) medical benefits were not deducted, (2) annuity deductions were not made, and (3) errors occurred in federal withholding calculations.

Each of the employees affected has been contacted, and this error has been explained. My staff has been working overtime to input all missing data, so that corrections can be made on the August 30 payroll run.

Had I double-checked the information before paychecks were run, this would not have happened. There is no excuse, but I can assure you that I have implemented a verification system that will ensure this does not happen again.

MEMO WRITER TIPS

1. Explain the error in as much detail as possible.

2. Explain why the error occurred, being sure to take ultimate responsibility for it, if that is appropriate.

3. Tell how the error is being corrected.

4. Give an assurance that you have implemented proper procedures to make sure the error does not recur.

PHRASING ALTERNATIVES

Paragraph 1

Several departments have been without essential supplies for the past 14 days, because some purchase requisitions were filed though the orders had not yet been placed.

The customer calls you received about billing errors have been researched. This billing error occurred because customer bills were calculated using an incorrect discount formula.

The food and beverage orders for the upcoming conference will have to be filled by another supplier since the original vendor was never given an order confirmation.

Paragraph 2

These supplies will be given rush priority and will arrive no later than the end of this week.

The correct formula has now been programmed into the computer, so all future bills will be calculated correctly.

The new vendor has assured us that adequate food and beverages will be available for the conference dinner.

Paragraph 3

I will personally supervise any future transactions to make sure this does not happen again.

Please accept my assurance that the problem has been resolved, adequate training has been instituted, and this situation will not arise again.

I can assure you adequate steps have been taken to resolve the matter.

EXPLAINING AN EMPLOYEE ERROR*

To:

From:

Date:

Subject: Error in Airline Reservations

I made an error in ordering tickets for your Dallas to Nashville flight on August 5. Instead of booking you on a non-stop flight, I booked you on a flight with three stops.

New, first-class travel arrangements have been made.

<u>Departure:</u>

Comstock Airlines, Flight #46

Leaves Dallas	August 5	1:00 p.m.
Arrives Nashville		5:10 p.m.

<u>Return Flight:</u>

Comstock Airlines, Flight #112

Leaves Nashville	August 7	2:42 p.m.
Arrives Dallas		6:23 p.m.

Thank you for bringing this error to my attention. Enjoy your trip.

MEMO WRITER TIPS

1. Explain what error was made and why.
2. Take responsibility for the error and explain how it has been corrected.

PHRASING ALTERNATIVES

Paragraph 1

The brochure you ordered, "Excellence in Education," has a number of typographical errors in it.

Instead of scheduling the staff meeting for Conference Room B, I put the meeting in the 4th floor conference room, which is already occupied on that date.

---

*This memorandum was written by a reservations clerk.

Dave Kendall was to have reported to Maxwell Company to repair their telephone system on January 15 at 3:00 p.m. Because of an error on the dispatch form, he reported to the wrong address.

Paragraph 2

If you will return the proofs of the brochure to the printing office, we will proofread the document again, make necessary corrections, and prepare a second set of proofs for your review—at no additional cost.

I regret any inconvenience the room assignment may have caused you, but I can assure your future assignments will be double-checked.

I have called the customer to explain what happened. Their equipment has been repaired, and they have been given a 20 percent discount on their bill to make up for the error. In the future, dispatchers will read addresses back to customers, to make sure dispatchers record the correct address.

HANDLING A DISCRIMINATION COMPLAINT

To:
From:
Date:
Subject: Discrimination Charge

I have received and reviewed the discrimination complaint you made regarding your supervisor, Mr. Edward Timmons. As per company policy, all allegations will be thoroughly investigated by the Equal Employment Opportunity Committee, whose next meeting is scheduled for Friday, October 10, 19____ . This committee will take approximately 30 days to interview parties involved and render its decision regarding your complaint. The decision of this committee is final and binding on both parties.

Let me assure you that this company is committed to equal opportunity for all employees, regardless of race, ethnic background, or national origin. Allegations of discriminatory practices are taken very seriously, and violations of equitable treatment policies, if found, are not tolerated.

Expect to hear from this office no later than November 11. Thank you for bringing this situation to my attention.

> **MEMO WRITER TIPS**
>
> 1. Follow company policy and directives when handling allegations of racial discrimination.
> 2. Acknowledge that the complaint has been received and review what steps will be taken to investigate the complaint.
> 3. Let the complainant know when he/she can expect to hear the results of the charges.
> 4. Assure the complainant that all necessary action will be taken to resolve the matter in a fair and equitable way.
> 5. Seek legal advice if necessary.

PHRASING ALTERNATIVES

Paragraph 1

Your complaint of adverse action based on racial discrimination has been received and is currently being investigated.

I have received your racial discrimination complaint. Be assured that the necessary steps are being taken to thoroughly research and investigate this matter.

I want to assure that you that the complaint you recently filed (Complaint #22-46) alleging actions of a discriminatory nature will be dealt with in the most fair and equitable way possible.

Paragraph 2

Section 29, Paragraph 3, of the Policy and Procedures Manual outlines the steps to be taken next. You can expect to know the results of this process no later than November 4.

After a thorough investigation of the charges by an impartial party, you will be notified of the results of the investigation within 30 days.

The thorough investigation of this matter will take approximately 45 days to complete, at which time you will be notified of the decision made by the Complaint Review Panel.

Paragraph 3

Our agency prides itself on its commitment to equal hiring and promotional practices, and any violations of this process will be dealt with swiftly and fairly.

This organization does not condone or tolerate racial and ethnic discrimination, and when charges such as yours are brought, we take those charges very seriously and want to resolve the matter as expeditiously as possible.

You can be certain that if racial discrimination practices can be substantiated, every effort necessary to eradicate these practices will be taken.

HANDLING A SEXUAL HARASSMENT COMPLAINT

To:
From:
Date:
Subject: Sexual Harassment Allegations

Your recent charges of sexual harassment are disturbing. An investigation into the allegations was begun today, and the results of that investigation should be available within 30 days.

During that time, you are being reassigned to the Pathology Laboratory, pending the outcome of these investigations. This should alleviate any reprisals that might result from filing such charges.

Be assured that this company neither condones nor tolerates violations of its fair practices policy. Your allegations, if substantiated, will result in whatever steps are necessary to rectify the problem, including criminal prosecution if it is warranted.

MEMO WRITER TIPS

1. Follow the established practices for dealing with issues of sexual harassment.

2. Acknowledge the receipt of the complaint and explain to the employee what steps will be taken to resolve the issue.

3. Let the employee know when he/she can expect to receive the results of the investigation.

4. Assure the employee that sexual harassment will not be tolerated.

PHRASING ALTERNATIVES

Paragraph 1

I have received and am in the process of reviewing your charges of sexual harassment.

Any charge of sexual harassment is taken seriously and evaluated thoroughly.

Your sexual harassment complaint has been received and is being processed by this office.

Paragraph 2

Your Employee Handbook outlines the steps to be followed when such allegations are made. As outlined there, you will be notified of the findings of the investigating body within 45 days.

Both employees involved will be interviewed, as will other employees who may have witnessed inappropriate actions. Following this, the Fair Practices Task Force will evaluate the complaint and all pertinent testimony and make a decision about the charges. Their decision is binding and will be rendered in a hearing to be held no more than 60 days from the date of the initial complaint.

The charges you have made will be thoroughly investigated and, if corroborated, will result in appropriate action. You should hear something in the way of findings no more than 30 days from now. If you have questions in the interim, feel free to contact me.

Paragraph 3

Harassment under any circumstances is a serious and disturbing matter and will be dealt with harshly.

This company values all its employees and makes no decisions based on matters of sex or race. The fair practices doctrine of the company will be upheld.

I can assure you that everything possible will be done to get to the bottom of this matter. Even the perception of sexual harassment episodes is something our organization can ill afford and will not tolerate.

HANDLING PREJUDICE AGAINST EMPLOYEES-OF-COLOR

To:
From:
Date:
Subject: Racial Incidents

A disturbing practice of using racial slurs and telling racial jokes has begun to develop. While this agency cannot control the opinions of its workers, it can control the actions of its workers. Any display of racial prejudice which hampers the work efforts of employees is strictly prohibited. The intimidation and/or harassment of minority employees of this firm will not be tolerated.

A series of racial awareness seminars will be conducted over the coming month. Each and every member of this plant WILL attend, and each and every member of this plant will work together harmoniously without any further incidents of racial bigotry or harassment.

I hope I have made myself VERY clear. Learn to work together or find work elsewhere.

MEMO WRITER TIPS

1. Episodes of prejudice are certain to occur in the workplace and must be dealt with quickly and forthrightly.

2. Let employees know where the company stands as far as racial incidents are concerned.

3. Make it clear what the consequences of continued racial problems are.

4. If necessary, schedule workshops or meetings to discuss this issue. The memorandum serves as simply a reminder since problems this serious cannot be dealt with on paper alone.

PHRASING ALTERNATIVES

Paragraph 1

Several members of minority groups have made complaints to me about your use of racial slurs and epithets. Let me assure you that such conduct will not be tolerated.

I take a very hard line when it comes to even the perception of unfair or harmful treatment based on race. Any behavior that interferes with the productivity of employees will be eliminated immediately.

You will refrain from any further behavior that demeans the character and background of the racial minorities employed by this organization.

Paragraph 2

I will be closely monitoring the conduct of workers in your section, and let me assure you any further racial incidents will be dealt with swiftly.

You will report to me weekly on the progress you are making in resolving racial problems.

I cannot believe that you made those remarks, and I know that you will not make them again.

Paragraph 3

This agency operates on a policy of fair treatment for all its employees. Either adhere to this policy or suffer the consequences of continued violations.

I am certain you will want to follow the equal treatment guidelines set forth by this organization.

I do not want to revisit this issue again. See to it that I don't have to.

MAINTAINING OPERATIONS DURING A STRIKE

To:
From:
Date:
Subject: Strike—Coverage of Work Details

Local 242 has announced a strike, effective at midnight tomorrow night. All managers will report for duty to handle operations during this strike. Managers should begin advertising for temporary workers, to replace those on strike.

I am confident a new agreement will be reached soon. In the interim, thank you for helping to make operations go as smoothly as possible.

MEMO WRITER TIPS

1. Tell when the strike action is effective.

2. Let managerial personnel know what their duties and responsibilities will be during the strike action. In many cases, this may involve a specific list of personnel by name and their assigned tasks.

3. Thank the employees for managing operations during the strike.

PHRASING ALTERNATIVES

Paragraph 1

A strike is slated to begin on Monday, September 3. Schools will be closed until this action can be resolved. All principals and assistant principals are to report to their schools as scheduled. During this time, you will be expected to answer telephone calls and inquiries from parents and community members.

Negotiations have not yet been reached on the nurses' new collective bargaining agreement. If a strike does occur at midnight on April 1, each of you will be called upon to do whatever is necessary to ensure the care of patients.

A strike of Local 65 seems unavoidable at this time. Supervisors will report for duty at 12:00 noon on Friday if this occurs, and work assignments will be distributed at that time.

Paragraph 2

The attached roster lists the work assignments of supervisory personnel: . . . Your efforts during this emergency are greatly appreciated.

I want to extend to you my warmest appreciation for your efforts to keep us operational during this crisis.

Thank you for your assistance. Hopefully, this strike will be over soon.

RESOLVING A DISPUTE BETWEEN ANTAGONISTIC SUBORDINATES

To:
From:
Date:
Subject: Co-Worker Cooperation

My repeated efforts to resolve the differences between you and Jamison have been largely unsuccessful. Report to my office on Monday, June 4. The three of us will sit down and work out a plan that will allow the two of you to work together. If we cannot do that, then we will have to discuss reassignments or other steps that may be taken to resolve this matter. See you Monday.

MEMO WRITER TIPS

1. Subordinates who do not get along is an issue that should be resolved in a face-to-face conference.
2. Use this memorandum to announce what steps you are planning to get the workers to cooperate.
3. Make it clear that you expect them to work out their differences.

PHRASING ALTERNATIVES

Paragraph 1

Your inability to work harmoniously is beginning to affect the overall operations of your section. This cannot be tolerated. I am giving you one more chance to sit down and discuss your differences and develop a plan that will allow you and Mr. Hanrahan to function in a cooperative spirit. I'll expect a report within two weeks on the outcome of your negotiations.

The differences Ms. Curry and you have are costing us time and money. Get your differences resolved and get on with it. If not, I will be forced to take measures to resolve this situation myself.

I have scheduled a conference on Wednesday so that you, Ken, and I can discuss the problems you are having working together. Draw up a list of your differences, as well as a list of potential solutions to these differences and bring them with you. We will meet at 3:00 p.m. in my office.

STEERING A SUBORDINATE TO THE EMPLOYEE ASSISTANCE PROGRAM

To:
From:
Date:
Subject: Employee Assistance Program

Our Employee Assistance Program offers a variety of counseling services aimed at helping employees with financial, personal, or stress challenges. I'm enclosing a copy of the brochure that outlines these services for your information.

Many of these services are provided either free of charge or on a sliding-fee schedule, based on your ability to pay. Your use of these services is strictly confidential.

I know that you have been under a great deal of stress lately and encourage you to take advantage of the assistance available through this program.

MEMO WRITER TIPS

1. Don't put the employee on the defensive by beginning this memo by talking about the employee's problems. Simply outline the services available through the assistance program and enclose other pertinent information that details the services.

2. Tell what kind of services the program offers and what the costs, if any, are.

3. Reassure the employee that confidentiality will be used to allay any fears the employee may have about using the services.

4. Close by saying you hope the employee will use the services, and include what led you to write this memorandum.

PHRASING ALTERNATIVES

Paragraph 1

Many fine problem-solving opportunities are available through the company's Employee Assistance Program (details enclosed).

I recognize that our employees work here as whole persons. The problem is, their personal lives can sometimes influence their on-the-job performance. For this reason, the company has contracted the counseling services available through its Employee Assistance Program.

Look over the information I've attached about our Employee Assistance Program. You may find the personal, confidential counseling services offered by licensed professionals helpful.

Paragraph 2

The initial consultation is free, and the other counseling sessions are offered at a reduced rate to company employees. All information discussed in these sessions is held in strictest confidence.

Employees can avail themselves of top-notch counseling at significantly lower rates than would be available if they sought out these services on their own. Using these services would in no way reflect negatively on their work here, since all dealings with the EAP company are strictly confidential.

Services are provided on a sliding-fee scale, and your confidentiality would be maintained throughout.

Paragraph 3

I suggest you look into the services provided by EAP. They may be able to help you get through a difficult period in your life.

Use these services if you think they'd be helpful.

I know you've been having some problems lately, and I think EAP might be able to help.

SUGGESTING CONFLICT-RESOLUTION TECHNIQUES

To:
From:
Date:
Subject: Conflict-Resolution Strategies

Conflict is often a constructive way to move past obstacles and derive new solutions to old problems. Conflict can also be destructive. Here are a few conflict-resolution techniques you might find helpful:

1. Identify the real source of conflict.
2. Brainstorm ways to promote a win-win outcome.
3. Talk face-to-face with the person with whom you're in conflict.
4. At the outset, stress that you are anxious to resolve the conflict.
5. Using "I" messages, say how the conflict has made you feel, such as "I feel really frustrated that we can't seem to work this out."
   or "I feel stupid when you speak to me in that tone of voice."
6. Often, asking questions rather than making statements facilitates resolution, such as "Why are you speaking to me in that tone of voice?"
   or "What is there about this issue that seems to be making you so angry?"
   or "What can I do to straighten this mess out?"
   or "What could I do to make this right for you?"
   Questions prompt us to be focused internally rather than externally.
7. Never resort to name calling or personal attacks. Address the issue, not the person. Remember, "A bell can never be unrung." Don't say things in anger you'll regret later.
8. Write down thoughts or suggestions.
9. Shake hands with the other person. Physical contact often diminishes barriers.

Remember, the goal is to reach viable solutions, even if one party has to agree to disagree about them. Make your conflict constructive by using these techniques.

SUMMARIZING LABOR NEGOTIATION PROCEEDINGS

To:
From:
Date:
Subject: Update on Labor Negotiations

Negotiators met with the leadership of Local 42 again today and here is the status of those negotiations:

1. Management offered a 4.3 percent pay raise; labor maintains its 7.8 percent raise demand. Progress is being made on this issue, however.
2. Labor agreed to drop the request for two additional paid holidays per year.
3. Some progress was made on the issue of healthcare benefits. Labor proposed that the company pay 80 percent of these benefits and employees pay 20 percent. Management is proposing a 60/40 split of these costs.

Meetings will resume tomorrow at 6:00 a.m. I will keep you up to date on proceedings as events occur.

MEMO WRITER TIPS

1. Let the reader know when meetings occurred.

2. Outline each point of negotiation and summarize what progress has been made on resolving each issue.

3. Let readers know when they can expect the next update.

PHRASING ALTERNATIVES

Paragraph 1

Here is a summary of negotiations held on Monday, August 24:

The list of union demands and the status of negotiations with regard to each are as follows:

Little progress has been made in the labor dispute as of 10:00 p.m. today. Management presented its latest proposal, but labor rejected it completely. No new negotiations have been scheduled.

Paragraph 2

Negotiations will continue through the night, and I'll prepare another update tomorrow morning.

Union membership is expected to vote on the latest package this evening. I will report the results of that vote as soon as they become available.

WARNING AN EMPLOYEE
ABOUT DRINKING ON THE JOB

To:
From:
Date:
Subject: Drinking on the Job

This is a warning that if you report for work while intoxicated again, you will be dismissed immediately. Drinking on the job cannot be tolerated, and this policy has been discussed with you twice before.

I assume that if you value your continued employment with this company you will come to work alcohol-free.

MEMO WRITER TIPS

1. Follow your company policy about handling incidents of this nature.
2. Make it clear to the employee that drinking on the job will not be tolerated.

PHRASING ALTERNATIVES

Paragraph 1

You are terminated immediately for drinking on the job. Previous discussions about this have not corrected the problem, and we can no longer keep you in our employ.

I have reason to believe that you were drinking on the job last evening. Though I cannot prove it, I will be watching you closely, and if I can find proof, you will be terminated immediately.

Drinking on the job is cause for immediate dismissal. Consider this a warning, but if any future incidents occur, you will be let go on the spot.

14

Model Memos about Quality-of-Life Issues

Enhancing employees' quality of life enhances their ability to work productively. Progressive businesses recognize how employee welfare issues affect overall job performance. As society changes, the modern workforce reports for work with a host of other concerns: caring for children or elderly parents, balancing work with play, meshing work life with family and personal concerns.

The model memoranda in Chapter 14 can help you communicate about such quality-of-life subjects as:

- Childcare concerns
- Social activities
- Sports events
- Carpools
- Flexible time (flex-time) schedules
- Job sharing
- Clean work environments
- Wellness/fitness programs

Most of these memoranda will convey your ideas; all you have to do is add your company's specifics to the models. Satisfactory quality of life yields satisfactory work performance. Use the model memos in this chapter to satisfy your agency's memo-writing needs, where quality of life is concerned.

ANNOUNCING A
COMMUNITY-SERVICE PROJECT

To:
From:
Date:
Subject: Adopt-a-School Project

This year, we have an opportunity to show our support for this community by participating in an Adopt-A-School Project. This project is jointly sponsored by the Board of Education, KPPM-TV (Channel 8), and the Do-Right Foundation.

The project involves the following opportunities for service:

- Helping with school clean-up and beautification projects
- "Adopting" one class, visiting the class once each month, and talking to students and teachers
- Mentoring one child by calling and/or taking the child on one outing each month
- Attending monthly parent/teacher/student association meetings
- Visiting a child's home once per month
- Providing technical assistance at teacher in-service meetings
- Preparing holiday baskets for needy school families

Each option requires a minimum of one to two hours per month and a one-year or one-semester commitment. Formal training will be provided for all volunteers. If you are interested in participating in this community service project or would like more information, call me at ext. 345. The project will begin September 15, 19/20____ and last until June 6, 19/20____ . Each of us can change the world, one child at a time.

MEMO WRITER TIPS

1. Describe the project in as much detail as possible.
2. Let prospective volunteers know how much time will be required.
3. Provide contact information.
4. Stress the rewards of volunteerism.

ANNOUNCING A COMPANY-SPONSORED SOCIAL ACTIVITY*

To:
From:
Date:
Subject: Annual Christmas Party—December 19, 19____

You and a guest are invited to attend Hope Franklin Enterprises' 19____ Christmas party on December 19 from 4:00 p.m. to 8:00 p.m.

    The party will be held at Crown Inn, 489 West 10th Street, Banquet Room C. A cash bar opens at 4:00 p.m. Dinner will begin at 5:30 p.m.

    Please R.S.V.P. to Marshall Tucker by December 12, 19____. Hope to see you all there.

MEMO WRITER TIPS

1. Include all the specifics in the announcement: day, date, time, and location of party.
2. Describe what activities will take place at the party and let employees know whether guests are welcome.
3. Include any special dress requirements.

PHRASING ALTERNATIVES

Paragraph 1

    This year's Christmas party will be held on Friday, December 18 from 6:00 p.m.–9:00 p.m., in the employee cafeteria.

    Come one, come all to the July 4 picnic. This year we'll have it at Broadway Park, 20th and Broadway. Mel Brown has a sign-up sheet for side dishes and paperware. The company will furnish meat and beverages.

    I'd like to extend a personal invitation for all of you and one guest to join me for our annual banquet. This year's banquet will be held at the Roadside Inn, Junction 4 and Bluff Roads, in the main dining room. A social hour will begin at 6:00 p.m.; dinner will be served at 7:00 p.m. Dancing will follow until ?????? Men are asked to wear suit coat and tie; ladies are asked to wear after-five attire.

---

*This memorandum was written by a vice-president of an educational corporation.

Paragraph 2

Call Jo (ext. 230) if you plan to attend.

A sign-up sheet has been posted in the staff lounge.

RSVP (regrets only) to John, ext. 62.

ANNOUNCING A COMPANY-SPONSORED SPORTS ACTIVITY

To:

From:

Date:

Subject: Softball Team

Brave souls are needed for this year's softball team. Those interested should meet in the employee lounge on Friday, June 30 at 4:00 p.m. to discuss a team name and upcoming games.

Softball experts need not apply!

MEMO WRITER TIPS

1. Tell what the sports activity is and who should participate in it.
2. Give particulars about meeting dates, times, locations.

PHRASING ALTERNATIVES

Paragraph 1

Any employee interested in participating in a golf tournament this June 14–17 should contact Ed Degard, ext. 94. I'm looking for professional golfers, but since we don't have any around here, anyone who's willing (and has their own clubs) can call.

Sign up for a day of fun in the sun, as we host this year's Games Day: Saturday, July 14, 10:00 a.m.–2:00 p.m., Rosewood Park. Refreshments will be provided, and guests (maximum 2 per employee) are welcome. A sign-up sheet is posted in the employee cafeteria.

Volunteers are needed to run in the Jarvis Run-for-Fun event on Saturday, August 2. This is a charitable event to raise funds for the McCook Public Library. Each runner will be asked to get a minimum of $50.00 in pledges. It promises to be a fun-filled day and a way for you to get to know the members of the community. Contact Mary Christian (ext. 21) if you're interested.

Paragraph 2

Be there or be square!

A good time will be had by all, so see you there.

Last year's fun day was a rousing success, and I hope we have an even bigger turn-out this year. See you next Saturday.

ANNOUNCING WELLNESS PROGRAM ACTIVITIES

To:

From:

Date:

Subject: Upcoming Wellness Activities

The following wellness activities have been scheduled for this month:

Tuesday, May 1, 19/20____	11:00 a.m.–12:00 noon	Mind, Body, Health Lecture
Wednesday, May 9, 19/20____	12:00 noon–1:30 p.m.	Low-Fat Lunch Buffet
Thursday, May 17, 19/20____	8:00 a.m.–9:00 a.m.	Yoga Session

(For yoga, wear loose clothing and bring a large towel or exercise mat.)

Friday, May 26, 19/20____	2:00 p.m.–3:00 p.m.	Massage Therapy

All sessions will be held in Room A, Fitness Center. The "Walk a Mile for Me" Club continues to walk each morning from 7:30 to 8:30 on the Fitness Center track. You may join the club at any time.

Get fit! Call me at the fitness Center, 234-5678, to register for sessions or to find out how you can improve your overall health.

MEMO WRITER TIPS

1. Describe the wellness activity in detail.

2. Discuss any special equipment or requirements.

3. Provide a contact name and telephone number.

ACQUAINTING A SUBORDINATE WITH CHILDCARE OPTIONS

To:
From:
Date:
Subject: Childcare Referral Service

A childcare referral service is another benefit offered to employees. The attached list contains descriptions of local childcare facilities. If you are interested in using one of these centers, you should contact them directly about the services they offer.

Placement on this list does not indicate company endorsement of individual childcare centers. Rather, I have simply listed the services available in this area. You must screen centers and come to your own conclusions about their suitability for your child(ren).

Since many employees use the facilities listed on this referral list, you might want to talk to several of them to find out whether or not they have been satisfied with their childcare placements.

If I can be of further assistance in this matter, call me at Extension 737.

MEMO WRITER TIPS

1. Briefly describe the childcare benefits your company offers. Today, many organizations have addressed the childcare needs of their workers either through referral services, on-site daycare, or payroll deductions for daycare services.

2. In the case of referral services, make it clear in your memo that the company assumes no responsibility for the quality of the services on the list, unless the company has screened daycare facilities.

PHRASING ALTERNATIVES

Paragraph 1

The attached list will familiarize you with daycare facilities currently being used by our employees. A childcare benefit option is available to new employees. You may have childcare costs deducted directly from your paycheck. When you pay 80 percent of the costs the company pays the other 20 percent. Contact the Human Resources Division if you are interested in this option.

Our on-site daycare center provides quality childcare to employees. Employees pay a standard fee of $80.00 per child per week (reduced rate for additional children). Contact the center director, Ms. Carolyn Franken, at ext. 433 for additional details.

A number of childcare facilities are within walking distance of our plant. Marge Drexel (ext. 12) maintains an up-to-date list of company-approved daycare centers. Contact her for additional information.

Paragraph 2

The company has pre-screened the facilities on the list, to ensure that they offer childcare consistent with minimal standards for daycare operation.

Our on-site facility currently has a six-month waiting list. If you are interested in using this center, sign up as soon as possible. In the interim, the center director can provide you with a list of neighborhood daycare facilities.

These centers have not been pre-screened. This is simply a referral list. Primary responsibility for determining the level of care offered by these facilities rests with each employee.

ACQUAINTING AN EMPLOYEE WITH ELDERCARE OPTIONS

To:

From:

Date:

Subject: Information about Eldercare

Here's the information on eldercare facilities and programs. As you can see, there are a number of programs, some close to our office. While I can't endorse a specific program, several employees have enrolled their parents in the program operated by Joiston Parks and Recreation (p. 3).

Most services provide either hourly, half-day, or all-day care for seniors. They also offer a broad range of activities, from water aerobics to community service. Each listing provides details about facilities, rates, activities, and medical services. Most fees are based on a sliding scale.

The programs listed in this brochure offer a 10 percent discount to our employees. I encourage you and your senior to visit the facilities that interest you before you select a program.

MEMO WRITER TIPS

1. Provide employees with specifics.
2. Discuss services and fees, if known.
3. Encourage employees to visit the eldercare programs themselves.
4. Refrain from endorsing a specific program.
5. Provide employees with a brochure or list of options.

ENCOURAGING EMPLOYEES TO CARPOOL

To:
From:
Date:
Subject: Employee Carpools

Our city's better-air campaign is now in full swing. All employees are encouraged to participate in carpools, in an effort to maintain a quality environment for us all. Carpools not only help to conserve fuel, promote clean air, and save money, but they also allow riders an alternative to fighting rush-hour traffic every day.

Carpool and ride-share lists are available in the Employee Relations Department. To offer a ride, become a member of an existing carpool, or start a new carpool, call Jan Brady, ext. 510.

Carpools work. Join one today.

MEMO WRITER TIPS

1. Discuss the benefits of carpooling.
2. Tell employees about existing carpools, whom they need to contact, and where they can sign up.
3. Close by offering a few final words about joining carpools.

PHRASING ALTERNATIVES

Paragraph 1

If you haven't looked into carpooling as a hassle-free way to get to work each day, do so today! We have operated a carpool referral service for the past three years, with very successful results.

Carpooling can provide you with a relaxing ride to work, for about 50 percent of what you are currently spending for fuel and other costs. Carpools keep the air cleaner, help co-workers get to know each other better, and relieve you of driving at least three weeks per month (in a four-person carpool). What more could you want?

Look into carpooling. It's a clean, safe alternative to the daily drudgery of driving to work alone.

Paragraph 2

A list of carpools is posted in the employee lounge, 1st floor. If you want to start a new carpool or join one that already exists, sign up on that list today.

The Regional Council of Governments (779-4833) offers a free carpool referral service, listing car- and vanpools originating from various points in the metropolitan area. Give them a call today.

Contact Pete Smyth, Room 42, about arranging a carpool or joining one.

Paragraph 3

Join a carpool today; you'll be glad you did.

Carpooling is encouraged. If you haven't thought about this option before, do so soon.

Investigate the benefits of carpooling today. What do you have to lose?

ENCOURAGING EMPLOYEE DONATIONS

To:
From:
Date:
Subject: Donations—Battered Women's Shelter

Transitions Battered Women's Shelter is in need of the following items:

- Deodorant, toothpaste, and soap
- Children's clothing and shoes

- Children's toys (new or used)
- Toilet paper, facial tissue, paper towels
- New or used women's clothing and shoes
- Overcoats

Please leave your donations in the drop-box outside Personnel, Room 304, by Friday, November 19. Whatever you can give will be greatly appreciated.

MEMO WRITER TIPS

1. Describe the organization requesting donations.
2. Detail where donations should be delivered.
3. Enlist employee support.

ENCOURAGING EMPLOYEE VOLUNTEERISM

To:
From:
Date:
Subject: Give Till It Helps!

Everyone wants to give around the holidays, but what about the rest of the year? There are many people in need in our community. And they don't always need money. Sometimes, they just need a little tender, loving care—a smile, a few moments, a conversation.

I have a list of dozens of community-service projects. And right now, I have more projects than I have volunteers. You could get involved in a mentoring program, a nursing-home visitation project, storytelling for preschoolers, or planting and painting projects. Most of the volunteer opportunities require minimal time, one to two hours per month.

All year round should be a season for giving. Won't you help? Call me at ext. 789 and volunteer. It will make a big difference in your life and in the lives of others.

MEMO WRITER TIPS

1. Stress the benefits of volunteerism.

2. Provide detailed information about volunteer opportunities.

3. Let interested employees know whom to contact.

INFORMING WORKERS ABOUT FLEX-TIME HOURS*

To:
From:
Date:
Subject: Flex-Time Work Hours

This is a reminder about the flex-time work schedule that goes into effect on Monday, September 1, 19_____. Employees may work either 6:00 a.m. to 2:30 p.m. or 8:00 a.m. to 4:30 p.m. You may report anytime between 6:00 a.m. and 8:00 a.m., working eight (8) hours from the time that you report for work. Core hours are 8:00 a.m. to 2:00 p.m. All employees are expected to be present (unless on authorized leave) during these hours.

We will pilot this program for the next 60 days to see how well it works and to correct any flaws in the system. Your cooperation as we offer this new option to employees is appreciated.

MEMO WRITER TIPS

1. Spell out the hours of work, indicating when employees may report for work, how long they must work each day, and when they may leave.

2. Be sure to point out what the "core" hours of operation are, those hours when all employees are expected to be on duty.

---

*This memorandum was written by a manager for a communications company.

PHRASING ALTERNATIVES

Paragraph 1

Our flexible-time (flex-time) work schedule goes into operation next Monday, October 15. Hours are as follows:

7:30 a.m.–9:00 a.m. Arrival time (You may come to work anytime between these hours.)

9:00 a.m.–3:00 p.m. Standard hours (All employees must be present.)

4:30 p.m.–6:00 p.m. Departure time (You may leave work during these hours, eight (8) hours from the time that you arrived.)

The new flex-time work hours, effective Monday, January 14, are listed below. Employees may choose the flex-time hours most convenient for them, but then must work this schedule each day. Notify your immediate supervisor if you would like to change your flex-time schedule.

We have worked out a flexible-hours (flex-time) schedule for arrival and departure times from work. This schedule will go into effect on Monday, August 4 and will continue throughout the test period, for the next 30 days. You may choose one of the following schedules:

6:00 a.m.–2:30 p.m.

6:30 a.m.–3:00 p.m.

7:00 a.m.–3:30 p.m.

7:30 a.m.–4:00 p.m.

8:00 a.m.–4:30 p.m.

8:30 a.m.–5:00 p.m.

Let your supervisor know which flex-time schedule you will be working.

INFORMING WORKERS ABOUT JOB-SHARING POSSIBILITIES

To:

From:

Date:

Subject: Job Sharing

A number of employees have requested information about job-sharing possibilities with the company. A task force was appointed to survey other companies that have such programs and work out a proposal for implementing similar opportunities at Fabrik Technologies.

A pilot job-sharing program will begin January 5, 19____ . Job sharing has been authorized for specific positions (see attached list). Two employees interested in sharing the responsibilities for one of these positions could both be authorized to work 20 hours per week. Benefits would be reduced to a part-time, permanent-employee level, and salary would be adjusted accordingly.

Employees interested in additional details about the program should contact me at ext. 4610 by November 1. I need to have the names of all personnel who will participate in this pilot job-sharing project by that time.

I think this represents an exciting opportunity to make work more compatible with family life, and I look forward to your participation in this new venture.

MEMO WRITER TIPS

1. Spell out the requirements for job sharing and let employees know which employees are eligible for such a program.

2. Describe how the job-sharing arrangement is to work.

3. Let employees know how they may find out additional information and whom they should contact if they are interested in sharing the responsibilities for their jobs.

PHRASING ALTERNATIVES

Paragraph 1

In an effort to continually upgrade the benefits offered to our employees, I am pleased to announce the new job-sharing option.

Several of you have inquired about job-sharing as an alternative to full-time employment. Such arrangements can now be made, but are limited to the positions listed on the attached list.

Any employee interested in part-time, job-share arrangements should contact me at ext. 422 for additional information.

Paragraph 2

Right now, opportunities for job sharing are limited to two employees performing the same job. These two employees, in accordance with procedures, would split the assignments of the job and work hours that would maintain an eight-hour-per-day work schedule. Of course, pay and benefits would be adjusted to the new 20-hour-per-week classification.

Interested employees, in conjunction with their managers, could design new work schedules—20 hours per week—and share the responsibilities of the job function.

The duties of approved job-sharing positions have been divided so that they could be handled by two workers. Pay and benefits would be changed accordingly.

Paragraph 3

Call me at ext. 26 if you are interested.

Employees interested in exploring this option should contact Bernice McKenna at Extension 21.

A meeting to discuss this new option has been scheduled for Friday, September 2, 19____, 2:00 p.m.–3:30 p.m., Room 101. All employees are welcome to attend.

MAINTAINING A CLEAN WORK ENVIRONMENT

To:
From:
Date:
Subject: Clean Work Areas

All employees are responsible for maintaining a clean work area, free of debris and litter, at all times. Equipment should be returned to storage lockers when you have finished using it. Any coffee cups, wrappers, and other paper items should be thrown away before you leave at the end of the day.

A clean work area reflects the pride I know each one of you has in the job you are doing. Your cooperation in keeping your work area clean is greatly appreciated.

MEMO WRITER TIPS

1. Remind employees that a clean work area is important.
2. Outline specifically what employees are responsible for doing.
3. Close by thanking employees for adhering to this policy.

PHRASING ALTERNATIVES

Paragraph 1

I need your cooperation in keeping the photocopier room clean. Please put any "bad" copies in the scratch paper bin. Return unused paper to the shelves so I can keep an accurate count of available stock.

Please make sure that your work area has been properly cleaned when your shift is over. I have received a number of complaints from second-shift workers about papers being left on the floor, machinery being left in the middle of the floor, etc. This should not happen.

Paragraph 2

Since customers constantly see our work areas, I want those areas to reflect the high level of professionalism we have in this firm. Making sure desks, floors, and wastebasket areas are litter-free will help project this image. Thank you.

I appreciate your assistance in maintaining a clean work environment for us all.

MOTIVATING EMPLOYEES TO USE WELLNESS-PROGRAM FACILITIES

To:
From:
Date:
Subject: Employee Wellness Facilities

Wellness facilities, including a gymnasium, racquetball courts, weight-lifting equipment, and stationary bicycles, have been installed for the benefit off all employees. In addition, aerobics classes are offered before and after work hours and during lunch hours. Wellness facilities, located on the 9th floor, are open from 6:00 a.m. until 7:00 p.m.

MEMO WRITER TIPS

1. Let employees know where the facilities are located, what the hours of operations are, and any special services that are offered.

2. Briefly describe the kind of services offered. Include a brochure, if one is available.

3. Close by letting employees know where they can call for more details.

Using these facilities can help you not only to keep fit but also to work off stress and have a healthier life. Call Ext. 340 to find out more.

PHRASING ALTERNATIVES

Paragraph 1

I am pleased to announce the grand opening of our new fitness center: Friday, June 12, 19____, 10:00 a.m., Suite 1146. Tours of the facility will be given, and sign-up sheets will be available for racquetball courts and exercise classes. Stop by and visit this latest addition to our health benefits package for employees.

The attached wellness program schedule outlines the schedule for our fitness center. Make use of these programs. They have been instituted to promote a healthier work environment for us all.

Paragraph 2

Connie Comstock is the Fitness Center Director. She can be reached at ext. 409 if you have questions or wish to sign up for special programs.

Contact Mitch Overton at ext. 2102 to find out how this fitness center can benefit you.

15

Report Memoranda

Memoranda provide a perfect package for the reports you have to write for your supervisor, your peers, or your subordinates. You'll research a specific topic or problem. You'll gather as much information—facts and figures—about that topic as you can. You'll analyze and interpret this information and then make recommendations or suggestions about how to improve what you discovered. Finally, you'll package your ideas in a memorandum report.

Often, you may use surveys or questionnaires to collect data for your report. One of the memoranda in Chapter 15 shows you how to write a transmittal memo for surveys or questionnaires. Sometimes, you'll have to prepare monthly, quarterly, or annual reports on work progress. You'll find a model memorandum to help you frame these progress reports as well. Other times, your work may involve site or branch store visits. A model site visit report has also been included in this chapter. There's a model report memorandum that discusses the progress of a task force or committee, as well as a model that asks subordinates for their reports.

Package your reports in memorandum fashion. The models provided in this chapter can help you do just that.

DISTRIBUTING A SURVEY*

To:
From:
Date:
Subject: Faculty Development Needs Assessment

The office of Instructional Services is in the process of determining faculty development needs for spring Semester and the coming academic year. Please take a few moments to let us know what kind(s) of training would be most useful to you.

Write your name (optional) and the subject you teach at the top of the form. For each item, circle the number that indicates your interest in the topic. Indicate "strong" interest in the topic by circling #1. Circle #2 if you have "some" interest in the topic and #3 if you have little or no interest in the topic.

Indicate whether you would attend a workshop on the topic by circling #4. If you would be willing to facilitate such a workshop, circle number 5.

Please return all completed questionnaires to the Office of Instructional Services no later than FRIDAY, OCTOBER 15, 19____ . A stamped, addressed envelope has been attached for your convenience, or you may return your completed survey to my office, Room 212.

Add any comments you care to; they are welcome. Thank you for your time and cooperation.

MEMO WRITER TIPS

1. In the first paragraph, let the reader know who is conducting the survey and why.
2. In the second paragraph, explain how the survey form should be filled out.
3. Let the reader know to whom and by when the survey should be returned.
4. Thank the reader for completing the survey.

---

*This memorandum was written by the Director of Faculty Development at a college.

PREPARING AN ANNUAL OR QUARTERLY REPORT FOR YOUR SECTION*

To:
From:
Date:
Subject: Annual Report 19____, Services Bureau

The following report outlines the accomplishments of the Services Bureau this year.

Word Processors

Word processors typed a total of 9,000 offense reports.

Cadet Program

During 19____, four (4) police cadets spent 7,800 hours in each of four (4) areas in the department:

1. Records/Communications—Duties in this area included records maintenance, forms inventory, records searches, guard license background checks, relief dispatching, counter service to citizens, mail runs, and miscellaneous errands.
2. Patrol—Cadets were involved in booking prisoners, taking counter reports, prisoner transport, patrol procedures, and patrol follow-up.
3. Photo Lab and Property Room—Cadets were involved in records maintenance, assistance at the firing range, crime and photo laboratory assistance, and property inventory.
4. Investigations—Cadets participated in records maintenance, photo file reorganization, contact-card file updates, the preparation of charts and graphs, and learning investigative techniques.

Evidence/Photo Crime Technician

1. Last year, 6,000 photographs and 1,700 mug shots were processed.
2. All property and evidence (212,000 pieces) was processed, stored, and released as necessary.
3. In addition, 150 unclaimed bicycles were donated to charitable organizations for distribution to needy children.

---

*This memorandum was written by an administrator of civilian personnel for a police department.

Records

1. Approximately 1,400 reports were sold to citizens, insurance companies, etc.
2. The records area was relocated and restructured to provide more efficient records service.
3. The Records Request Form was redesigned.
4. Hours for fingerprinting, guard licenses, and other services were standardized.
5. Also, 9,048 offense reports were processed and filed.
6. A new power file was purchased, resulting in faster records storage and retrieval.

Communications

1. A Regency 2152 phone system was purchased and installed.
2. The dispatch area was reconstructed to provide adequate security and greater efficiency.
3. A new Incident Report format was adopted, decreasing the time it takes to complete this initial call report by 1.7 minutes.
4. A Kodak ektagraphic map system was installed, to make the location of addresses, particularly in trailer parks, easier to find.
5. New warrant and arrest ledger procedures were implemented.
6. Court assumed bonding duties, Monday through Friday from 0800 to 1700 hours, relieving dispatch of this function.
7. City Council approved the second phase of radio equipment upgrade— a continuous, tone-coded squelch system—and the addition of simplex.
8. Eight certified dispatchers made it possible to operate with a full dispatch complement for the first time in the department's history. Officers were dispatched to a total of 35,362 incidents. Fire and ambulance equipment was dispatched to 2,208 incidents.
9. A class in Transactional Analysis and communications skills was conducted.
10. The Association of Public Safety Communications Officers Technical Assistance Program conducted an assessment of dispatch activity (copy attached).

My department has had its most productive year ever, and I am pleased to be able to report our achievements.

MEMO WRITER TIPS

1. Structure the report according to each of the major functions in your section or department.

2. List each of these functions/departments and provide a one- to two-sentence description of its accomplishments.

3. Use specifics wherever possible, i.e., "sold $56,803.00 and goods and services," rather than "sold considerable amounts of goods and services."

4. In most instances, you will want to list major accomplishments first and rank accomplishments in decreasing order of significance.

5. Structuring the report in list fashion will make it easier to read.

PREPARING A STATISTICAL REPORT

To:
From:
Date:
Subject: 19_____ Personnel Costs—Janitorial Staff

The 19_____ personnel costs for janitorial workers are listed below:

Employee	Base Salary	Fringe	Uniform Allow.	Annual Costs
DeSoto	$10,128.	$ 2,532.	$ 240.	$12,900.
Murphy	9,300.	2,325.	240.	11,865.
Johns	9,300.	2,325.	284.	11,909.
Curtis	9,300.	2,325.	204.	11,829.
Anderson	9,300.	2,325.	204.	11,829.
Kendricks	9,300.	2,325.	224.	11,849.
Bacchus	11,016.	2,754.	240.	14,010.
TOTAL	$67,644.	$16,911.	$1,636.	$86,191.

If you need additional information, let me know.

MEMO WRITER TIPS

1. The information for statistical reports can easily be tabulated and presented in columnar form.

2. Decide which areas need to be reported, structure the report according to these classifications, and list your findings in this way.

3. Should you need to make interpretations of the statistical data, report the findings first and then write a section called "Interpretations" or "Findings" based on this information. Write your interpretations in narrative form.

PREPARING A SITE VISIT REPORT

To:

From:

Date:

Subject: Site Visit—Midwest Region Stores

On my February visit to the Midwest Region, I visited 30 stores. The following information details my findings.

Findings

1. The new manager at Kenosha has completed on-the-job training and is scheduled for training at the home office, beginning March 15. She has hired and is in the process of training a new assistant manager. Two second assistants are fully trained.

2. The housekeeping problems we were having at the Haygood store have been corrected through the designation of a cleaning team for each crew. These procedures seem to be working well. The store was spotless, well-lit, and the parking lot was free from litter on my last, unannounced visit.

3. I have made arrangements for the Security Manager to visit the Thorgood operation, since it continues to experience a high pilferage and waste rate. The Security Manager will instruct the store manager in correct security procedures, report his findings to me, and I will follow up with the store manager in approximately 45 days.

4. Overall sales in the region increased by 12.4 percent during the last quarter (breakdown attached). This increase seems to be due, in part, to the "Fifties Giveaway" promotion targeted for this region.

5. All stores now have copies of the new training procedures for salads and specialty sandwiches. Selected crew personnel will begin training on these items next week, and I will be in contact with each store manager to follow up on their reactions to this training.

MEMO WRITER TIPS

1. Say when/where your visit took place.

2. Handy categories for reporting on your visit include "Observations," "Findings," "Recommendations," "Conclusions."

3. Use other categories if these are more consistent with the areas you know your manager is interested in finding out about. These categories might include "Revenues," "Management," "Training," "Costs."

4. Keep the report brief, using one to three sentences to report what you observed and how you handled the situation.

REPORTING SURVEY RESULTS

To:
From:
Date:
Subject: Needs Assessment Survey Results

The needs assessment conducted last month has yielded these results. Of the 100 surveys distributed, 69 were completed and returned. Responses to survey items were as follows:

[TALLY FINDINGS AND REPORT THEM ON THE SURVEY FORM HERE.]

Summary

The greatest interest seems to be in areas of stress management, time management, and employee wellness. Those topics employees seem least interested in include business ethics, telephone procedure, and the billing process.

Of the survey returns, 67 percent of employees rate this year's training efforts as "excellent." Another 22 percent say the program is "good." Overall, it would seem that we are offering those classes employees are most interested in taking and that sessions are conducted with a hands-on approach that involves participants in the training process.

A major suggestion coming out of this survey indicates some workers would be interested in training sessions held after work, if these could be offered for either college or C.E.U. (Continuing Education Unit) credit. I will look into both these possibilities and, in planning next quarter's training, offer at least one course during evening hours.

If you need additional information about survey results, please call me at ext. 388.

MEMO WRITER TIPS

1. The most efficient way to report survey findings is to fill the results in on a copy of the survey instrument used. Calculate the percentages of responses, or simply give the total number of responses or both. Include this as part of the report itself.

2. After you have reported the results in tabular form, summarize them, highlighting the strongest areas of response (both positive and negative). Pinpoint any suggestions or recommendations you would make as a result of the survey information you have obtained.

REPORTING TASK FORCE/COMMITTEE PROGRESS*

To:
From:
Date:
Subject: Final Report—Shared Governance Committee

Introduction

The Shared Governance Advisory Committee held its first meeting on May 18, 19_____ . At that time, this committee was charged with (1) discussing the shared governance process (as outlined in State Board Policy 2-20), (2) garnering input from members of the various college constituencies, (3) developing recommendations for a college shared governance process, and (4) submitting recommendations to the College President and College Council for review and approval.

This report has been prepared to outline this committee's recommendations for the establishment of a shared governance process at this institution.

---

*This report memorandum was written by a member of a college committee.

Name For Shared Governance Body

This committee recommends the shared governance body be called the College Assembly.

Structure of Shared Governance Body

After careful study and deliberation, it is our recommendation that the Assembly provide equal representation for all major college constituencies: administration, faculty, students, and classified staff. Each of these constituencies would elect three (3) representatives, two regular representatives and one alternate.

Terms of Service

To establish continuity, it is suggested that the first terms of members be one and two years: six members shall have one-year terms, and the other six, two-year terms.

Assembly Process

The Assembly shall establish by-laws to govern its operation. These by-laws would be approved by the College President, the College Council, and the constituencies of each representative.

The Assembly should meet not less than once a month during fall and spring semesters. Meetings should not be scheduled during the summer session unless deemed necessary by the Assembly chair or his/her designee.

The Assembly shall make recommendations directly to the President and, through him/her, to the College Council. The Assembly shall be an officially recognized advisory body to the President.

Scope of Involvement

The scope of involvement of the Assembly shall be consistent with State Board Policy 2-20: ". . . including matters of grievance procedure and due process, employee welfare, employee evaluation, budget, educational program and facility development, institutional role and philosophy, academic freedom and responsibility, and codes of conduct."

These recommendations are respectfully submitted by the Shared Governance Advisory Committee.

_____   _____
Chairperson   Members

MEMO WRITER TIPS

1. Review the purpose and charge of the committee or task force in the opening paragraph. This will frame the discussion to follow by letting the reader know what the report will include.

2. List and explain the findings and/or recommendations of the task force.

REQUESTING REPORT INFORMATION FROM SUBORDINATES

To:

From:

Date:

Subject: Report on New Evaluation Procedure

The new performance appraisal procedure was recently completed. Please prepare a report of how this new procedure worked in your area and what problems, if any, you found with using it.

Specifically, I am interested in knowing (1) how employees responded to the new procedure, (2) whether this process was easier to administer than the previous system, (3) how long it took to complete all evaluations in your unit, (4) how results from the new process compare with previous performance appraisal results for employees.

I'd like to have your final report no later than Friday, July 16.

MEMO WRITER TIPS

1. Request the report and state its purpose in a general way.

2. Itemize specific areas you'd like to see covered in the report, as well as any specifics related to structure.

16

Memoranda: The "Write Stuff"

Effective memoranda, as well as effective business letters and reports, have the "write stuff." What's the "write stuff?" It's the "stuff" that makes your reader say, "I see what you mean; I understand," rather than "Huh????" It's the "stuff" that communicates your ideas to someone else THE FIRST TIME, so you don't have to write a second or third memo, or sit down with people face-to-face to explain what they thought you meant, which wasn't what you thought you'd said.

Chapter 16 outlines the "write stuff" your memoranda should have. Standard memoranda headings—the "To, From, Date and Subject" lines—and what they should/should not contain are discussed. A number of formats for memoranda headings are displayed.

Sometimes, you may have to adapt a model memorandum for your specific needs. At these times, you may find yourself suffering from a common writer's "disease" called "White Paper Shock." The "POWER" Writing Process discussed in this chapter may help you conquer "White Paper Shock," once and for all.

Modern business language helps you convey your message in simple, informal terms. You'll find a list of specific phrases and clichés that you should avoid, if you want to purge your memoranda of wordy, outdated language.

Editing your memoranda effectively polishes them and enables you to project the image you want to portray. Whether you like it or not, your business writing conveys much more than its message. Misspelled words, punctuation errors, shattered sentences, and poor grammar may make your reader reach negative conclusions about who you are and what abilities you have. Write your memoranda "right," or someone may get the wrong impression about you.

This chapter's comprehensive section on Effective Editing will help you create the "write" impression. You'll be able to write clear, complete sentences free of convoluted "therewhichits" and unnecessary prepositional phrases. You'll also find specific strategies for curing another writer's malady—"commatosis"—the generous sprinkling of commas in writing, whether the writing

408

needs commas or not. You'll find guidance for when to write "it's" and when to write "its." And when to write "bosses" and when to write "boss's." Translating technical language is also discussed briefly.

Sometimes, "one memorandum is worth a thousand conversations." Often, you must decide whether/when a memo should be written. This chapter also outlines and discusses when you should talk and when you should write. Some issues need to be discussed in person or on the telephone, and this section gives you practical suggestions for deciding which form of communication—written or oral—will work best for you.

Finally, a "Write Stuff" Memorandum Checklist provides you with an easy way to evaluate how well your memoranda communicate your ideas. Check your memos for audience, purpose, organization/accuracy, language/tone, sentence structure, grammar/punctuation/spelling, appearance, and follow-up by using this handy checklist.

The suggestions in Chapter 16 will help you make sure your memos have the "write stuff." If they do, they'll communicate your ideas to someone else clearly and concisely—the first time.

Here's hoping all the memoranda you write will have the "write stuff."

MEMORANDA FORMATS

Memoranda headings contain five standard pieces of information:

1. A "TO" line—names the person to whom the memorandum is written. For the sake of consistency, if the "To" line contains a job title, so should the "From" line.

2. A "FROM" line—names who wrote the memorandum.

3. A "DATE" line—shows the date on which the memorandum was written.

4. A "SUBJECT" line—describes the main idea or topic of the memorandum. By reading the "Subject" line, the reader should be able to tell what the memorandum is about. In many cases, the "Subject" line determines whether the reader will read the entire memorandum or not.

When you write the "Subject" line, think of your purpose for writing. What is it you want your reader to know? What is it you want your reader to do? Thinking of your purpose will often pinpoint how you should phrase your "Subject" line.

Often, your "Subject" line is typed/word-processed in capital letters only; this calls attention to it.

5. Writer Initials—Write your initials at the end of the "From" line. This indicates that you have read the memorandum and have approved its contents. An example of where you should write your initials follows:

Date: January 3, 19_____
To: Marilyn Thompson
From: John Bradley *JB*
Subject: Production Quotas

If you prefer, type your name or initials two lines below the last line of the memorandum.

MEMORANDA HEADING FORMATS

Headings for memoranda can be structured in a variety of ways. Each is acceptable, depending upon standard practice in your organization. Usually, a company or agency will adopt a standard memo heading that is then used by all its employees. In some cases, memo headings may be pre-printed or stored in a computer, in order to save time.

Standard formats for memoranda headings include the following:

FORMAT #1   FORMAT #2   FORMAT #3
TO: DATE: DATE:
FROM: TO: TO:
DATE: FROM: FR:
SUBJECT: SUBJECT: RE:

FORMAT #4   FORMAT #5
TO: DATE: To: From:
FROM: SUBJECT: Department: Department:
                             Subject: Date:

FORMAT #6   FORMAT #7   FORMAT #8
To: To: March 3, 19__
From: From: To:
Subject: RE: From:
Date: Date: Re:

STANDARD MEMORANDUM PREPARATION

While any of these formats may be used, some standard rules apply.

The information that completes each line of the heading should be aligned vertically at the left. Few things look less professional than heading information, each line of which begins at a different place. Examples follow:

CORRECT FORM

TO:	Margaret Donnelly
FROM:	Jack O'Hara
DATE:	March 3, 19____
SUBJECT:	PERFORMANCE APPRAISALS

INCORRECT FORM

TO: Margaret Donnelly
FROM: Jack O'Hara
DATE: March 3, 19____
SUBJECT: PERFORMANCE
APPRAISALS

The message of your memorandum begins on the third line below the last heading line.

Memoranda are used to communicate within an agency. They are rarely sent to companies or individuals outside your organization. Letters are used to communicate with these companies, individuals, or agencies.

Generally speaking, memoranda have three main parts:

1. An Introduction—conveys the main idea of the memorandum, unless this main idea is "bad news" which should be explained first. If "bad news" is delivered at the beginning of the memorandum, your reader is apt to stop reading here and then call you for an explanation. When "bad news" is being delivered, it is often best to explain first and give the actual "bad news" later.

2. A Body—explains the main idea in more detail and provides the reader with specifics that illustrate, explain, give examples of, or clarify the main idea of your memorandum.

3. A Conclusion—tells the reader what action she/he should take, what results you expect, or thanks the reader.

   In memo writing, shorter is generally better. Tell the reader what you want him/her to know, and be as brief and concise as possible.

Memoranda are brief documents that communicate your ideas to someone else in your organization. They should not take the place of face-to-face communication, but have the advantage of recording your ideas, long after voice communication has disappeared into thin air.

OVERCOMING "WHITE PAPER SHOCK": THE "POWER" WRITING PROCESS

When you write at work do you attempt to think, write, edit, and revise as you go along? If you do, you may find you suffer from a common writing disorder, "White Paper Shock." This malady is characterized by trauma: the trauma that sets in when you must write something, but no ideas will come. Clear symptoms signal the onset of "White Paper Shock." You stare at a blank sheet of paper or a blank CRT screen; the blank sheet of paper/screen stares back at you.

The model memoranda in this book have been provided to help you combat "White Paper Shock." Most of the model memoranda will meet your needs. Phrasing alternatives provide you with several different ways to say the same thing.

Sometimes, you may have to adapt a model memo to fit the specialized demands of your industry or organization. If you do, use the "POWER" Writing Process: **P**lan, **O**rganize, **W**rite, **E**dit, **R**evise/Rewrite.

Using this process can make you more comfortable with the act of writing a memorandum, letter, or report—and ease the symptoms of "White Paper Shock," as a result. Start with the model memoranda in this book. If you need to adapt them, follow the steps in the "POWER" Writing Process, one step at a time:

1. PLAN

(1.1) Analyze Your Reader(s)

Who will read your memorandum? Your "White Paper Shock" will only get worse if you concentrate on what YOU need to do, on what YOU need to say, on how YOU need to write the memorandum. The most critical factor in the entire writing process is THE READER(S)—who THEY are, how well THEY know you, what THEIR response is likely to be. Take the first step in overcoming "White Paper Shock" by taking the focus off of you and putting it where it belongs—on THE READER.

Look at the model memorandum and choose the best phrasing alternative for your reader. Or rephrase the model memorandum, if necessary, to target your specific reader.

(1.2) Establish a Purpose

Why are you writing? What are the main points you must cover in your memorandum? What is it you are trying to get your reader to do, understand? Write the purpose of your memorandum—BEFORE you begin to write.

Find the purpose that most closely matches yours in the Table of Contents. Use the model memorandum as is or add to it if it does not address your purpose entirely.

(1.3) Collect Everything You Will Need

What information will you need to achieve your purpose? Collect all documents, files, facts, figures, and computer printouts—BEFORE you begin to write. Add these specific details to your model memorandum. But once you begin to write, you won't want to break your train of thought by having to get up to collect information, talk on the telephone, or meet with others.

(1.4) Brainstorm Ideas

THINK BEFORE YOU WRITE! List your ideas BEFORE you begin to write the memorandum. Look at your purpose. Now, on a sheet of paper, jot down every idea related to your purpose that comes to mind.

Although writing can often help you think, writers who suffer from "White Paper Shock" are usually paralyzed further by having to come up with ideas while in the midst of writing.

Consider your needs and jot down any additional ideas not covered in your model memorandum.

2. ORGANIZE

(2.1) Put Ideas In Order

Once you have brainstormed, edit your list of ideas. Cross off those that won't help you achieve your purpose. Organize what's left. Put #1 next to the main idea of your memorandum. Then number the rest of your ideas, in decreasing order of importance. The last idea should be the least important.

Use your model memorandum as a base and decide where additional ideas should be placed.

3. WRITE

(3.1) Write Your First Draft

You are now ready to begin the actual writing. Remember, though, your first draft is just that—a draft; it need not be perfect. Don't edit as you write; that comes later.

Merge added ideas with your model memorandum.

4. EDIT

(4.1) Edit Your Draft

Here's where you begin to take your writing apart. Be very critical of your first draft. Does your memorandum accomplish your purpose? Does it say what you mean and mean what you've said? Is it organized? Are words spelled correctly? Is your grammar okay? These are the questions you ask yourself as you edit. Mark anything you need to check or correct.

5. REVISE/REWRITE

(5.1) Revise/Rewrite Your Draft

Correct your draft. Once you've made your corrections, you're ready to write your final memorandum.

(5.2) Proofread Final Draft

Once your final memorandum has been typed/word-processed, proofread it to make sure everything is correct, initial your memorandum and send it on its way.

Using the model memoranda in this book and following the "POWER" Writing Process can help you write more effectively, with a minimum of "White Paper Shock." Of course, PERFECT PRACTICE MAKES PERFECT. These steps may take more time at first, but once you get used to the process of writing, the steps will become second nature. With practice, POWER, and your model memoranda, you may find you've cured your case of "White Paper Shock."

USING MODERN BUSINESS LANGUAGE

Today's business writing is more informal than ever. Your memoranda should say what you need to say, using as few words as possible: Let one or two words do the talking of many.

A case in point . . .

Pursuant to our recent telephonic communication of August 21, please find enclosed three copies of the report you requested.

What does this mean in modern business language?

Here are three copies of the report you wanted.

Use simple words to convey your ideas clearly. Modern business language will give your writing more power, save you time, and help you communicate more effectively with your readers.

USE	INSTEAD OF
about, on, of	regarding, with regard to
about	with reference to, in reference to
agree	concur, in agreement with
as we said/discussed	as per our telephone conversation
because, since	due to the fact that
buy	purchase
by (a specific date)	as soon as possible
can	has the capability
consider	take into consideration
enough	sufficient
except	with the exception of
for	for the purpose of
get	obtain
give, send	furnish
here is	attached herewith is, enclosed please find
here	herein
I/We recommend	It is recommended . . .
if, when	in the event that
in, on, through, by	via
instead of	in lieu of
I've noticed OR (leave out)	It has come to my attention . . .
keep	retain
(leave out)	It is . . .
(leave out)	I think, I feel . . .
(leave out)	Permit me to say . . .
(leave out)	Please be advised . . .
now, today	at the present time
past, earlier	previous
please	It is requested . . .
revise	make revisions
rush	expedite
saw	witnessed
send	transmit, forward
send out	disseminate

USE	INSTEAD OF
separately	under separate cover
so	therefore
tell	notify, advise
to	in order to
try	attempt
we, us	this office

EDITING EFFECTIVELY

The EDITING phase of the writing process is where you begin to take your first draft apart. Follow this process when editing:

READ SILENTLY

Read the entire document through silently. Check to make sure it makes sense. Read your memo as you think your reader might. Be sure your memorandum achieves your purpose.

READ ALOUD

Read the entire memorandum ALOUD, pointing at each word as you read. since your mind will see what it wants to see, you may miss errors when you read silently. Reading aloud will help you pinpoint errors your mind may not want to see.

CHECK SENTENCES

Make sure all sentences are complete. A complete sentence has a naming part (the subject—who or what the sentence is about); a telling part (the verb—tells what the subject does, has done to it, or is); and sense. A complete sentence makes sense—NO SENSE, NO SENTENCE! (EXCEPTION: Fragments, incomplete sentences, convey stronger impact. "So why the continued delay" is stronger than "Why do you continue to delay?" You may *deliberately* use fragments *sparingly* when your message needs greater impact.)

CONQUER "COMMATOSIS"

"Commatosis," or the generous use of unnecessary commas, is a common fault of business writers. If you're not sure you need a comma, leave it out.

USE A COMMA TO

1. **Signal the end of a complete sentence when it is joined to another complete sentence by** *and, but, or, for, nor, so,* **or** *yet.*

   Examples:

   The letters are ready for editing, but the final report still needs work.

   You asked me to set up the appointment, yet you had already scheduled a meeting for the same time.

2. **Separate introductory groups of words from the complete sentence.**

   Examples:

   After years of hard work, she was finally promoted.

   After she worked hard for many years, she was finally promoted.

3. **Separate non-essential expressions from the rest of the sentence. Commas act like "hooks." Generally speaking, what's between the "hooks" can be removed from the sentence without affecting the meaning of the sentence.**

   Examples:

   James, the office manager, was promoted.

   Your projects, however, are right on target.

   Nevertheless, I still need those figures by 9 a.m.

4. **Separate three or more items in a series.**

   Examples:

   Bring your files, computer printouts, and sales figures to the meeting.

   Sam, Donna, and Jeffrey are supposed to attend.

5. **Separate the main elements (day of the week, day of the month, and year) of a complete date. Put a comma after the year if another word follows it in the sentence.**

   Examples:

   We will meet on Monday, January 4, 19____, at 3:00 p.m.

   The meeting will be held on Friday, December 23, 19____, in the executive conference room.

6. **Separate the main elements of an address (street address, city, state). Put a comma after the state or zip code if anything follows it in the sentence. Do not separate the state and zip code with a comma.**

   Examples:

   The package was sent to 3999 East Lansing Street, Denver, Colorado, on the 4th of January.

   The client's address is 401 Hancock Lane, San Diego, California.

   Mail the computer run to Dorsey Enterprises, 234 Abbott Drive, Suite 310, Chicago, IL 60612, by 5:00 p.m. today.

7. **Address someone directly.**

   Examples:

   The sales figures, Mrs. Hampstead, were lower than last month's.

   Jack, meet me in my office at 2:00 p.m.

8. **Separate equal adjectives (descriptive words). You should be able to reverse the adjectives and insert "and" between them, if they are equal.**

   Examples:

   She was a loyal, diligent employee.

   That was a clear, concise presentation.

MAKE SUBJECTS AGREE WITH VERBS

Make sure your subject agree in number with your verb. [In that sentence, the subject and verb don't agree.] If your subject is singular (about one item, person), the verb must be singular; if the subject is plural (about two or more items, persons), the verb must be plural.

Examples:

members of the committee ARE, not is

neither my supervisor nor Mr. Jones HAS, not have

my supervisor and I HAVE, not has

Here ARE the documents. ("Documents" is the subject.)

Here IS the file. ("File" is the subject.)

CHECK "SELF" PRONOUNS

Double-check all "SELFS"—myself, himself, ourselves. "Self" pronouns are often used incorrectly. "My associate and myself checked your account." is WRONG, WRONG, WRONG. The sentence should read, "My associate and I checked your account." Would you say, "Myself checked the account"? Probably not.

TRAMPLE "THEREWHICHITS"

Beware of "THEREWHICHITS." Make these wordy sentences shorter and more direct by getting rid of "there," "which," or "it." Examples follow:

"Therewhichit" : There were five members of the department at the meeting.

Should Read : Five department members attended the meeting.

"Therewhichit" : There are several employees in this department who will receive merit increases.

Should Read : Several department employees will get merit increases.

"Therewhichit" : The memo which I sent to you last week explained the procedure.

Should Read : Last week's memo explained the procedure. **(OR)**

The memo sent to you last week explained the procedure.

"Therewhichit" : The meeting which was canceled last week has been rescheduled.

Should Read : The meeting canceled last week has been rescheduled. **(OR)**

Last week's canceled meeting has been rescheduled.

"Therewhichit" : It has come to my attention that people are taking 25-minute breaks.

Should Read : People are taking 25-minute breaks.

"Therewhichit" : It is recommended that the sales projections which were discussed at our August 3 meeting be revised.

Should Read : The sales projections discussed at our August 3 meeting should be revised.

PURGE UNNECESSARY PREPOSITIONAL PHRASES

Check for unnecessary prepositional phrases (phrases beginning with words like *at, of, to, for, up, down, between, around,* etc.). These also pollute writing.

Each member of the committee was asked to brief department heads on the new procedure at their monthly meeting.

Some prepositional phrases (OF the committee, ON the new procedure, AT their monthly meeting) could be eliminated by writing:

Each committee member explained the new procedure at his/her department's monthly meeting.

Examples	Becomes
1. the head of the department	department head
2. the vice-president of the company	the company vice-president
3. the management class for supervisors	the supervisors' management class
4. the subordinate with innovative ideas	the innovative subordinate

Some prepositional phrases cannot be eliminated from sentences. Those that can be, should be: your sentences will be more direct, less wordy, more effective.

USE APOSTROPHES (') CORRECTLY

Make sure apostrophe marks (') are used correctly. Often, writers think apostrophe marks make words plural (mean more than one). Apostrophe marks don't make words plural. Apostrophes make words possessive (show ownership) or shorten two words into one (make contractions).

USE POSSESSIVES TO SHOW OWNERSHIP

The general rules for forming possessives are these: If a singular noun (about one item, person) does not end in "s," add an apostrophe (') mark plus "s" to make the noun show ownership.

a man's wallet

the operator's voice

a doctor's diagnosis

the supervisor's skill

If a singular noun does end in "s," add an apostrophe (') plus "s" if another syllable (word part) is created when the possessive is formed.

Mr. Jones's office

my boss's appointment

Dr. Barnes's class

the class's test scores

If a plural noun (about two or more items, persons) does not end in "s," add the apostrophe (') plus "s" to make the noun show ownership.

my children's teacher	the women's suits
the men's ties	the people's choice

If a plural noun does end in "s," add only the apostrophe (') mark to make the noun show ownership.

both secretaries' machines	countries' leaders
three bosses' messages	both Barneses' offices

The following chart illustrates the differences among singulars, plurals, singular possessives, and plural possessives:

SINGULAR	PLURAL	SINGULAR POSSESSIVE	PLURAL POSSESSIVE
man	men	man's wallet	men's wallets
doctor	doctors	doctor's diagnosis	doctors' diagnoses
operator	operators	operator's voice	operators' voices
Mr. Jones	both Joneses	Mr. Jones's office	both Joneses' offices
boss	bosses	boss's message	bosses' messages
supervisor	supervisors	supervisor's skill	supervisors' skills
woman	women	woman's suit	women's suits
secretary	secretaries	secretary's machine	secretaries' machines

USE CONTRACTIONS TO SHORTEN TWO WORDS INTO ONE

Sometimes pronouns (its, their, your) and contractions (it's, they're, you're) that sound just like these pronouns get confused:

PRONOUNS: their/theirs = belonging to them

Their skills are needed.

Theirs are on this table.

CONTRACTION: there's = there is

There's [There is] the file you were searching for.

they're = they are

They're [They are] going to be late for the meeting.

PRONOUN: its = belonging to it

Its levers are broken.

Its language is confusing.

CONTRACTION: it's = it is

It's [It is] time for lunch.

You know it's [it is] late.

PRONOUN: your = belonging to you

Your office called.

I'll screen your calls.

CONTRACTION: you're = you are

You're [You are] next in line for the promotion.

If John calls, should I say you're [you are] out?

Pronouns that show ownership (his, hers, theirs, yours, ours) NEVER have apostrophe marks.

WATCH FOR WORDS COMMONLY CONFUSED

Check the spellings of words that sound alike and are, therefore, often confused:

accept—Please accept my apology.

except—Everyone except you came to the meeting.

affect—How will this plan affect your department?

effect—The effects of this change are not yet known.

choose—If you choose to join us, we'll see you there.

chose—I chose not to apply for the position.

further—We can discuss this further tomorrow.

farther—The new plant is farther from the main office than the old one was.

loose—The bolt on the machine is loose.

lose—Did you lose the report?

personal—You shouldn't have opened that letter; it was personal.

personnel—Our department has 320 personnel.

right—Her office is on the right-hand side of the hall.

write—Please write the memo.

stationary—Affix this so it's stationary; I don't want it moving around.

stationery—I designed the new logo for our company stationery.

to—Plan to attend the meeting.

too—Will you need a copy, too?

two—Make two copies of the report.

TRANSLATE TECHNICAL JARGON

Make sure any technical language you use can be readily understood by your reader. If you're not sure your reader will understand a technical term or phrase, choose a more commonplace word instead.

Checking each of these areas will help you edit more effectively.

WHEN TO TALK; WHEN TO WRITE

Written words have several advantages over spoken words:

- When you write, you create a permanent record of your ideas.
- Writing a memorandum allows you to communicate with many people; telephoning them personally would take time.
- Memos provide readers with reference sheets for your ideas; people don't have to memorize what they think you've said.
- Writing helps you think. Often, by putting your ideas down on paper, they become clearer to you and, thus, clearer to your reader.
- You can organize written words much better than you can organize spur-of-the-moment conversations.

With all these advantages, however, sometimes talk works more effectively. You should probably talk, rather than write

1. When the message you want to convey is complex. Consider your reader when you make this decision. You know what you know, but will the reader?

2. When the person to whom you are writing may be angered by your message, **or when you're writing a memo in anger.** Cool off, then go talk.

3. When you've had conflict with your reader in the past. Writing may only prolong the inevitable. Don't avoid face-to-face confrontation by volleying back and forth in a memo tennis match.

4. When you've already written two memos about the same subject.

5. When there's a chance your message may be misunderstood.

6. When your reader is totally unfamiliar with the language you use or the work you do.

7. When you don't need/want a written record of your message and a telephone call or visit could convey your message more quickly.

8. When you're changing a major procedure or process. Clarify it in writing, but then follow-up with talk.

9. When your memo (other than a report memorandum) is more than one page long. If you need a permanent record, write the memo. If you're conveying lots of information, talk about it, as well.

10. When your reader doesn't need the information in your memo.

A "WRITE STUFF" MEMORANDUM CHECKLIST

Use this checklist to make sure your memorandum has the "write stuff."

YES   NO

☐   ☐   1. Is this memorandum necessary? Would a face-to-face conversation or telephone call be better? Do I need/want a written record? Is a memorandum the best way to communicate these ideas? Am I writing this memo only to avoid face-to-face conflict?

- -

IF YOU DON'T NEED TO WRITE A MEMO, STOP HERE. CALL OR VISIT THE PERSON AND COMMUNICATE YOUR IDEAS IN PERSON OR OVER THE TELEPHONE.

- -

AUDIENCE

☐   ☐   2. Is this memorandum written for its intended reader? Who is the reader? How familiar is the reader with the memo topic? What job does the reader have in my organization—superior, peer, subordinate? How well do I know the reader? How's the reader likely to react? How do I want the reader to react?

YES   NO

PURPOSE

☐   ☐   3. Does the memorandum have a clear purpose? What is it?

☐   ☐   4. Can my reader tell what the purpose is?

ORGANIZATION/ACCURACY

☐   ☐   5. Is my message organized? Do my most important ideas come first?

☐   ☐   6. Does each paragraph have one central idea? Does each sentence in that paragraph support that main idea?

☐   ☐   7. Do I use clear transitions (signal words like but, then, next) between each sentence/paragraph?

☐   ☐   8. Have I checked all the facts, dates, and figures in my memo?

☐   ☐   9. Do I explain bad/unpleasant news before telling what the bad news is, if appropriate?

☐   ☐   10. Have I used bullets and lists to spell out step-by-step procedures, highlight important facts and details, or itemize key points?

LANGUAGE/TONE

☐   ☐   11. Is my reader familiar with the language I've used?

☐   ☐   12. Will my reader readily understand technical words I've used?

☐   ☐   13. Is the tone of the memo conversational?

☐   ☐   14. Have I used active rather than passive voice appropriately (The manager wrote the letter, rather than The letter was written by the manager)?

☐   ☐   15. Have I used passive voice (The decision was made by the committee, rather than The committee made the decision) to de-emphasize the subject of the sentence or soften bad/unpleasant news?

☐   ☐   16. Have I used action rather than "to be"—is, are, was, were, been—verbs (Jack agrees rather than Jack is in agreement)?

YES   NO

☐   ☐   17. Does one word do the talking of many?

☐   ☐   18. Have I used modern business language?

☐   ☐   19. Is the memo clear and concise?

☐   ☐   20. Have I used non-sexist language: she/he or him/her rather than him; sales personnel rather than salesmen?

SENTENCE STRUCTURE

☐   ☐   21. Are all my sentences complete? (or Have I *deliberately* used incomplete sentences, fragments, for greater impact?)

☐   ☐   22. Have "therewhichits" been eliminated?

☐   ☐   23. Have I gotten rid of unnecessary prepositional phrases?

GRAMMAR/PUNCTUATION/SPELLING

☐   ☐   24. Is each word spelled correctly?

☐   ☐   25. Does the subject of each sentence agree in number with its verbs (members ARE).

☐   ☐   26. Are commas (,) used correctly?

☐   ☐   27. Are apostrophe marks (') used to form possessives (supervisor's meeting) or contractions (it's [it is])?

☐   ☐   28. Are other punctuation marks used correctly?

☐   ☐   29. Are "self" pronouns used correctly?

APPEARANCE

☐   ☐   30. Are my memo headings correct and complete?

☐   ☐   31. Does my memo have adequate "white space"—blank space to unclutter its appearance and make it more visually appealing to the reader?

☐   ☐   32. Have I proofread and initialed my memorandum and sent it to a member of my organization?

FOLLOW-UP

☐   ☐   33. Have I followed up, if necessary, to make sure my message was communicated?

Index